TRATTORIA
ITALIA

TRATTORIA
ITALIA

A Gastronomic Tour of Italy

RIZZOLI NEW YORK

First published in the United States of America in 1999 by
Rizzoli International Publications, Inc.,
300 Park Avenue South,
New York, NY 10010

© 1999 RCS Libri S.p.A.

ISBN 0-8478-2174-9

LC 98-68687
Printed and bound in Italy

Graphics and cover: Elena Pozzi
Layout: Flavio Guberti
Editor: Monica Floreale
Regional Introductions: Monica Floreale
Useful Addresses: Sergio Negrini
Photographic Research: Roberta Graberini
Production: Ready-made, Milan
Translation from the Italian: Rhoda Billingsley

Photo Credits
Farabolafoto: p. 8 (Giorgio Oddi); p. 20 (Michele D'Ottavio); p. 44 (Curzio Baraggi);
p. 68 (Lucio Bracco); p. 82; p. 122 (Coppola); p. 132 (Riccardo Musecchio); p. 144
(Stefano Chieppa); p. 158 (Giorgio Oddi); p. 186 (Giovanni Rinaldi); p. 200
(Giovanni Rinaldi); p. 224 (Marco Melodia). Agenzia Stradella Milano: p. 32 (D.
Ceresa); p. 58 (D. Ceresa); p. 94 (F. Giaccone); p. 108 (F. Giaccone); p. 172 (Amedeo
Vergani); p. 210 (Amedeo Vergani). Archivio fotografico R.C.S.

Prices given in restaurant listings represent the approximate cost of a two-course
meal and dessert for one person, without drinks.

Preface

What characterizes Italian cooking? The foods that immediately come to mind are spaghetti and pizza, the two Italian dishes that are known throughout the world. And yet, if anything distinguishes Italian cuisine, it is its variety. What do the typical dishes of Piedmont and Lombardy have in common with those of Calabria and Sicily? And doesn't the gastronomy of a region not only exploit its local resources but also reflect its own particular history – which in the case of Italy was often marked by invasions of peoples from distant lands who brought their own traditions along with them? Herein lies the point: there is no such thing as a national Italian cuisine. What does exist, however, is an Italian regional cuisine or, better yet, an infinite variety of dishes linked to each of the country's geographical areas and cultural settings, each one influenced by the different eating habits of its people. Recipes for traditional regional dishes, information about typical local products, suggestions for serving wines, together with a list of recommended trattorias and restaurants, are presented here simply as a starting point for a long journey through Italy, whose gastronomy represents only one of many fascinating aspects to be explored and enjoyed.

Contents

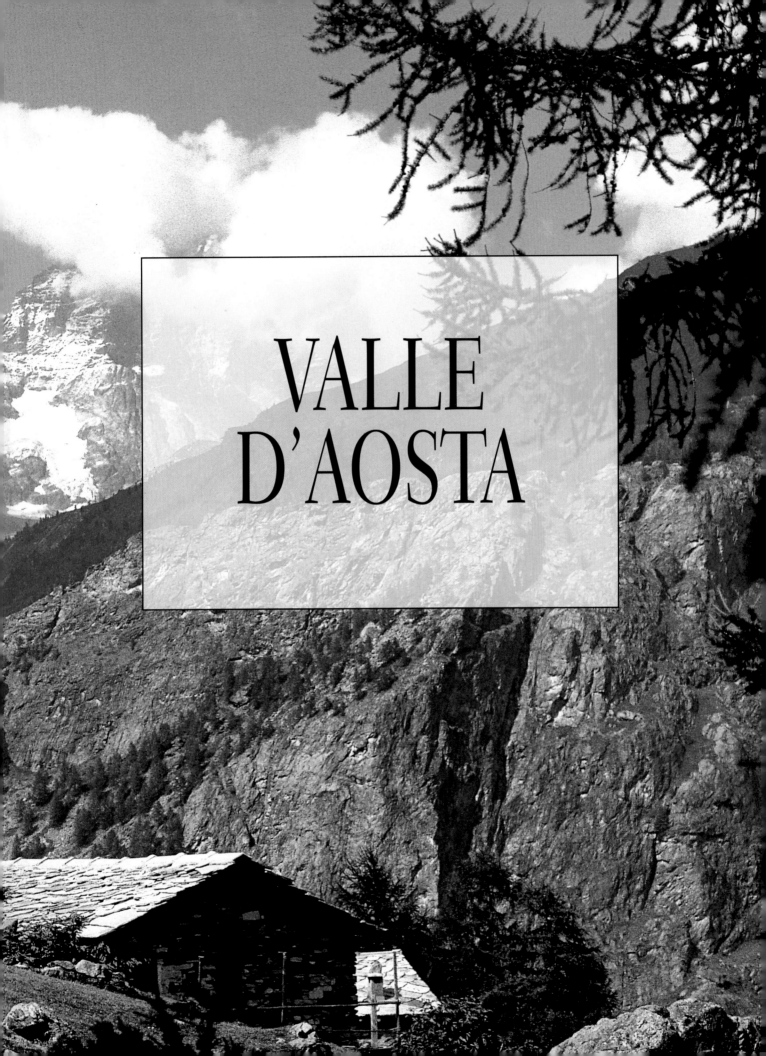

VALLE D'AOSTA

From the summer alpine pastures to fontina

Enclosed on the north by Mont Blanc, the highest and most famous of the European Alps, and barricaded on the east and west by the equally magnificent mountains of Monte Rosa and Gran Paradiso, the region of Valle d'Aosta almost seems to flaunt its isolation and autonomy. Its rugged mountains, snow-covered during the long winters, have not curbed the spirit of initiative of its inhabitants. In the long valley bathed by the Dora Baltea River, the sunniest slopes have been terraced and planted with vines. Farther north, in summer, the cows are brought to the alpine pastures so that their milk will have the fragrance of the mountain meadows. Given such a premise, what could characterize the Aostan gastronomy better than those dishes that exploit its wonderful dairy products?

Fonduta, the famous cheese fondue made with fontina and eaten with toasted bread.

The queen of the Aostan cuisine is *fontina*, the famous cheese produced in the high summer alpine pastures that surround Aosta. The principal ingredient of the famous *fonduta*, it is also served with *polenta concia*, is practically always added to the great variety of soups that characterize the individual valleys, and is an essential ingredient in the preparation of potato *gnocchi*, or dumplings.

The Castle of Fénis, built in the fourteenth century by the lords of Challant.

In addition to its cheeses, which include tasty alpine *tome* and *robiole*, the Valle d'Aosta is known for preserving a wide variety of foods.

In order not to be caught unprepared in winter when there were heavy snowfalls and they were isolated for long periods of time, the inhabitants of the alpine chalets would bake their black bread, made of wheat and rye flours, just once or twice a year. They kept it dry in special cupboards and served it in the thick, hot winter soups. Like bread, meat also had to last as long as possible, and so *mocetta* came into being. This chamois meat is air dried like prosciutto and often served as an antipasto today, but once it was eaten very sparingly so as to last until spring.

Like mocetta, beef was mixed with spices and salted, and salt pork was also a staple. The specially produced salt pork from Aosta literally melts on toasted slices of rye bread as well as enhancing the flavors of polentas and soups.

The fair of Sant'Orso, which takes place in Aosta on January 30 and 31, is a must for those who wish to know more about the region's traditions. One of the oldest fairs in Europe, it is still today a showcase for traditional wooden agricultural implements: milking stools, shovels, rakes, ladders, baskets, sledges, butter molds, together

Mont Blanc seen from the Val Veni, a glacial valley that extends from the Col de la Seigne to Entrèves near Courmayeur.

worth the effort! For nature lovers, the Gran Paradiso National Park offers a variety of trails for hiking and mountain biking. And if you are lucky, you will catch a glimpse of the ibex, or mountain goats, which are almost extinct in other parts of Europe, as well as chamois, partridges, golden eagles, and marmots.

The town of Cogne is the perfect place for setting off into the park, and it is also an important center for the production of honey. Any restaurant in this area will be sure to have *soupetta alla cogneintze* on its menu: a soup based on rye bread, cubes of fontina cheese, rice, and meat broth. In order to complete one's gastronomic picture of the region, a visit to Gressoney on the Piedmont border is recommended. Here the local population, which is of German stock, has preserved a culinary tradition comparable to that of the region of Alto Adige. Their *knölle*, big dumplings made from cornmeal, are very similar to the Alto Adige *canederli*, and the tables are always laden with platters of speck, *crauti* (sauerkraut), and potatoes.

A young ibex on the rocks of Gran Paradiso National Park.

with wooden carvings and knick-knacks, and the characteristic *grolle*, the small pots with many spouts which, filled with coffee, grappa, and lemon peel, are passed around at the end of an Aostan dinner.

If you would also like to see how the nobles lived, then a little time should be dedicated to visiting at least one of the seventy castles that are located between Aosta and St. Martin. The most interesting is perhaps the castle of Fénis, an almost fairytale construction that today houses the Valle d'Aosta Museum of Furniture. The only thing that might be missing from this atmosphere of culture and medieval refinement is a plate of *capriolo*, or venison cooked in the Aostan manner: after three days in a marinade of red wine, bay leaves, cloves, thyme, cinnamon, juniper berries, and minced onion, garlic, parsley, celery, and carrot, the venison is cooked in oil and grappa. The preparation is long, but well

Before leaving the region, one must sample the delicious *tegole d'Aosta*, crisp hazelnut biscuits, accompanied by a glass of Genepy, the typical liqueur of the valley.

Prugne valligiane
(Stuffed Prunes Wrapped in Bacon)

Preparation time
15 minutes plus
soaking time

Cooking time
15 minutes

Difficulty
easy

Serves 6
- 18 dried prunes
- 18 almonds, skinned
- 18 bacon slices
- dry white wine

Mellow, aromatic white wine.
Recommended:
- Valle d'Aosta Chambave Moscato
- Oltrepò Pavese Cortese

1 Rinse the prunes in cold water, place them in a bowl, and cover them with dry white wine. When they are soft, drain them, reserving the wine. Remove the pits and place an almond in each cavity. Wrap a slice of bacon around each prune, fixing it with a toothpick.

2 Preheat the oven to 425°F. Place the prunes in a baking dish and pour the reserved wine on them. Bake for about 15 minutes, turning them once.
Remove from the oven, set aside for 10 minutes, and serve.

Soupetta a' la cogneintze
(Cogne-style Soup)

Preparation time
15 minutes

Cooking time
30 minutes

Difficulty
easy

Serves 4
- ½ cup butter
- 8 slices Italian bread
- 4 cups meat broth
- 1 cup rice
  pinch of cinnamon
- 8 ounces fontina cheese, thinly sliced
- ½ cup dry white wine

Light red wine.
Recommended:
- Valle d'Aosta Nus Red
- Merlot del Piave

1 Preheat the oven to 425°F. In a frying pan, melt 3 tablespoons of the butter. Add the bread in batches and fry until golden. Remove from the pan and keep warm. Bring the broth to a boil.

2 Melt 2 tablespoons of the butter in a saucepan. Add the rice and stir with a wooden spoon until the rice is toasted. Sprinkle with the wine and, as soon as this is absorbed, add the broth by the ladleful, making sure it has been absorbed before adding more broth.

3 When the rice is *al dente* and creamy add the cinnamon, stir, and remove from the heat. In a 8-inch souffle dish, make layers of the bread, the risotto, and the fontina, ending with risotto and fontina. Melt the remaining butter and drizzle it over the top. Place in the oven for a few minutes before serving.

Fontina is a tender cheese, made from the whole milk of cows, which can only be produced in the Valle d'Aosta region, its name and origin being controlled (DOC).

13

Carbonada
(Braised Beef and Onions)

Preparation time
15 minutes

Cooking time
1 ½ hours

Difficulty
easy

Serves 4
- 2 pounds boneless beef chuck, cut into small pieces
- flour
- 4 tablespoons butter
- 1 pound onions (about 4 medium), thinly sliced
- salt and pepper
- 2 cups red wine
- freshly ground nutmeg

Light red wine.
Recommended:
- Enfer d'Arvier
- Dolcetto

1 Dredge the meat in flour and shake off the excess.

2 Melt the butter in a deep pot and brown the meat, stirring with a wooden spoon so that it does not stick to the bottom. When it is uniformly brown, remove it to a platter.

3 Add the onions to the same pot, add salt, and cover, cooking them very slowly on low heat. When the onions are soft, add the meat and 1 cup of the red wine.
Season with a pinch of salt and freshly ground pepper and cook over medium-low heat for about one hour, adding red wine from time to time as it is absorbed.

4 The sauce should be thick and rather dark. Season to taste and add nutmeg. Serve with polenta.

In the past, this recipe was made with beef that had been preserved with salt and aromatic herbs. A similar dish, *carbonnades*, found in Flemish cuisine, calls for beer instead of wine.

Torta di mele rovesciata
(Upside-Down Apple Tart)

Preparation time
30 minutes

Cooking time
40 minutes

Difficulty
medium

Serves 6 to 8
- 1 7-ounce package frozen puff pastry
- 2 pounds Renette apples or other cooking apples (about 5 medium)
- lemon juice
- 6 tablespoons butter
- ¾ cup sugar
- cream (optional)

Dessert wine.
Recommended:
- Valle d'Aosta Chambave Moscato
- Moscato di Strevi

1 Thaw the frozen pastry and preheat the oven to 425°F.

2 Peel, halve, and core the apples. Sprinkle them with lemon juice so they do not discolor.

3 Melt the butter in a 9-inch round cake pan (if possible a tin-lined copper one) with 2-inch sides over medium heat. Stir in the sugar and as soon as it begins to color, arrange the apples on it. Turn them carefully so that they are covered with the syrup.

4 Remove the cake pan from the heat, and place it in the oven for 10 minutes. Remove it from the oven and let cool.

5 Roll out the pastry dough into a disk that is about 10 inches in diameter and 1 inch thick. Place it over the apples, taking care to seal the dough against the sides. Return the tart to the oven for 30 minutes until golden brown.

6 Turn the tart carefully onto a serving dish so that the caramelized apples are on top. Serve at room temperature accompanied by a pitcher of cream or a bowl of whipped cream, if desired.

VALLE D'AOSTA

Chalets in the Gressoney Valley

SPECIALTIES

Antipasti (Appetizers)
Lardo di Arnad, Mocetta, Prosciutto crudo di Saint Marcel, Sanguinaccio (Boudin), Tetetta.

First courses
Crespelle alla valdostana, Fonduta alla valdostana, Gnocchi di ortiche, Polenta alla valdostana, Soupetta cogneintze, Soupa valpellineintse.

Entrées
Camoscio in civet, Carbonade, Scaloppa alla valdostana, Soça di Cogne.

Desserts
Crema di Cogne con tegole, Meculin, Blanc manger.

TYPICAL RESTAURANTS
Cime Bianche
Loc. La Vieille, Breuil-Cervinia
Tel. 0166/948061, Closed Monday
Prices: Lire 60,000/75,000

Les neiges d'antan
Fraz. Cret de Perrères 10, Breuil-Cervinia
Tel. 0166/948852
Prices: Lire 80,000/100,000

Lou Ressignon
Rue des Mines 22, Cogne
Tel. 0165/74034, Closed Monday evening
and Tuesday
Prices: Lire 40,000/65,000

Hotel Dolonne
in Dolonne, Strada della Vittoria 24
Courmayeur
Tel. 0165/846671,
Closed Wednesday
Prices: Lire 60,000/70,000

Maison de Filippo
in Entrèves, Via Passerin d'Entrèves
Courmayeur
Tel. 0165/869797,
Closed Tuesday
Prices: Lire 60,000/70,000

Pierre
Via Martorey 43, Verrès
Tel. 0125/929376, Closed Tuesday
Prices: Lire 70,000/90,000

Hostellerie de la pomme couronnée
Frazione Resselin 3, Gressan
Tel. 0165/251010, Closed Tuesday
Prices: Lire 35,000/70,000

Soupa Valpellineintse

Typical products from the Valle d'Aosta

WINES

White
Blanc de Morgex et de la Salle, Malvasia di Nus, Moscato di Chambave, Peitite Arvine.

Red
Arnad-Montjovet, Chambave rouge, Donnaz, Enfer d'Arvier, Fumin, Gamay, Petit rouge, Torrette.

Dessert wine
Passito di Chambave, Passito di Nus.

CHEESES
Fontina, Formadzo, Toma, Rebleque di Gressoney.

SHOPPING FOR TYPICAL PRODUCTS

Wines
Enoteca La Croix Blanche
Allein

Enoteca La Cave
Via Festaz, Aosta

Co. Pro. Val.
Frazione Trepont 16, Villeneuve

Caves Cooperatives di Donnas, *Donnas*

Cheeses
Latteria Gerard Lale
Via De Sales 14, Aosta

Co. Pro. Val.
Frazione Trepont 16, Villeneuve

Azienda agrituristica Les Ecureuils
Homené Dessus, Saint-Pierre

Maison du Fromage
Via Roma 120, Courmayeur
(Ascoli Piceno)

Cold Meats
Macelleria Bertolin
Strada Statale 6, Arnad

Co. Pro. Val.
Frazione Trepont 16, Villeneuve

Macelleria Marco Jeantet
Via Grappein 38, Cogne

Cooperativa La Kiuwa
Arnad

Lardo (*salt pork*)

For centuries salt pork has been one of the most popular seasonings in cooking. Although it lost its popularity during the dark days of fats, it has recently been rediscovered by connoisseurs of fine foods. Salt pork is produced throughout Italy, but the regions of Valle d'Aosta and Tuscany produce particular varieties that literally melt in the mouth!

Salt pork is rarely mentioned when processed pork products are discussed, as if it were unworthy, yet its use dates back to ancient times. It certainly is not considered mainstream since popular tastes run to light or low-fat products. But, while it is rejected by some, it can now be found on the menus of exclusive restaurants and in the pantries of gourmets.

CHARACTERISTICS
Salt pork comes from the back of the pig, from the adipose layer directly under the pig's skin, while the softer fat beneath this is rendered into lard.

Good salt pork must be of a certain thickness, and come from the so-called 'heavy' hogs, which are distinguished from those defined as 'fattening' or 'lightweight'. In Italy, 70 percent of the swine population is of the heavy variety. However, these proportions are inverted abroad, which explains the presence in foreign cuisines of fresh pork cuts like baking hams, for example, which are almost nonexistent in Italy. The 'lightweight' hogs weighing un-

der 220 pounds are destined for the fresh meat market, while the heavier variety, weighing from 350 to 450 pounds and more, are destined for the pork processing factories. It is interesting to note that the heavy hogs are that way constitutionally and not because they have been fattened. As a matter of fact, in order to make good processed pork products, there should be a higher proportion of lean meat to fat meat. Satisfactorily thick salt pork comes only from big hogs, and thin salt pork from lightweight hogs is not suitable for aging, and would never be as 'sweet' or soft as the top-quality products.

The methods for producing salt pork vary from region to region. In general, large square or rectangular pieces are cut and layered in special tubs with salt, aromatic herbs, garlic, and spices. The pork is then covered with brine and weighted down. After a period of three or more months, the salt pork is ready for consumption.

BUYING SALT PORK

• Choose salt pork that is at least two inches thick.
• Salt pork with a straw-yellow color is not as sweet as better-quality salt pork and tends to be rancid. The white variety with a slight pink gradation is preferable.
• The odor should be delicate and enhanced by the aroma of the seasonings.
• It should be flavorful and slightly salty. It has a decidedly 'sweet' taste, vaguely reminiscent of fresh walnuts.

SERVING SUGGESTIONS

As with good olive oil, the delicate flavor of salt pork is best savored as a spread or seasoning. Added to sauces or roasting meats, it gives an extra richness of flavor.

Cut the salt pork into cubes, fry them, and when they have melted and are crisp, serve them together with the cooking fat over a salad of curly endive dressed with a little salt and vinegar.

Cut and cook the salt pork as above, toss with wide tagliatelle (fresh egg noodles), and season with freshly ground black pepper.

Salt pork can be substituted for bacon when making pasta alla carbonara.

Mince the salt pork and serve it on slices of hot grilled polenta.

Mince the salt pork with garlic and a little hot red pepper and sauté it with chopped onion, carrot, and celery as a base for minestrone or other vegetable soups.

Melt the salt pork with sage leaves and garlic, and add it to pizzoccheri (buckwheat noodles) instead of butter.

Serve thinly sliced salt pork on toasted bread with freshly ground black pepper.

Chop salt pork together with aromatic herbs, spread the mixture on filet steaks, and broil them.

VARIETIES OF SALT PORK
The most famous salt pork in Italy comes from Arnad and Colonnata.

The salt pork from Arnad (Valle d'Aosta) is produced from big hogs. Once the skin has been removed, it is placed in receptacles in three layers with salt and herbs between the layers: bay leaves, pepper, sage, rosemary, cloves, cinnamon, juniper berries, nutmeg, and garlic. It is then completely immersed in water that has been boiled with herbs and salt and then cooled. If the pork is to be brined for a long time, white wine is often added. The receptacle is closed with a weighted lid. Brining can last from three months to one year.

The salt pork from Colonnata in the Apuan Alps (Tuscany) comes from hogs that often weigh up to 350 pounds. The pieces of salt pork are seasoned with pepper, cinnamon, cloves, sage, rosemary, and garlic, and aged in traditional nonporous marble basins that are usually rubbed on the inside with garlic.

THE RIGHT WINE
White wines like Valcalepio, Montecarlo, or Arneis are preferable.

IN SEARCH OF SALT PORK

In Valle d'Aosta, go to Arnad. There, at the Salumificio Bertolin on Via Nazionale 11, Frazione Extraz, you will find a sweet salt pork that will melt in your mouth, one you can eat uncooked like butter on bread.

At Carrara, at Lia Rossi, Via del Commercio 5, you will find an excellent salt pork from Colonnata, which is cured in the traditional marble basins.

PIEDMONT

Truffles and wines for fussy palates

The real character of the Piedmontese can be discovered at the table. If it is true that the inhabitants of this region are traditionally shy and loath to show their feelings, it is also true that a Piedmontese menu is indicative of a serious yet joyful participation in the pleasures offered by a tableful of friends. In Piedmont, what the earth hides is brought to light to please fastidious palates. The famous white truffles of Alba are shaved onto risottos and a variety of pastas or used to enhance the flavor of partridge and quail; they also can make a simple omelette unforgettable. Any great gourmet (with a pocketful of money) must absolutely go to Alba to taste truffles with anchovies. Layers of that precious tuber are covered with a sauce of butter, rosemary, sage, and anchovies, baked in a wood-burning oven, and served with squares of bread fried in butter. Since you are already in the famous Langhe, it is worth having a look at its equally renowned wines. The hills in this area produce Dolcetto, Nebbiolo, Grignolino, Barolo, and Barbaresco.

Not far from the Langhe is Monferrato, where industry has not succeeded in invading the countryside, so that the hills are still dotted with ancient hamlets, castles, and towers. This land, too, is renowned for its wines: Barbera del Monferrato, Barbera d'Asti, Freisa, and Moscato. And the town of Asti produces a wonderful spumante to sip with a dessert of baked peaches filled with almonds, *amaretti*, sugar, and cocoa, which has followed a main course of *fritto misto* (a mixture of fried meats and vegetables, like calf's brains, pig's liver, boletus mushrooms, zucchini, eggplant, apples, and amaretti). A walk around the city will help the digestion, and a visit to the Romanesque baptistery of San Pietro, the cathedral, and the Piedmontese Gothic Collegiata di San Secondo is certainly worthwhile.

Monferrato is also the valley in which the best *bagna caöda* is made, because it is where the sweetest, softest cardoons grow. However, if you prefer onion to garlic, then a valid alternative is the *cipollata rossa monferrina* (a sauce made of *robiola* or cream cheese, sweet red pepper, spring onions, hot red pepper, and paprika) spread on oven-toasted slices of country bread brushed with oil.

Above: A detail of the Romanesque baptistery of San Pietro in Asti. Right: Vegetables stuffed with rice and meat.

Farther north in Valsesia (the valley encompassing the provinces of Vercelli and Novara) they make *uberlekke*, a variation of the usual mixed boiled meats. It is a dish that can be found almost everywhere in Piedmont but has become

most famous in this particular area. *Uberlekke* includes a variety of beef cuts, calf's head and tongue, pork spareribs, mutton, pork sausage, liver, mortadella, and ham hocks. It is accompanied by boiled potatoes, turnips, carrots, and horseradish sauce.

The biggest rice market in Europe is in the Vercelli area, which is one good reason not to leave before you have tasted *panissa*, a rice

and bean dish that was once the traditional food of the poor people who worked in the rice fields. It is eaten with water hens, migratory swamp fowl as big as pigeons which feed on the almost-ripened rice. They are wrapped in bacon and pan roasted with chopped vegetables and bay leaves.

Before leaving the rice fields, make a stop at Novara to taste the fried frogs' legs done in the Novara style, and visit the Basilica of San Gaudenzio, whose dome by Alessandro Antonelli is a direct descendant of the famous Mole Antonelliana in Turin.

The dishes in the Piedmontese capital of Turin are more elaborate and usually stuffed with meat and vegetables. Worth trying are the stuffed veal (filled with minced veal, tongue, salt pork, mushrooms, truffles, bread, egg, Parmesan cheese, garlic, and parsley), and the rice-filled peppers. After a visit to the city, if there is still time, have a look at the Egyptian Museum, whose collection is second only to those of the Cairo Museum and the Louvre in Paris.

In a last nod to the city, buy a box of *gianduiotti*, those delectable chocolates that owe their name to Gianduia, the Piedmontese commedia dell'arte character created by the puppeteer Sales at the beginning of the nineteenth century.

Wine-seller's sign in Alba, a town famous for wines and truffles.

The Basilica of Superga in Turin, built by Filippo Juvarra in the first half of the eighteenth century.

Bagna caöda
(Hot Vegetable Dip)

Preparation time
30 minutes

Cooking time
30 minutes

Difficulty
medium

Serves 4
- 8 to 10 salted anchovy fillets, rinsed, dried, and boned
- 8 to 10 cloves garlic, thinly sliced
- 1 cup extra virgin olive oil
- 3 tablespoons butter

Raw vegetables
- Cardoons cut in pieces
- Carrots, cut in sticks
- Sweet peppers, seeded and cut into strips
- Savoy cabbage, inner leaves only
- Jerusalem artichokes
- Belgian endive
- Radicchio from Chioggia or Treviso

Cooked vegetables
- Baked whole onions
- Roasted peppers
- Beets

Light red wine.
Recommended:
- Barbera del Monferrato
- Colli Piacentini Bonarda

1 Place the anchovies and garlic in a small earthenware dish, add the oil (it should cover them) and cook for 30 minutes over very low heat, mixing from time to time. The garlic should cook without discoloring, and the anchovies should dissolve. The mixture should barely simmer.

2 When the *bagna caöda* is ready, add the butter and, as soon as it melts, place the dish on an alcohol burner so that the dip stays warm. Everyone at the table dips the different raw or cooked vegetables into the sauce, accompanying each mouthful with country bread.

In Piedmont, the *bagna caöda* is served in the *s'ciônfeta*, an earthenware pot that has its own little burner.

Rabaton alessandrini
(Bread and Swiss Chard Dumplings)

Preparation time
30 minutes

Cooking time
5 minutes

Difficulty
medium

Serves 4 to 6
- 1 slice stale bread without crust
- ½ cup milk
- ¾ pound Swiss chard or spinach leaves, boiled briefly and squeezed dry
- 1 fistful parsley leaves, chopped
- 2 tablespoons chopped fresh marjoram or thyme
- 1 scant cup ricotta cheese
- 3 eggs
- 1 cup grated Parmesan cheese
- bread crumbs
- flour
- 4 tablespoons butter

Dry white wine.
Recommended:
- Roero Arneis
- Gambellara

1 Soak the bread in the milk. Squeeze out the excess milk and pass the bread and the chard through a food mill into a bowl. Add the chopped herbs, ricotta cheese, eggs, ⅔ cup of the grated Parmesan cheese, and enough bread crumbs to make a soft homogeneous mixture. Mix well. To make the *rabaton*, shape a spoonful of the mixture quickly into a ball in your lightly floured hands.

2 Drop the *rabaton* into boiling salted water. As soon as they rise to the surface, push them down to the bottom with a slotted spoon. When they return to the surface, remove them with the slotted spoon to a serving platter, sprinkle them with the remaining grated Parmesan cheese, and dot them with the butter. Serve immediately.

In the Alessandria area, the *rabaton* are boiled in a meat or vegetable broth for greater flavor, and then placed in the oven for 10 to 15 minutes before serving.

25

Fritto misto alla piemontese

(Piedmontese Mixed Fried Meat)

Preparation time
1 hour

Cooking time
30 minutes

Difficulty
medium

Serves 8

- 3 ½ ounces brains
- 3 ½ ounces sweetbreads
- 3 ½ ounces marrow
- 7 ounces mixed calf's and pig's liver
- 3 ½ ounces Italian link sausage
- 8 baby lamb chops
- 1 ½ pounds zucchini, zucchini blossoms, and boiled cauliflower florets
- 1 apple
- lemon juice
- 8 amaretti cookies
- ½ cup milk
- 8 squares *frittura dolce* (see recipe facing page)
- 2 to 3 eggs
- flour
- 2 ½ cups bread crumbs
- vegetable oil for frying
- salt

Light red wine.
Recommended:
- Dolcetto d'Acqui
- San Colombano

1 Drop the brains, sweetbreads, and marrow in boiling water, drain, and rinse under cold water. Eliminate the membranes and cut into pieces. Slice both types of liver and pat dry with a paper towel. Cut the sausage into pieces.

2 Trim, wash, and dry the zucchini and cut them lengthwise into matchsticks. Remove and discard the stamens and stems from the zucchini blossoms.
Wash the blossoms under cold water and drain them on a towel.

3 Peel and core the apple, cut it into round slices, and sprinkle with lemon juice. Soften the amaretti slightly in the milk.

4 Beat the eggs in a bowl with a pinch of salt. For all the meats, vegetables, apple, and amaretti: dredge in flour, dip in the beaten eggs, and then roll in the bread crumbs. The *frittura dolce* squares are fried without coating.

5 Preheat the oven to 350°F. Heat 2 tablespoons oil in a small skillet and fry the pieces of sausage without letting them dry out, drain on paper towels, and transfer to a towel-lined baking sheet in the oven.

6 Heat about ¼ inch of oil in a large skillet and fry all the other ingredients in batches. Drain them and place them alongside the sausage, changing the paper towels frequently. After everything has been fried, transfer the lot to a warm serving platter, sprinkle with salt, and serve immediately.

The ingredients can vary according to individual tastes and the seasons, but the *frittura dolce* and amaretti are a must in any mixed fry.

Frittura dolce
(Sweet Fried Polenta)

Preparation time
10 minutes

Cooking time
30 minutes

Difficulty
easy

Serves 4
- 2 cups milk
- ¼ teaspoon salt
- 3 tablespoons granulated sugar
- 1 strip lemon zest
- ¾ cup semolina
- 1 egg
- 1 cup bread crumbs
- 4 tablespoons butter
- ½ cup confectioner's sugar

1 In a saucepan, mix the milk with the salt, sugar, and lemon zest, and bring to a boil. Add the semolina slowly, whisking constantly, and cook over moderate heat for about 10 minutes. Remove from the heat and remove and discard the lemon zest.

2 Wet a large, flat platter. To the semolina mixture, add the egg and stir energetically. Pour the mixture onto the platter, level it out to about 1 inch high, and let it cool.

3 Cut the semolina into rhomboid shapes or squares and dredge in bread crumbs, shaking off the excess crumbs. In a frying pan, melt the butter. Add the coated semolina pieces and fry on both sides. Drain, dust with confectioner's sugar, and serve.

Monte Bianco
(Puréed Chestnuts and Whipped Cream)

Preparation time
40 minutes plus cooling time

Cooking time
1 hour 15 minutes

Difficulty
easy

Serves 4 to 6
- 2 pounds chestnuts in shells
- ½ vanilla bean
- 4 cups milk
- ¾ cup granulated sugar
- ¼ cup rum
- 2 cups whipping cream, chilled
- ⅓ cup confectioner's sugar
- whole marrons glacés, for decoration

1 Make a cut on the flat side of the chestnuts with the point of a knife and boil them in slightly salted water for 25 minutes. Drain them and peel while they are still hot, removing the inner skin as well. Transfer them to a saucepan. Add the vanilla bean and milk. Simmer over low heat for about 45 minutes. The chestnuts should be soft but not mushy. Drain and purée through a food mill using the disk with the smallest holes. Add the granulated sugar and rum and stir energetically with a wooden spoon. Let the mixture cool.

2 Just before serving, purée the mixture again (this time using the disk with the largest holes) onto a serving platter, letting the purée form a mountain.

3 In a deep bowl, whip the cream, sifting the confectioner's sugar into it as you whip it. Cover

the mountain with the cream, using a spatula or a pastry bag. Decorate it with marrons glacés, and serve immediately.

PIEDMONT

Uberlekke (Mixed boiled meats)

SPECIALTIES

Antipasti (Appetizers)
Acciughe al verde, Acciughe in bagnet ross, Bagna caöda, Insalata di carne cruda, Ovoli in insalata, Salam dla duja.

First courses
Agnolotti dal plin, Capunet, Fonduta, Miacce, Panissa, Polenta concia, Rabaton, Ravioli al brasato, Tajarin, Tapulon.

Entrées
Bollito misto, Brasato al barolo, Finaziera, Fricandò di vitello, Fritto misto, Pollo alla cacciatora, Vitello tonnato.

Desserts
Bonet, Monte Bianco, Panna cotta, Zabajone.

TYPICAL RESTAURANTS
Porta S. Martino
Via Luigi Einaudi 5, Alba (CN)
Tel. 0173/362335, Closed Monday
Prices: Lire 60,000

Arcimboldo
Via Legnano 2, Alessandria
Tel. 0131/52022, Closed Sunday
Prices: Lire 60,000

Gener neuv
Lungo Tanaro 4, Asti
Tel. 0141/557270, Closed Sunday evening and Monday
Prices: Lire 90,000/110,000

Pio V
Via S. Pio V 41, Bosco Marengo
Tel. 0131/299666, Closed Sunday evening and Wednesday
Prices: Lire 60,000

Boccondivino
Via Mendicità Istruita 14, Bra (CN)
Tel. 0172/425674, Closed Sunday and Monday at noon
Prices: Lire 55,000

Gardenia
Corso Torino 9, Caluso (TO)
Tel. 011/9832249, Closed Thursday and Friday at noon
Prices: Lire 70,000

Scoiattolo
Casa del Ponte 3/B, Carcoforo (VC)
Tel. 0163/95612, Closed Monday
Prices: Lire 50,000/70,000

Italia
Via Moretti 19, Ceva (CN)
Tel. 0174/701340, Closed Thursday
Prices: Lire 45,000

Osteria della Chiocciola
Via Fossano I, Cuneo
Tel. 0171/66277, Closed Sunday
Prices: Lire 50,000

Belvedere
Piazza Castello 5, La Morra (CN)
Tel. 0173/50190, Closed Sunday evening and Monday
Prices: Lire 55,000/60,000

Lu Taz
Via San Maurizio 5, Limone Piemonte (CN)
Tel. 0171/929061, Open only in the evening, closed Tuesday
Prices: Lire 70,000/80,000

Contea
Piazza Cocito 8, Neive (CN)
Tel. 0183/67126, Closed Sunday evening and Monday
Prices: Lire 100,000

Vecchia Cooperativa
Via Nazionale 54, Nucetto (CN)
Tel. 0174/74279, Closed Monday evening and Tuesday
Prices: Lire 55,000

Il Borgo
Via Roma 120, Ormea (CN)
Tel. 0174/391049, Closed Monday
Prices: Lire 35,000

Alla Torre
Via I Maggio 75, Romagnano Sesia (CN)
Tel. 0163/826411, Closed Monday
Prices: Lire 60,000

Agrifoglio
Via Accademia Albertina 38d, Turin
Tel. 011/837064, Closed Sunday and Monday
Prices: Sampling Lire 40,000, menu Lire 60,000

Tre Galline
Via Bellezia 37, Turin
Tel. 011/4366553, Closed Sunday
and Monday at noon
Prices: Lire 50,000

Real Castello
Via Umberto I 9, Verduno (Cuneo)
Tel. 0172/470125
Prices: Lire 90,000

WINES
White
Arneis, Cortese dei colli tortonesi,
Cortese dell'alto Monferrato, Cortese
di Gavi, Erbaluce di Caluso, Favorita
delle Langhe, Pelaverga di Verduno.

Red
Barbaresco, Barbera d'Alba, Barbera
d'Asti, Barbera dei colli tortonesi,
Barbera del Monferrato, Barolo, Boca,
Brachetto d'Acqui, Bramaterra, Carema,
Dolcetto delle Langhe, Dolcetto del
Monferrato, Dolcetto d'Acqui, Dolcetto
d'Alba, Dolcetto d'Asti, Dolcetto di
Diano d'Alba, Dolcetto di Ovada, Fara,

Freisa d'Asti, Freisa delle Langhe, Freisa
del Monferrato, Freisa di Chieri,
Gattinara, Ghemme, Grignolino d'Asti,
Grignolino del Monferrato casalese,
Lessona, Malvasia di Casorzo d'Asti,
Malvasia di Castelnuovo Don Bosco,
Nebbiolo d'Alba, Nebbiolo delle Langhe,
Roero, Rubino di Cantavenna, Ruché
di Castagnole Monferrato, Sizzano.

Dessert wine
Asti spumante, Caluso passito, Moscato
d'Asti, Moscati di Strevi.

CHEESES
Bettelmatt, Brusso, Castelmagno,
Raschera, Robiola di Roccaverano, Toma
di Bra, Toma di Murazzano.

SHOPPING FOR TYPICAL PRODUCTS
Wines
Enoteca Fracchia
Via Vernazza 9, Alba (Cuneo)

Grandi vini
Via Vittorio Emanuele, Alba (Cuneo)

Bottega Comunale dei Quattro Vini
Piazza Italia, Neive (Cuneo)

Enoteca Regionale
Castello, Grinzane Cavour (Cuneo)

Cantina Comunale
Via Carlo Alberto 2, La Morra (Cuneo)

Enoteca Regionale del Monferrato
Piazza del Popolo, Vignale Monferrato
(Alessandria)

Panissa (Rice and beans)

Cheeses
Salumeria centrale
Corso Italia 15, Acqui Terme

Elvira Ponzo
Piazza Caranti - San Bartolomeo
Chiusa Pesio (Cuneo)

Luciana Camerini
Borgata Sprella 21c
Feisoglio (Cuneo)

Caseificio Alta Valsesia
Via Varallo 5, Piode (Vercelli)

Buttiero & Dotta
San Gerolamo Roccaverano (Asti)

Caseificio San Martino
Corso Piemonte 129
Saluzzo (Cuneo)

Caseificio Cooperativo Elvese
Borgata Serre, Elva (Cuneo)

Cold Meats
Piero Rosso
Via Gioberti 36, Asti

Salumeria Canonica
Via Roma 39, Barolo (Cuneo)

Salumeria Barcellini
Via Arona 43, Borgomanero (Novara)

Giovanni Chiapella
Piazza Caduti della Libertà 15
Carrù (Cuneo)

Douja d'Or
Via Gozzano 46, Ivrea (Turin)

Borgiattino
Via Cernaia 32, Turin

Tartufi (truffles)

Truffles add a touch of class to the humblest of dishes. These edible subterranean fruiting bodies of fungi live in symbiosis with certain trees. Their colors and dimensions vary, and they are veined on the inside. They have a very characteristic odor that is both intense and penetrating.

CHARACTERISTICS

The law controlling truffles relates to seven of the numerous species of truffles, two of which are particularly famous: the white truffle and the black truffle.

The Tuber magnatum, Pico, or white truffle is of a light color with gradations that tend toward yellow, hazel, or gray. It is finely veined with a pink, beige, or light brown tonality on the inside. Its odor is distinct, strong, and pleasant; and its taste, though intense, has a particular delicacy. It is always served raw because it loses some of its characteristics in cooking. It is sliced directly onto the food it is served with, in thin shavings with a special truffle shaver. Individual truffles can weigh almost a pound, although they are usually smaller. They are in season from October until the end of December.

The prized black truffle, Tuber melanosporum, Vittadini, has a wart-like, hard outer covering. When sliced, the inner part is black in color with purplish reflections and has white streaks that turn pink in contact with the air, and black when cooked. Black truffles' perfume is intense and full, as is their flavor, even when cooked. Black truffles are often used in fillings, and in baked pastas, gratinéed dishes, sauces, and souf-

flés. They can be over a pound in weight, but are rarely larger than a tangerine. They are in season from mid-November until mid-March.

The other five types of truffles are less precious, but deserve to be mentioned.

The Tuber brumale, Vittadini, known as

the 'winter truffle', has a wart-like dark red outer skin that turns black when mature. The inner gray-black part, streaked with white, turns chocolate-colored in cooking. It is in season from January through March.

The Tuber melanosporum, var. moschatum, De Ferry, called the 'nutmeg truffle', has a wart-like black skin and a dark inside veined with white. It is in season from February to March.

The Tuber aestivum, Vittadini, commonly called the 'summer truffle', has a black, warty skin; the inside is a yellowish bronze with light veining that disappears in cooking. It is in season from June to November.

The Tuber mesentericum, Vittadini, known as the 'ordinary black truffle', has a wart-like outside and is yellow inside with light-colored veining. It is in season from September through the first part of May.

The Terfezia leonis has a smooth skin that tends toward brown; its inside is a reddish pink. It is in season during summer and autumn.

BUYING TRUFFLES

It is generally advisable to buy the best-quality truffles, even if they are the most expensive, since they offer a better return and greater satisfaction. Be careful, however, not to buy a lesser-quality truffle for a top-quality price. When buying, keep in mind the above descriptions and the seasons in which each is available.

Make sure the truffle is fresh: it should have a pleasant odor and be firm to the touch. If it is tough, it is dry; if it is soft to the touch, it is old.

Beware of truffles with soil clinging to them, not only because it is dishonest to sell soil at the going price of a truffle, but also because there are those who do not think twice about patching up a broken truffle (which is of lower commercial value) with a bit of mud. If you want to purchase more than one truffle, check each one carefully.

SERVING SUGGESTIONS

The color of a truffle determines how it will be used in cooking: white truffles are only served raw on top of food in order to fully express their aroma; on the other hand, black truffles are better cooked.

Shave a white truffle on top of a salad of boiled shellfish.

Season pappardelle *(broad egg noodles) with butter, grated Parmesan cheese, and a black truffle that has been grated, sliced, or julienned, and gratinéed for a few minutes in the oven.*

Dice a black truffle and blend it into the ricotta cheese and spinach filling for tortelli *(ravioli-like dumplings).*

Beat egg yolks and cream and add a chopped black truffle. Pour the mixture into ramekins and set them in a pan of boiling water. Bake until firm.

Sauté a chopped black truffle in butter together with trout fillets, and serve the fish with the truffled butter.

Serve soft-boiled eggs with minced white truffle.

Season gnocchi *(potato dumplings) with fontina cheese and sliced white truffle.*

Shave a black truffle onto vol-au-vent *filled with mushrooms.*

STORING TRUFFLES

If you have bought a truffle and do not intend to eat it immediately, you may keep it for a week (as long as it is fresh) in the following way: wrap it in a piece of paper, then cover this with two pieces of damp paper, and lastly three pieces of dry paper, and place in the vegetable bin of the refrigerator.

Do not freeze truffles under any circumstances because they will lose their aroma.

The popular idea of keeping a truffle in rice is valid if it is kept there for just one day, otherwise it will dry out quickly.

THE RIGHT WINE

The choice of wine depends on the other ingredients in the truffled dish. In general, full-bodied aromatic white wines are recommended, like a Müller Thurgau from Trentino, a Sylvaner from Alto Adige, or a fruity Traminer from Friuli.

IN SEARCH OF TRUFFLES

The most famous centers for white truffles are Alba, in the province of Cuneo, and Acqualagna, in the province of Pesaro-Urbino.
The capital of the black truffle is Norcia, in the province of Perugia. Every Saturday morning, at the truffle market in Alba, the dealers sell the truffles they have found during the night. The Fair of White Truffles, held in Alba from October 6 to 27, is a major attraction for all those involved with these delicacies.

LIGURIA

A *region of sailors and gourmets*

Squeezed between the Apennines and the Tyrrhenian Sea, Liguria could be one of the more difficult places to live in Italy – but the love and perseverance of its inhabitants have made it one of the most enchanting. Whoever visits Liguria is struck by the enormous effort that has gone into terracing its slopes in order to plant vineyards and olive trees. The effort is even more praiseworthy since Liguria's natural setting has remained untouched, and its cities and towns are an integral part of some of the most spectacular panoramas in Italy.

Above: The thirteenth-century church of San Pietro at Portovenere, a village on the Gulf of La Spezia. Below: The typical spiny artichokes of Liguria.

Throughout the centuries, the resourceful Ligurians have rolled up their sleeves and exploited the possibilities of the region, taking care to maintain their own independence. And this is also evident in their cuisine, an array of dishes whose main ingredients have been grown and harvested locally. Here, basil plays a leading role, especially in Liguria's gift to the rest of Italy: *pesto*, a sauce of basil, pine nuts, pecorino cheese, garlic, and oil. Flour, water, and eggs are worked together with a variety of herbs to make the dough for *picagge* (lasagne) and *pansotti* (ravioli) which are then filled in different ways and served with a walnut sauce. For an idea of the wealth of the edible herbs that abound on Ligurian soil, go to the marketplaces of Genoa and ask for *preboggion*, a bunch of greens that varies from season to season, in which a kind of Savoy cabbage, borage, Swiss chard, and wild *radicchio* occupy first place. You can make anything with preboggion, from the filling for the above-mentioned pansotti to vegetable soups and sauces for tasty first courses. Perhaps the dish that best symbolizes Liguria is the *cappon magro,* a platter of fish and vegetables based on an old and complicated recipe that unites the land and the sea. Those who love fish will want to try the soups and fries of *gianchetti* or *bianchetti* (whitebait), and the many different and delicious ways that *stoccafisso* (dried cod), although not typical of the Ligurian sea, has been interpreted in this region of sailors and gourmets. The most interesting personal touch may be 'codfish in the Genoese manner', in which the fish is cooked with tomatoes, potatoes, raisins, and pine nuts.

A visit to Camogli in early May provides a wonderful opportunity for tasting Ligurian

fish and seeing the Riviera of the Levante. The brightly colored houses of this little, old fishing village are built on top of one another around the picturesque port where the fishermen come and go in their boats. At the Festival of Fish, held on the second Sunday of May, the fishermen use a gigantic pan to fry an enormous quantity of fish, which they then offer to the public.

If you are there at another time of the year, go to nearby Recco, where the delicious cheese focaccia is made of a very thin layer of dough filled with a creamy Ligurian cheese. And from Recco, you can take the panoramic Via Aurelia that unwinds along the coast and passes through one jewel of a village after

another: Portofino, Santa Margherita Ligure, and farther south in the direction of La Spezia, the Cinque Terre. These five tiny villages (Monterosso, Vernazza, Corniglia, Manarola, and Riomaggiore) between the mountain and the sea are connected to one

another by one of the most beautiful footpaths in the region.

Cappon magro, a delicious platter of fish and vegetables.

As you head inland from the coast, you will come across local specialties that once again bear witness to the resourcefulness of the Ligurians in using what the land has to offer: rabbits, chickens, lambs, and goats, which are prepared with olives, spiny, flavorful artichokes, and the mushrooms that abound in the chestnut woods that cover the slopes almost down to the sea.

An entire study could be made of the diverse ways of cooking snails in this region – a Ligurian delicacy that dates back in time, and each village has its own special recipe. Perhaps the most traditional is one from medieval times in which the snails are cooked with onion, tomato, parsley, basil, celery, walnuts, hazelnuts, capers, and pecorino cheese.

Lastly, before leaving this region, a world of wonderful sweets can be sampled in the pastry shops. First and foremost is the Genoese *pandolce*, a bread enriched with butter, raisins, candied fruit, pine nuts, and fennel seeds. There are also *canestrelli*, made of short pastry, *biscotti del legaccio*, and the soft and delicate *sciumette*, which are always served in Ligurian homes at Christmas and carnival.

Vernazza, one of the villages of the Cinque Terre, seen from the sea.

Panissa
(Fried Chickpea Polenta)

Preparation time
10 minutes plus
cooling time

Cooking time
50 minute

Difficulty
easy

Serves 4 to 6
- 2 ¼ cups chickpea flour
- vegetable oil for frying
- salt

Dry white wine. Recommended:
- Riviera Ligure di Ponente Pigato
- Bianco Vergine Valdichiana

1 Place the chickpea flour in a large saucepan and dilute it little by little with 5 cups lukewarm water, beating the mixture constantly with a whisk. Mash any lumps that form with a wooden spoon.
Season with salt and cook over low heat for about 30 minutes or until the mixture becomes thick and smooth and pulls away from the sides of the pot.

2 Pour the *panissa* onto a slightly wet, flat surface, spread it evenly to a thickness of not more than ½ inch, and let it cool completely.

3 Cut the *panissa* into diamond-shaped pieces of the same size and fry in 1 inch oil. When the pieces are crisp, drain them on paper towels and serve immediately from a warm serving platter.

Panissa can also be cooked in a special electric kettle. If you prefer not to fry it, cut it into pieces and serve it hot, covered with sliced new onions, oil, and freshly ground black pepper.

Torta di zucca
(Pumpkin and Spinach Pie)

Preparation time
30 minutes

Cooking time
1 ½ hours

Difficulty
medium

Serves 6
- 3 pounds pumpkin or similar winter squash
- 1 pound spinach
- salt and pepper
- 4 tablespoons grated Parmesan cheese
- 1 teaspoon chopped fresh marjoram leaves
- freshly grated nutmeg
- 3 eggs, one separated
- 2 ½ cups flour
- 3 tablespoons extra virgin olive oil

Dry white wine.
Recommended:
- Colline di Levanto Bianco
- Trebbiano di Romagna

1 Preheat the oven to 350°F. Halve the squash, remove and discard the rind, seeds, and filaments, place in a shallow baking dish, and bake until soft. Clean, wash, and cook the spinach with a pinch of salt and just the water that clings to the leaves. Drain after 10 minutes, squeeze it dry, chop it, and place it in a bowl.

2 Pass the squash through a food mill directly onto the spinach. Add the Parmesan cheese, marjoram, nutmeg, 2 whole eggs and 1 yolk, salt and pepper.

3 Increase the oven heat to 425°F and grease a 10-inch pie dish. Sift the flour onto a board and mix it with the oil and enough water to obtain a smooth dough. Divide the dough into two pieces, one slightly larger than the other. Roll out the dough with a rolling pin into two thin disks. Line the greased pie dish with the larger disk, and pour the vegetable mixture into it, covering it with the second disk. Brush the top crust with the beaten white of an egg. Seal the edges of the two disks by folding the larger over the smaller, then flute the edge with your fingers. Bake for about 45 minutes until golden. Let cool slightly.

Mandilli de saea
(Lasagne with Pesto)

Preparation time
30 minutes plus 30
minutes resting time

Cooking time
20 minutes

Difficulty
medium

Serves 6
- 4 cups flour
- 5 eggs
- 30 basil leaves
- coarse salt
- 1 clove garlic
- 1 tablespoon pine
  nuts
- 1 tablespoon grated
  pecorino cheese
- 1 tablespoon grated
  Parmesan cheese,
  plus extra for garnish
- 6 tablespoons olive
  oil
- butter
- salt

Dry white wine.
Recommended:
- Riviera Ligure di
  Ponente
- Cortese dell'Alto
  Monferrato

1 Sift the flour onto a board, shaping it into a mound. Make a well in the center and break the eggs into it. Beat them with a fork, and then slowly mix them with the flour, using your fingers. Make sure they don't spill out. When all the flour has been incorporated, but the mixture is still granular, start kneading the dough with your hands until it becomes smooth and elastic. Shape it into a ball, cover it with a cloth, and let it rest for 30 minutes.

2 In the meantime, wash and dry the basil leaves and place them in a marble mortar with a pinch of coarse salt. Using a wooden pestle, press but do not pound the ingredients against the side of the mortar. Add the garlic, pine nuts, and then, little by little, both the grated cheeses. When the mixture is uniform, transfer it to a bowl and slowly add about 4 tablespoons of the oil, mixing constantly with a wooden spoon until the sauce is creamy.

3 Flour the board and rolling pin. Flatten the dough with the palms of your hands and roll it out, stretching it into a regular shape. From time to time, wrap it around the rolling pin, and roll it out in the opposite direction. When it is very thin, cut it into 4-inch squares.

4 Bring a large pot of water to a boil and add the remaining 2 tablespoons olive oil and some salt. Drop a few *mandilli* in at a time, removing them when they are *al dente*. Alternate them in layers with the pesto in individual pasta plates. Dot them with butter and sprinkle with the remaining grated Parmesan.

This pasta is so light that in the Ligurian dialect its name means 'silken handkerchiefs'.

Triglie con i capperi
(Red Mullet with Capers)

Preparation time
20 minutes

Cooking time
20 minutes

Difficulty
medium

Serves 4
- 8 red mullets (about 8 ounces each)
- 6 tablespoons extra virgin olive oil
- $^3/_4$ cup dry white wine
- $^3/_4$ cup lemon juice
- salt and pepper
- 1 tablespoon capers, rinsed and drained

Dry white wine. Recommended:
- Colline di Levanto Bianco
- Montescudaio Bianco

1 Scale and clean the mullets, then wash and dry them.

2 Heat the oil in a frying pan, add the mullets in one layer, and pour over them $^1/_2$ cup of the wine and $^1/_2$ cup of the lemon juice. Season lightly with salt and pepper and distribute the capers on top.

Cook for 6 minutes over low heat. Turn the mullets once, adding the remaining wine and lemon juice, and cook for another 6 minutes. Transfer the mullets to a serving platter and keep warm.

3 Pour the sauce over the mullets and serve immediately.

LIGURIA

SPECIALTIES

Antipasti (Appetizers)
Cappon magro, Capponada, Mosciame, Torta di bianchetti, Torta pasqualina.

First courses
Corzetti alla polceverasca, Farinata, Mesciüa, Panigacci, Pansotti, Piccagge matte, Risotto al nero di seppia, Sardenaira, Testaroli, Trofie al pesto.

Entrées
Buridda di stoccafisso, Cima alla genovese, Cozze alla marinara, Fegato all'aggiada, Fritto misto, Muscoli alla lericina, Seppie in zimino, Totani ripieni, Vitello all'uccelletto, Zuppa di pesce.

Desserts
Cubaita, Marocca, Pan di Spagna.

TYPICAL RESTAURANTS
Palma
Via Cavour 5, Alassio
Tel. 0182/640314, Closed Wednesday
Prices: Lire 150,000

Antica osteria dei leoni
Via Mariettina Lengueglia 49, Albenga
Tel. 0182/51937, Closed Monday
Prices: Lire 60,000/70,000

Mussel sauce

Familiare
Piazza del Popolo 8, Albissola Marina
Tel. 019/489480, Closed Monday
Prices: Lire 50,000

Pironcelli
in Montemarcello
Via delle Mura 45, Ameglia
Tel. 0187/601252, Closed Wednesday
Prices: Lire 45,000

Antica trattoria La Baita
Via Lucifredi 18, Borghetto d'Arroscia
Tel. 0183/31083, Closed Monday, Tuesday and Wednesday
Prices: Lire 60,000/70,000

Hotel Miramonti
Via 5 Martiri 6, Calizzano
Tel 019/79604, Closed Monday
Prices: Lire 40,000/50,000

Nonna Nina
in San Rocco
Via Molfino126, Camogli
Tel. 0185/773835, Closed at noon
Prices: Lire 60,000

Frantoio
in Rivarola, Via Conturli 2, Carasco
Tel. 0185/350230, Closed Monday
Prices: Lire 40,000

Al Castello da Marco
Via Provinciale 247, Castelnuovo Magra
Tel. 0187/674214, Closed Monday
Prices: Lire 50,000

Da Armanda
Piazza Garibaldi 6, Castelnuovo Magra
Tel. 0187/674410, Closed Wednesday
Prices: Lire 65,000

Serafino 2
Via Matteotti 8, Cervo
Tel. 0183/408185, Closed Tuesday
Prices: Lire 50,000

Dria
Via Costaguta 27, Chiavari
Tel. 0185/323699, Closed Sunday evening and Monday
Prices: Lire 60,000

Ca' del Moro
Frazione Gorra
Via per Callizzano 34, Finale Ligure
Tel. 019/696001, Closed Tuesday evening and Wednesday
Prices: Lire 65,000

Antica osteria della Foce
Via Ruspoli 72-74r, Genoa
Tel. 010/5533155, Closed Sunday and Saturday at noon
Prices: Lire 20,000/30,000

Bruxaboschi
in San Desiderio, Via Mignone 8, Genoa
Tel. 010/3450302, Closed Sunday evening and Monday
Prices: Lire 60,000

Da Maria
Vico Testadoro 14r, Genoa
Tel. 010/581080, Closed Monday evening and Saturday
Prices: Lire 15,000

Genio
Salita San Leonardo 61r, Genoa
Tel. 010/588463, Closed Sunday
Prices: Lire 50,000

Negrao
in Negrao
Via Genova 428, La Spezia
Tel. 0187/701564, Closed Monday
Prices: Lire 35,000

Da Fiorella (früher Da Cappelletta)
Via Case Sparse 5, Ortonovo
Tel. 017/66857, Closed Thursday
Prices: Lire 40,000

Locanda Cervia
in Nicola
Piazzetta della Chiesa, Ortonovo
Tel. 0187/660491, Closed Monday
Prices: Lire 40,000/50,000

Puny
Piazza Martiri dell'Olivetta 5, Portofino
Tel. 0185/269037, Closed Thursday
Prices: Lire 110,000

Taverna del Corsaro
Calata Doria 102, Portovenere
Tel. 0187/790622, Closed Thursday
Prices: Lire 80,000/90,000

Giancu
in San Massimo, Rapallo
Tel. 0185/260505, Closed Wednesday,
and at noon
Prices: Lire 60,000

La Baita
Via Alpini d'Italia 8, Recco
Tel. 0185/792625, Closed Monday,
and at noon
Prices: Lire 50,000

Ligurian *canestrelli*

Manuelina
Via Roma 278, Recco
Tel. 0185/74128, Closed Wednesday
Prices: Lire 70,000

Ripa del Sole
Via De Gasperi 19, Riomaggiore
Tel. 0187/920143, Closed Monday
Prices: Lire 45,000/55,000

Paolo e Barbara
Via Roma 47, San Remo
Tel. 0184/531653, Closed Thursday noon
and Wednesday
Prices: Lire 150,000

Pescatori
Via Bottaro 43, Santa Margherita Ligure
Tel. 0185/286747, Closed Wednesday and
Thursday
Prices: Lire 80,000

Chiapparino
Via Colle Caprile 35, Uscio
Tel. 0185/91297, Closed Thursday
Prices: Lire 40,000

Gambero Rosso
Piazza G. Marconi 7, Vernazza
Tel. 0187/812265, Closed Monday
Prices: Sampling Lire 55,000
Menu Lire 70,000

WINES
White
Bianco dei Colli di Luni, Cinque Terre,
Pigato, Vermentino.

Red
Ormeasco, Rossese di Dolceacqua.

Dessert wine
Sciacchetrà.

CHEESES
Bruzzu di Triora, Caprino di Pieve di
Teco, Toma di Calizzano.

SHOPPING FOR TYPICAL PRODUCTS
Wines
Enoteca Bisson
Corso Ciannelli 28, Chiavari (Genoa)

Casa del Vino
Via Biassa 65, La Spezia

Enoteca Marone
Via S. Francesco 61, San Remo (Imperia)

Cheeses
Arte Bianca
Via Sapri 79, La Spezia

Consorzio Cooperativo Valle Stura
Via Roma 69, Moasone (Genoa)

Cold Meats
Salumificio Parodi
in Berti, Sant'Olcese (Genoa)

Cooperativa Casearia Val di Vara
Loc. Perazza, Varese Ligure (La Spezia)

Focaccia

Focaccia was known to the ancient Romans, but over the centuries a variety of ingredients were added to it so that variations developed in different parts of the country. The Ligurian focaccia is the most famous, and although it is now made in the rest of Italy, the secret of its fragrance remains a mystery.

Focaccia is made from the same dough as bread; it is usually savory, but at times can be sweet. Though available in many regions, that of Liguria is the softest and most fragrant and flavorful. To all appearances it is simple to make, but inferior focaccia can often be dry, mealy, and lacking in fragrance. The reasons for this are many and depend not merely on the quality of the ingredients, the water, the recipe, rising time, oven temperature, and baking time, but primarily on the hands of the baker.

CHARACTERISTICS

The preparation of focaccia is based on two steps: one for making the dough and one for preparing the mixture (equal parts of oil and water plus salt) that goes on top of it.

The ingredients for making the dough are flour, water (an amount equal to 55 percent of the weight of the flour), extra virgin olive oil, yeast, salt, and often malt. These are kneaded together, the salt being added at the end. The dough is left to rise for at least 30 minutes, then divided into as many pieces as there are pans to fill.

The pans, usually rectangular in shape with low sides, are greased with oil, and the dough is flattened into them using the palms of the hands.

The characteristic dimples on focaccia are made by pressing one's fingertips into the dough.

The dough is left to rise again for about an hour, and is then baked in a 425°F oven.

Focaccia can be seasoned with herbs such as rosemary, or covered with onions, olives, or fresh tomatoes. Recco is famous for its cheese focaccia, which should be eaten piping hot, straight from the oven.

BUYING FOCACCIA

Very few, if any, know the secret of Ligurian focaccia. Bakeries in other regions that successfully reproduce breads that are not of local tradition rarely obtain the same results when they attempt to make the Ligurian focaccia.

At the time of purchase, make sure that the focaccia is thin, about $1/2$ inch high, with well-marked dimples.

The surface must be of a light golden brown color, not pale like undercooked bread. In addition, it should be covered with an even film of oil, and not be opaque like bread, nor too oily.

The surface of the focaccia should be smooth, and the inside porous. It should be very soft, and have a distinct but not overpowering taste of extra virgin olive oil and salt.

A crisp, brittle variety of focaccia is the *schiacciatina*, which has the consistency of a cracker.

SERVING SUGGESTIONS

Focaccia is wonderful for breakfast, with coffee and milk. Filled with ham, cheese, or vegetables, it makes a simple, savory snack. Unlike bread, it is not eaten with butter.

Freshly made focaccia is usually eaten for breakfast wherever it is part of the local tradition. Some people may turn up their noses at the idea of combining focaccia and caffelatte *(coffee with milk), but the contrast of the two is particularly flavorful.*

Fill the focaccia with a soft cheese like taleggio *or* brie, *heat it in the oven until the cheese melts, and serve.*

Fill warm focaccia with ham.

Slice the focaccia in half lengthwise. Place sliced tomatoes, mozzarella, and basil on the cut halves, sprinkle with salt and freshly ground pepper, and drizzle a little olive oil on top.

Break schiacciatina *into pieces and use these instead of croutons in vegetable soups, cream soups, and salads.*

Rub the schiacciatina *with a clove of garlic and serve it in fish soup.*
Serve the focaccia cut into squares, together with bread. Or serve it as a snack. Unlike bread, it is not eaten with butter.

STORING FOCACCIA

The same rules apply for keeping focaccia as for small loaves of bread or rolls. Since focaccia slowly loses its fragrance once it is removed from the oven, it is best to eat it on the same day it is baked. It can be frozen and reheated in a hot oven.

THE RIGHT WINE

Like bread, focaccia does not go with any particular wine; the wine is chosen on the basis of the dish it accompanies. If it is eaten alone, choose a delicate white wine like Gavi, Lugana, or Ribolla Gialla.

IN SEARCH OF FOCACCIA

You can find good focaccia at any bakery in Liguria. If you want to be extra sure, try one of the following places.
At La Spezia, go to Farinata La Pia, Via Magenta 12, where they make *farinate* (a kind of focaccia made with chickpea flour), and also excellent hot focaccias.
At Monterosso al Mare in the Cinque Terre, at the bakery on Via Roma 61, the focaccia is particularly good, as at Pieve di Teco, in the province of Imperia, at the Panetteria Odetto, Via de Filippi 1.
At Ventimiglia, also in the province of Imperia, try the focaccia at the Panetteria Meineri, Via Genova 128.

LOMBARDY

A *vast variety of dishes*

From a gastronomical point of view, Lombardy is probably the most heterogeneous region in Italy, since every one of its cities has specialties that seem to be ignored just a few miles away. A reason for this may be the diversity of the territory. It is hard to know which best represents this region: the plains of the Po River with their rice fields and peat bogs, the lake country, the many rivers, or the mountains. There is also a great difference between the lifestyle in a metropolis like Milan and in a smaller city like Pavia or Bergamo. One thing is certain, however: rice takes pride of place over pasta, be it an addition to vegetable soups, a first course served with butter and Parmesan cheese, or a side dish colored yellow with saffron and served with ossobuco (veal shanks), or with sausages and all kinds of vegetables. Naturally, every city has its own specialty. In Mantua, for example, rice is seasoned with *salamelle* (a pork sausage) or other sausage, or is served as *risotto alla pilota*, which was invented by the people who husked (*pila*) the rice.

Other typical Mantuan fare includes *tortelli di zucca* (ravioli-type pasta Filled with pumpkin), *pasta rasida* (a bean and potato soup with fresh egg pasta), and *bigoli con sardelle* (a kind of homemade spaghetti with sardines). Food for the eyes in this region would include a visit to the Palazzo Te, a splendid and beautifully preserved example of sixteenth-century architecture with magnificent frescoes in its Sala di Psiche and Sala dei Giganti. Also, take time to see the Ducal Palace with the Camera degli Sposi, which was frescoed by Mantegna in the second half of the fifteenth century.

Another leading player in the regional cuisine is polenta, and here too the varieties are infinite, starting from the kind of flour used. One is a flour of *fràina*, also known as *grano saraceno* or buckwheat flour, which is used for *polenta taragna* and *polenta in fiur* (with milk), both of which are specialties from the Valtellina. Another is a yellow cornmeal (often coarse-grained) that is transformed into the simple polenta that usually accompanies different kinds of meat or vegetables, or is made into *polenta pasticciata*, which is a kind of polenta pie.

Above: Fresco in the Sala dei Giganti in the Palazzo Te in Mantua. Right: *Risotto alla milanese con zafferano* (Milanese rice with saffron).

Buckwheat flour is also the principal ingredient of *pizzoccheri*, another Valtellina specialty, which is served with butter and cheese, and is guaranteed to restore energy after a day in the mountains!

Leaving the Alps behind and moving to the lake country, one is faced with an embarrassment of riches, for Lombardy is blessed with (and shares with other regions) two of the largest lakes in Italy, Lake Maggiore and Lake Garda. How best to exploit this abundance of fresh water? Here the local fare is based on eel, carp, perch, pike, whitefish, and tench. One of the specialties in the area around Lake Como is *missoltitt in gratella*, which is made with the shad-like fish that are caught in May and June, dried in the sun, and preserved in layers with bay leaves. Another delicacy is fillet of perch, which is floured, dipped in egg and bread crumbs, and fried in bubbly hot butter. In addition to a visit to nearby Lecco and Como, the short walk from Civate to the Romanesque abbey of San Pietro al Monte is a must for any visitor.

Let's combine this gastronomic itinerary that extends from the lakes to the cities of the Po Valley with a series of stopovers in the name of the Sforza family, the dynasty that held one of the most brilliant courts in Europe, and which introduced the cultivation of rice to Lombardy. Our first stop is the Castello Sforzesco in Milan, which houses Michelangelo's Pietà Rondanini, and then Vigevano, which has one of the most beautiful piazzas in Italy, the Piazza Ducale, designed by Bramante for Ludovico il Moro. And while we are there, we can have an excellent *risotto alla milanese* (cooked with onion, bone marrow, meat broth, and saffron) accompanied by the classic *ossobuco* and a good Barbera wine.

Our next stops are at the Certosa di Pavia, where the tombs of the Sforza family are to be found, and Lodi, where, under the porticoes of the city, *büsecca*, or tripe, is offered on January 19 in honor of the patron saint of the city. Those not lucky enough to be there on that day can treat themselves to *zuppa alla pavese* (vegetable soup served with fried bread and an egg) or *risotto alla certosina* (rice with crayfish, frogs' legs, and fish broth).

Our last, but not least, homage to the Sforza is *torrone*. This nougat was created in 1441 for the wedding banquet of Bianca Maria Visconti and Francesco Sforza and was served to more than six thousand guests in the piazza of the Cathedral of Cremona.

Left: Facade of the Charterhouse of Pavia; the construction of this famous abbey began at the end of the fourteenth century.

Above: A box of Vergani Torrone from the early twentieth century showing a view of Cremona.

Tortelli di zucca
(Tortelli Filled with Pumpkin)

Preparation time
1 hour plus 1 hour resting time

Cooking time
30 minutes

Difficulty
medium

Serves 4
- 3 pounds pumpkin or similar winter squash
- 5 ounces amaretti (about 6 cookies)
- 3 ½ ounces *mostarda* (preserved fruits in mustard sauce)
- salt
- freshly ground nutmeg
- 4 eggs
- 8 tablespoons Parmesan cheese
- 2 ¾ cups flour
- ¼ cup butter, melted

1 Preheat the oven to 350°F. Peel the pumpkin and remove the seeds and filaments. Cut it into pieces and place in a shallow baking dish. Bake for about 20 minutes, or until the pulp is soft and dry. Crush the amaretti and cut the *mostarda* into small pieces.

2 Purée the pumpkin through a food mill, using the disk with the smallest holes. Add the amaretti, *mostarda*, salt, nutmeg, 1 of the eggs, and 4 tablespoons of the grated Parmesan cheese. Mix well and then cover the bowl and let the mixture rest for about 30 minutes.

3 Sift the flour onto a board and form a mound. Make a well in the center and break the remaining 3 eggs into it. Mix well, adding water if necessary, until the dough is homogeneous and firm. Run the dough through a pasta press to produce a thin sheet, and cut this into 2 ½-inch squares. Place ½ teaspoon of the pumpkin mixture in the center of each square and fold the dough into a triangle, sealing it by pressing the edges with your fingers. Fold the triangle again and press the two ends together to form a little bundle. Cover these with a cloth and let them rest for an hour or two.

4 Bring a large pot of water to a boil and add salt and the *tortelli*. Boil gently for 6 minutes or until filling is heated through. Remove them with a slotted spoon and place them on a warm serving platter. Sprinkle with the remaining grated Parmesan cheese and the melted butter and serve immediately.

For an important dinner, serve the *tortelli* in a hollowed-out pumpkin.

Dry white wine.
Recommended:
- Oltrepo Pavese Riesling
- Trebbiano di Aprilia

Mac del varesotto
(Rice and Chestnut Soup)

Preparation time
15 minutes plus soaking time

Cooking time
3 hours

Difficulty
easy

Serves 4
- 7 ounces dried chestnuts
- 1 bay leaf
- salt
- 4 cups milk
- ½ cup rice

Rosé wine.
Recommended:
- Chiaretto del Lago d'Iseo
- Biferno Rosato

1 Soak the chestnuts in lukewarm water for about 8 hours. Drain them. Remove their skins and rinse them. Place them in a large saucepan with just enough water to cover. Add the bay leaf and salt and cook over low heat until the chestnuts are soft and have absorbed almost all the water. Remove the bay leaf, and mash the chestnuts in the liquid with a fork.

2 Add the milk and bring the soup to a boil. Add the rice and cook for 15 minutes, stirring frequently. Taste and adjust seasoning. Serve in a tureen or individual bowls.

Polenta pasticciata
(Polenta Pie)

Preparation time
20 minutes plus the time to cook and cool the polenta

Cooking time
1 ½ hours

Difficulty
medium

Serves 4
- 3 cups cornmeal
- 1 ounce dried mushrooms
- 4 tablespoons butter, plus extra for greasing
- 1 large onion, chopped
- 1 stalk celery, chopped
- 5 ounces Italian sausage, peeled and crumbled
- 1 15-ounce can tomato purée
- salt and pepper
- ¾ cup grated Parmesan cheese
- 3 ½ ounces Bel Paese-type cheese (mild and semi-soft), sliced

Light red wine. Recommended:
- Castelchiaro Rosso
- Colli Piacentini Bonarda

1 Fill a deep saucepan with 8 cups water and add a fistful of coarse salt. As soon as the water comes to a boil, add the cornmeal in a thin stream while whisking vigorously. As soon as the polenta starts to bubble, lower the heat and continue to stir periodically with a wooden spoon for at least 45 minutes, or until the polenta pulls away from the side of the pan. Pour the hot polenta onto a large wooden cutting board and let it cool.

2 Soak the dried mushrooms in tepid water for 15 minutes. Squeeze dry and chop. In a skillet, melt 2 tablespoons of the butter. Add the onions and celery and sauté until softened. Add the sausage, mushrooms, and tomato purée and cook over moderate heat for about 20 minutes. Season with salt and pepper.

3 Preheat the oven to 425°. Butter a baking dish with high sides. Cut the polenta into ½-inch-thick slices. In the prepared dish, layer the polenta, the tomato sauce, the Parmesan cheese, and the sliced cheese, ending with a layer of sauce and Parmesan cheese. Dot the top with the remaining butter.

4 Bake for about 20 minutes, until a crust forms on top. Serve directly from the baking dish.

Brasato
(Braised Beef)

Preparation time
20 minutes

Cooking time
3 hours

Difficulty
easy

Serves 4 to 6
- 2 slices bacon
  ($\frac{1}{8}$-inch thick)
- 2 pounds beef pot
  roast
- 1 clove garlic
- 2 onions, chopped
- 4 carrots, chopped
- 3 stalks celery,
  chopped
- 1 bay leaf
- 3 cloves
- 2 tablespoons
  butter, cut into
  pieces
- salt

*Full-bodied red
wine.
Recommended:*
- Valtellina Superiore
- Sassicaia

1 Cut the bacon into strips and lard the beef, inserting the garlic into the meat. Place the beef, onions, carrots, and celery into a heavy-bottomed or cast-iron Dutch oven with a tight-fitting lid. Add the bay leaf, cloves, butter, and salt. Cover and simmer over low heat for 3 hours. Turn the meat two or three times during this time and adjust the salt at the end of cooking.

2 When the meat is tender, slice it and serve with the vegetables as they are, or pass them through the food mill. Serve the dish with polenta or mashed potatoes.

This recipe is typical of Milan; in the area around Brianza, chopped or puréed tomatoes are added to the sauce.

Asparagi alla milanese
(Asparagus, Milanese Style)

Preparation time
20 minutes

Cooking time
30 minutes

Difficulty
medium

Serves 4
- 3 pounds asparagus
- 2/3 cup grated Parmesan cheese
- 4 tablespoons butter
- 4 eggs
- salt and pepper
- chopped hard-boiled egg for garnish

Dry white wine.
Recommended:
- Valcalepio Bianco
- Bianco della Valdinievole

1 Snap off the tough ends of the asparagus, and pare the spears with a peeler. Wash and drain them. Tie them in bunches, making sure the spears are of the same height.

2 Drop them into boiling salted water, leaving the tips uncovered. Cook, covered, for about 8 minutes, until they are tender but not soft. Drain, untie, and transfer to an oval serving platter, or arrange the spears on four individual plates, keep-ing them close together. Sprinkle with the Parmesan cheese and keep warm.

3 Melt the butter in a skillet and fry the eggs until the whites are firm and the yolks are still soft. Salt and pepper them and place them on the serving platter (or the individual plates), spooning the melted butter on top. The eggs will look better if they are fried one at a time in a small skillet. Serve with chopped hard-boiled egg sprinkled on top.

Budino di panettone
(Panettone Pudding)

Preparation time
45 minutes plus
cooling time

Cooking time
45 minutes

Difficulty
medium

Serves 6
- 3 cups milk
- ³/₄ cup sugar
- a piece of
  cinnamon stick
- grated zest of
  1 lemon
- 1 pound stale
  panettone
- 2 eggs
- 4 egg yolks
- 5 tablespoons rum
- 5 tablespoons
  Marsala
- 4 ¹/₂ ounces
  semisweet
  chocolate, finely
  chopped

1 In a saucepan, simmer the milk with the sugar, cinnamon, and lemon zest for about 10 minutes. Remove from the heat and let cool. Butter an 8-cup mold with high, smooth sides. Fold aluminum foil three to four times, forming two long strips about 2 ¹/₂ inches wide. Press them into the mold, crossing them on the bottom, with their ends hanging over the sides. Cut the panettone into thin slices, and line the bottom and the sides of the mold.

2 Beat the eggs and the yolks in a bowl. Strain the tepid milk and add it slowly to the eggs. Mix the rum and the Marsala in a cup and brush the slices of panettone in the mold with the mixture. Sprinkle pieces of chocolate on the bottom, and cover them with more slices of panettone, repeating the layers to 1 inch from the top of the mold. Pour the egg-milk mixture very slowly over the layers so that it is absorbed.

3 Preheat the oven to 350°F. Set the mold in a pan of boiling water that reaches up to 2 inches from the top of the mold, and bake for about 35 minutes, or until a knife inserted into the pudding comes out clean. Cool the pudding, then unmold it onto a plate, using the strips of foil to loosen it. It can be served with zabaglione or a hot chocolate sauce.

LOMBARDY

SPECIALTIES

Antipasti (Appetizers)
Bresaola, Missoltitt, Salame d'oca.

First courses
Agnoli in brodo, Casonsei, Gnocchi al gorgonzola, Marubini, Minestrone, Paniscia, Pizzoccheri, Polenta taragna, Riso alla 'pilota', Risotto al salto, Risotto alla certosina, Risotto alla milanese, Risotto con gli aurtiz, Tortelli dolci di zucca, Zuppa alla pavese.

Entrées
Busecca, Cassoeula, Costoletta alla milanese, Ossobuco alla milanese, Polenta e osei, Pollo alla Marengo, Rane fritte, Rustin negàa, Rustisciada, Sciatt.

Desserts
Bisciola, Brassadei, Büselà, Panettone Torrone, Torta sbrisolona, Tortionata.

TYPICAL RESTAURANTS

Benedetto Girelli
Via Nazionale 17, Barghe (BS)
Tel. 0365/84140, Closed Tuesday
Prices: Lire 80,000

Antica Trattoria della Colombina
Via Borgo Canale 12, Bergamo
Tel. 035/261402, Closed Friday
Prices: Lire 40,000

Torrazzetta
Frazione Torrazzetta 1, Borgo Priolo (PV)
Tel. 0383/871041, Closed Monday
Prices: Lire 50,000

Passerini
Via Dolzino 128, Chiavenna (SO)
Tel. 0343/36166, Closed Monday
Prices: Lire 80,000

Mellini
Via Bissolati 105, Cremona
Tel. 0372/411803, Closed Sunday evening and Monday
Prices: Lire 55,000

Aquila Negra
Vicolo Bonacolsi 4, Mantua
Tel 0376/327180, Closed Sunday evening and Monday
Prices: Lire 90,000

L'Ochina bianca
Via Finzi 2, Mantua
Tel. 0376/323700, Closed Monday and Tuesday at noon
Prices: Lire 55,000

Cutlets, Milanese style

Crotasc
Via Don Lucchinetti 63, Mese (SO)
Tel. 0376/410030, Closed Monday and Tuesday
Prices: Lire 65,000

Alfredo Gran San Bernardo
Via Borghese 14, Milan
Tel. 02/3319000, Closed Sunday
Prices: Lire 80,000/100,000

La Madonnina
Via Gentilino 6, Milan
Tel. 02/89409089, Closed Sunday
Prices: Lire 40,000

Masuelli San Marco
Viale Umbria 80, Milan
Tel. 02/55184138, Closed Sunday and Monday at noon
Prices: Lire 60,000/75,000

Matarel
Via L. Solera Mantegazza 2 Ecke Corso Garibaldi, Milan
Tel. 02/654204, Closed Tuesday and Wednesdays at noon
Prices: Lire 65,000

Trattoria Milanese
Via Santa Maria 11, Milan
Tel. 02/86451991, Closed Tuesday
Prices: Lire 80,000

Colombi
Frazione di Loglio di Sotto I, Moltù Beccaria (PV)
Tel. 0385/60049
Prices: Lire 70,000

Osteria del Crotto
in Madonna, Morbegno (SO)
Tel. 0342/614800, Closed Sunday
Prices: Lire 60,000

Vecchio Fiume
Contrada Cima alle case 1, Morbegno (SO)
Tel. 0342/610248
Closed Tuesday evening and Wednesday
Prices: Lire 60,000

Trattoria Volpi

Bresaola with *bitto* cheese

Frazione Nosadello, Via indipendenza 36
Pandino (CR)
Tel. 0373/90100, Closed Sunday evening
and Monday
Prices: Lire 55,000

Antica Trattoria Lisetta
Via Benzoni 36, Palazzo Pignano (CR)
Tel. 0373/982400, Closed Wednesday
evening and Thursday
Prices: Lire 40,000

Antica Osteria del Previ
Via Milazzo 65, Pavia
Tel. 0382/26203, Closed Wednesday
Prices: Lire 60,000

Via Vai
in Bolzone, Via Libertà 18
Ripalta Cremasca (CR)
Tel. 0373/268232
Closed Tuesday and Wednesday
Prices: Lire 55,000

Antica Trattoria delle Rose
Via Gasparo da Salò 33, Salò (BS)
Tel. 0365/43220, Closed Wednesday
Prices: Lire 60,000

Italia
Via Garibaldi 1, Torre de' Picenardi (CR)
Tel. 0375/94108, Closed Sunday evening
Prices: Lire 75,000
Fulmine

Via Carioni 12, Trescore Cremasco (CR)
Tel. 0373/273103, Closed Sunday evening
and Monday
Prices: Lire 80,000/100,000

WINES
White
Chiavennasca, Cortese, Franciacorta,
Lugana, Pinot, Riesling, Tocai,
Valcalepio, Verdea.

Rosé
Chiaretto del Garda, Pinot rosato.

Red
Barbacarlo, Barbera, Bonarda,
Botticino, Buttafuoco, Capriano
del Colle, Cellatica, Franciacorta,
Grumello, inferno, Rosso di San
Colombano, Sassella, Sforzato,
Valcalepio, Valgella.

Dessert wine
Moscato, Sangue di Giuda.

CHEESES
Bagoss, Bitto, Branzi, Caprino di
Montevecchia, Casera, Gorgonzola,
Grana padano, Mascarpone, Mascherpa,
Quartirolo, Salva, Scimudin, Stracchino,
Taleggio.

SHOPPING FOR TYPICAL PRODUCTS
Wines
Cantina Sociale di Casteggio
Via Emilia, Casteggio (Pavia)

Enoteca Marino
Via Dolzino 66, Chiavenna (Sondrio)

Fratelli Ciapponi
Piazza 3 novembre 23, Morbegno
Sondrio

Enoteca Pi Due
Via Trieste, Ecke Via B. Campi,
San Colombano al Lambro
(Milan)

Cold Meats
Pozzi
Via Roma 39, Bormio (Sondrio)

Salumeria Saronni
Corso Mazzini 38, Cremona

Gastronomia Gatti
Darfo (Brescia)

Salumeria Carra
Via Tassoni 1, Mantua

Cheeses
Ol Formager
Piazzale Oberdan 2, Bergamo

Gastronomia Bonetti
Via Fratelli Dandolo2, Brescia

Nuova Casa del Formaggio
Via Roma 81, Lecco

Fratelli Ciapponi
Piazza 3 novembre 23, Morbegno
(Sondrio)

Panettone

The origins and etymology of this cake, which by now has become emblematic of Christmas, are unknown. What is known is that it was created in Milan, and that it soon conquered the tables of the rest of Italy. Delicious on its own, it also lends itself to myriad variations.

Although Milan was its birthplace, panettone has now become the national Christmas cake par excellence, and practically every Italian household consumes at least one during the holiday season. Tradition has it that it came into being by mistake: a baker's boy accidentally poured a cake batter with candied fruit and sultana raisins onto some bread dough, and so created a cake that became the pride of the town. There are also numerous possible interpretations regarding the etymology of the name. Some say that it simply means 'big bread' (pane = bread, tone = the suffix denoting bigness); others that it comes from Pan de Toni (Tony's bread), from the name of the first baker who made it; and others that it might originate from pan de ton (important bread), meaning a bread that was served on important occasions. In any case, small panettone used to be eaten in Milan during the year, while the big ones were baked for Christmas in memory of the 'pan grande' (big bread) that the head of the family used to slice on Christmas Day and give to his wife and children in order to insure good health and luck.

CHARACTERISTICS
Panettone is made of a dough which undergoes several risings, and to which is

added melted butter, sugar dissolved in water, beaten eggs, and egg yolks. Sultana raisins and pieces of candied fruit are worked into the dough, which is then kneaded until it becomes smooth and homogeneous. It is left to rise for a long time and then baked in the oven.

STORING PANETTONE
Panettone should be kept in its original wrapping paper and box in a cool place once it has been opened. It should be warmed slightly before serving so that the butter in the cake softens, thus making it more delicate to the taste.

BUYING PANETTONE

Many different kinds of panettone are available during the Christmas season, some produced by big companies, and others with lesser-known names. Those made in bakeries are usually the most expensive, but they are also the best. Generally, the well-known name brands are dependable and guarantee good quality; it is risky to buy lesser-known ones since they may be of inferior quality. One should therefore be careful not to be attracted by cheaper products inasmuch as they generally do not contain quality ingredients. Rather than buying those products, wait until after Christmas to buy a good panettone when the shops often put their leftover stock on sale.

SERVING SUGGESTIONS

A *fixed presence at toast-making time during the holidays, panettone has also won fans on non-festive occasions. Loved by the young and old alike, it is delicious for breakfast, or combined with other ingredients as a dessert or as a snack.*

Make a custard filling, folding in the necessary gelatin, and add raisins, candied fruit, and cubed panettone. Distribute in individual dessert cups and chill for several hours in the refrigerator before serving.

Dissolve 1 part sugar in 2 parts freshly squeezed orange juice. Boil for 4 minutes and then add 3 tablespoons of orange liqueur for every cup of liquid. Cool and serve with panettone.

Cut the panettone into equal-sized slices and use these instead of ladyfingers or sponge cake in making a charlotte.

Buy a small panettone, 8 inches in diameter, slice it horizontally into disks less than an inch thick, and top each of these individual portions with a dollop of whipped cream mixed with chopped marrons glacés.

Crumble leftover panettone and soften it in warm milk. Add 1 or 2 beaten eggs and enough flour to give the mixture consistency. Drop by the spoonful into hot oil and fry. Sprinkle these panettone fritters with sugar and serve.

THE RIGHT WINE

It has become common to uncork a bottle of dry spumante or champagne when panettone is served, but this choice of wine is questionable. First, a dessert should harmonize with the wine that accompanies it: a sweet wine enhances a sweet dessert. Thus a dry wine will take on an almost bitter taste and alter the flavor of the panettone. Second, it is bet-ter not to serve yeast-based cakes like panettone with fermented wines like spumante. Therefore, choose a sweet wine like Moscato d'Asti, Albana di Romagna, or Verduzzo di Ramandolo.

If, however, you want to make toasts with a sparkling wine, then choose a good Asti or an extra-dry Cartizze (that is, slightly sweet), or a Spumante Classico Demi-sec or a Champagne Demi-sec.

IN SEARCH OF PANETTONE

Commercially produced panettone is available everywhere. For those who wish to taste artisanal products, there is a wide choice of bakeries, particularly in a city like Milan. The Pasticceria Ambrosiana is one of the best in Milan, as is the Pasticceria Cova (some say this is where panettone was first made), as well as that of Sant'Ambroeus. The Pasticceria Marchesi makes a delicious panettone Filled with a delicate *crème chantilly* for those who prefer panettone with a filling.

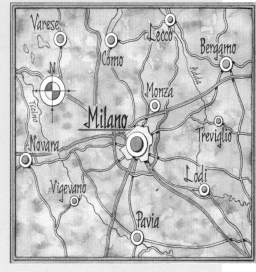

TRENTINO-ALTO ADIGE

A border gastronomy

There are historical reasons for the differences between the typical dishes of Trentino and those of Alto Adige, which are much closer to Austrian and German culinary traditions. The gastronomy of the former Austrian South Tyrol includes a variety of pork products, sauerkraut, dumplings, and meats, often combined with sweet sauces, while that of the province of Trento is based primarily on polenta, potatoes, soups, and wonderful cakes filled with jams or dried fruit.

That the cuisine of the Alto Adige is not very Italian is confirmed by the fact that pasta and rice are served as side dishes and not as first courses accompanied by different sauces. Soups made with barley, sauerkraut, meat, and, above all, *canederli*, or dumplings, are preferred to pasta as a first course. The dumplings are made of dried bread, milk, flour, and eggs to which are added speck, liver, vegetables, or herbs. Foods like these reflect the culture of the *masi*, the age-old farms of the Val d'Ultimo (Ultental), where the inhabitants are used to producing everything they need to lead a completely independent existence. They have their own land to farm, their own mill for flour, their own woods for building materials, horses for transporting the wood,

Above: Masi in Val di Rabbi, connected to the Val d'Ultimo by the passo di Rabbi. Top: Strudel, typical cake of Trentino.

and so on. In the Val d'Ultimo, there are other things to try besides the dumplings: goulash made with game, salsify soup with toasted *panpepato*, and especially the local desserts: *krapfen* (cream puffs filled with ground poppy seeds), strudels, *granten nudel* (made of flour, yeast, blueberry jam, and vanilla cream), and *kaiser schmarrn* (a sweet omelette made with blueberry jam).

For a tasty contrast, visit the Val Venosta, which extends from the sources of the Adige River to Merano in a landscape of medieval fiefs. It is worth stopping at Sluderno to admire the Castel Coira (Churburg), one of the region's most important examples of castle architecture.

On the other hand, at Merano, after a visit to the cathedral, castle, and Via dei

Portici in the old part of the city, one can indulge in a typical South Tyrolean dinner: *camoscio alla tirolese* (chamois Tyrolese style, in which the meat is marinated for five or six days in wine, vinegar, onions, celery, bay leaves, cloves, and ginger, and then cooked in red wine and sour cream), venison with blueberry sauce, beef goulash, or veal shank, and vegetables like red cabbage Merano style (that is, cooked with onions and Renette apples). In keeping with the theme of castles, a visit should be made to the Castle of Toblino, built on an island in the lake of the same name, not far from Trento. On August 9, an elegant dinner is held in costume at this picturesque castle, which is privately owned. Traditional dishes based on ancient recipes are served.

In Trentino, polenta plays a leading role in the menu, and it is always a rather special polenta. Potatoes, cheese, bacon, or sautéed onions are added to the standard coarse-grained cornmeal; or a black polenta is made

The characteristic Via dei Portici in Merano, in the old part of the city.

with buckwheat flour, and sauced with anchovies cooked in butter. This dark flour is also a basic ingredient of *smacafam*, a traditional country dish which, as its name indicates, is guaranteed to sate anyone's hunger. It consists of a rather creamy polenta which is poured into a greased baking dish and covered with a layer of sliced sausages. A sweet version of *smacafam* is traditionally prepared during carnival, substituting pine nuts, walnuts, raisins, and aniseed for the sausages.

Another popular carnival sweet is *chifelini*, made with a potato and flour dough and filled with jam. These delicious sweets are especially good served with a cup of hot cocoa and whipped cream. On Christmas Day, *zelten* is to be found on holiday tables. It is a rich cake filled with dried figs, raisins, dates, candied citron, walnuts, and pine nuts and covered with honey, almonds, and candied fruit.

View of the Castel Coira, at Sluderno, in Val Venosta.

61

Antipasto di mele
(Apple Appetizers with Beef Tartare)

Preparation time
30 minutes plus
resting time

Difficulty
medium

Serves 4
- 3 ½ ounces lean ground beef
- ½ cup fresh-squeezed lemon juice
- salt and pepper
- 1 clove garlic, halved
- 4 Red Delicious apples
- 1 head curly endive
- 1 tablespoon extra virgin olive oil

Soft, aromatic white wine. Recommended:
- Alto Adige Sauvignon
- Cortese dei Colli Tortonesi

1 Mix the meat with 2 tablespoons of the lemon juice and season with pepper. Push the garlic into the center of the meat. Cover and let sit for an hour or so. In the meantime, wash and dry the curly endive, cut it into strips, and wrap it in a towel.

2 Wash and dry the apples. Cut the top off each one as follows: place the apple on the work table and, at about ³/₅ of its height, insert a sharp, pointed knife at an angle, and cut around the apple in zig-zag fashion as shown in the photograph.

3 Separate the two pieces and sprinkle the cut edges with lemon juice. With a melon baller, remove the pulp from inside the apples. Remove any core material and brush the apple balls with lemon juice. Smooth out the insides of the apples.

4 Just before serving, remove the garlic from the meat. Mix the meat with salt, the olive oil, and the apple balls. Fill the bottoms of the apples with this mixture and cover them.

5 Arrange the filled apples on beds of curly endive on individual plates. Serve immediately.

Canederli

(Dumplings)

Preparation time
30 minutes

Cooking time
30 minutes

Difficulty
medium

Serves 4

- 5 ounces stale bread without crust
- 15 tablespoons hot milk
- 1 tablespoon extra virgin olive oil
- 3 ½ ounces bacon or speck, diced
- 1 small onion, minced
- 2 ounces sausage meat, skin removed, crumbled
- 1 egg
- nutmeg
- 1 fistful parsley leaves, chopped
- flour
- 4 cups meat broth
- grated Parmesan cheese to taste
- freshly ground black pepper

Rosé wine.
Recommended:
- Alto Adige Lagrein Rosato
- Arborea Sangiovese Rosato

1 In a mixing bowl, crumble the bread into the hot milk and mash together.

2 In a small skillet, heat the oil. Add the bacon and cook over low heat until it is soft but not crisp. Add the onion and cook until transparent. Add the bacon and onion to the bread and milk. Add the sausage, egg, a pinch of nutmeg, the parsley, and enough flour to make a soft mixture, mixing it thoroughly.

3 Bring the meat broth to a boil. Wet your hands and shape the mixture into round balls about the size of an egg (there should be about a dozen). Drop the balls gently into the boiling broth and simmer them over low heat for about 15 minutes.

4 Serve the dumplings in the broth, sprinkling them with abundant grated Parmesan cheese and freshly ground pepper.

The *canederli*, or *Knödel*, can also be served as a side dish with boiled or stewed meat, or alone accompanied by sauerkraut.

Arrosto di maiale alle prugne
(Roast Pork with Prunes)

Preparation time
30 minutes

Cooking time
1 ¼ hours

Difficulty
medium

Serves 4
- ½ pound pitted prunes
- hard cider
- 2 to 2 ½ pounds pork loin
- salt and pepper
- 4 tablespoons extra virgin olive oil
- 1 bay leaf, broken into pieces
- 6 cloves
- 2 tablespoons butter
- 1 teaspoon mustard

Full-bodied red wine.
Recommended:
- Teroldego Rotaliano
- Vino Nobile di Montepulciano

1. Rinse the prunes, place them in a small bowl, cover them with cider, and let them soak for about 30 minutes. Preheat the oven to 425°F.

2. With a sharp knife, cut the meat away from the ribs, leaving them bare.

3. Using a long knife with a rounded tip, open the meat like a book, first with a horizontal cut, and then with an oblique one, so as to reach the bone near the ribs.

4. Place one row of prunes under the bone, then fold the meat back towards the ribs and place another row there. Chop the remaining prunes and set aside.

5. Roll the meat back onto itself, tying it with white string between the ribs. Season the roast with salt and pepper. Place it in a roasting pan, drizzle the oil over it, and cover it with pieces of bay leaf and the cloves.
Roast for at least an hour, basting it from time to time with the pan juices. The roast is done when you prick it with a skewer and its juices run clear.

6. When the roast is done, brown the butter in a small skillet, and stir in the mustard. Add the remaining prunes and a tablespoon or two of cider and cook over low heat for 2 minutes.

7. Transfer the roast to a warm serving platter. Strain the juices from the roasting pan and add them to the skillet, stirring well. Untie the meat and slice it. Pour the prune sauce over it and serve.

The cider typically used in this dish would be hard cider, or fermented apple juice. Dry white wine may be substituted, in which case add a sliced apple to the prunes when they are soaking.

Bozner Schnitten

(Chocolate Slices)

Preparation time
30 minutes plus
chilling time

Cooking time
30 minutes

Difficulty
easy

Serves 6 to 8
- $^1/_2$ cup butter, at
  room temperature
- $^1/_2$ cup sugar
- 3 $^1/_2$ ounces
  semisweet
  chocolate, melted
- 3 eggs
- 1 $^1/_4$ cups flour
- 1 $^1/_2$ teaspoons
  baking powder
- 6 tablespoons plus
  2 teaspoons milk
- $^1/_2$ cup blueberry
  or plum preserves
- whipped cream

1 Butter a 9 x 5-inch loaf pan and preheat the oven to 425°F. In a bowl, beat the butter with the sugar. Add the chocolate and the eggs, one at a time, beating well after each addition. Sift the flour and baking powder into the bowl, and then pour the milk in slowly, mixing constantly.

2 Pour the mixture into the loaf pan and bake in the middle of the oven for 30 minutes. Remove from the oven, invert the cake onto a rack and let it cool. When the cake is cool, cut it in half hori-zontally. Spread jam on the lower layer and replace the top. Cover the cake with whipped cream using a pastry bag or a spatula so that it is about $^1/_2$ inch thick, and make lines on it using a fork. Serve the cake sliced.

Blueberry or plum preserves complement the chocolate nicely, but any flavor preserves may be used.

TRENTINO-ALTO ADIGE

SPECIALTIES

Antipasti (Appetizers)
Carn salada, Lucanica, Sisam, Speck.

First courses
Canederli, Caronzei, Gnocchi alle ortiche, Orzotto, Schlutzkrapfen, Strangolapreti, Zuppa d'orzo, Zuppa di funghi.

Entrées
Capriolo con polenta, Gulash di vitello, Stinco di maiale al forno, Tafelspitz, Tonco di pontesel.

Desserts
Kaiserschmarren, Omelette con frutti di bosco, Strudel, Torta di carote, Torta di fregoloti, Zelten.

TYPICAL RESTAURANTS

Belvedere
Via Serafini 2, Arco (TN)
Tel. 0464/516144, Closed Wednesday
Prices: Lire 45,000

Stroblhof
Via Piganò 25, Appiano (BZ)
Tel. 0471/662250, Closed Monday
Prices: Lire 60,000

Zur Rose
Via J. Innerhofer 2, Appiano (BZ)
Tel. 0471/662249, Closed Sunday and Monday at noon
Prices: Lire 90,000/100,000

Il Picchio
Piazza Mercato - Terme di Comano Bleggio - Lomaso (TN)
Tel. 0465/702170, Closed Wednesday
Prices: Lire 50,000

Castel Toblino
Via Caffaro 1, Calavino (TN)
Tel. 0461/864036, Closed Tuesday
Prices: Lire 60,000

Mildas
Via Antonio Rosmini 7, Giustino (TN)
Tel 0465/502104, Closed Monday and Sunday
Prices: Lire 65,000

Steinbock
Via Flora 9, Glorenza (BZ)
Tel. 0473/831495, Closed Monday
Prices: Lire 50,000

Montana
Via Cima Nova 31, Luserna (TN)
Tel. 0464/789704, Closed Thursday
Prices: Lire 45,000

Malga Montagnoli
in Montagnoli
Madonna di Campiglio (TN)
Tel. 0465/443355, Closed October, November, May, and June
Prices: Lire 60,000

Conte Ramponi
Piazza San Marco 38, Malè (TN)
Tel. 0463/901989, Closed Monday, always open during high season
Prices: Lire 60,000

Malga Panna
Via Costalunga 29, Moena
Tel. 0462/573489, Closed Tuesday, always open during high season
Prices: Sampling Lire 70,000, menu Lire 95,000

Dorfnerhof
in Casignano 5, Montagna (BZ)
Tel. 0471/819798, Closed Monday
Prices: Lire 25,000/35,000

Patscheiderhof
in Signato 178, Renon (BZ)
Tel. 0471/365267, Closed Tuesday
Prices: Lire 55,000

Borgo
Via Garibaldi 13, Rovereto (TN)
Tel. 0464/436300, Closed Sunday evening and Monday
Prices: Lire 100,000

Jagerhof
Via Passo del Giovo 80
San Leonardo in Passiria (BZ)
Tel. 0473/656250, Closed Monday
Prices: Lire 50,000/60,000

Moleta
Via Nazionale 28, Spiazzo - Borzago (TN)
Tel. 0465/801059, Closed Monday
Prices: Lire 50,000/60,000

Beef goulash

Mezzosoldo
in Mortaso, Spiazzo (TN)
Tel. 0465/801067, Closed Thursday
Prices: Lire 65,000

Piè di Castello
in Cologna, Tenno (TN)
Tel. 0464/521065, Closed Tuesday
Prices: Lire 75,000

Al Vo'
Vicolo del Vo' 11, Trento
Tel. 0461/985374, Closed Sunday
Prices: Lire 50,000

Due Spade
Via Don A. Rizzi 11, Trento
Tel. 0461/234343
Closed Sunday and Monday at noon
Prices: Lire 95,000

WINES
White
Chardonnay, Gewürztraminer, Müller-Thurgau, Nosiola, Pinot bianco/Weißburgunder, Pinot grigio/Rulander, Riesling Italico/Welschriesling, Riesling Renano/Rheinriesling, Sylvaner, Terlaner, Terlaner Sauvignon, Valdadige, Veltliner.

Rosé
Lagrein Kretzer, Moscato rosa.

Red
Cabernet, Cabernet Sauvignon, Kalterer See, Lagrein Dunkel, Marzemino, Merlot, Pinot nero/Blauburgunder, Schiava/Vernatsch, St. Magdalener, Teroldego Rotaliano.

Kaiserschmarrn

Dessert wine
Moscato giallo/Goldenmuskateller, Vino Santo.

CHEESES
Casolet, Graukäse, Hochpustertaler Poina, Puzzone di Moena, Spressa Toblach, Vezzena.

SHOPPING FOR TYPICAL PRODUCTS
Wines
Enoteca Vinum
Via Brennero 28
Bozen

Enoteca Schondoerf
Via Centrale 55
Bruneck (Bozen)

Vinothek
Via dell'Oro
Kaltern (Bozen)

Cantina Sociale di Toblino
Sarche di Calavino (Trento)

Cold Meats
Macelleria Sighel
Via C. Battisti 35
Baselga di Piné (Trento)

Salumificio Riccadonna
Bleggio Superiore (Trento)

Salumeria Bernardi
Via Centrale 36
Bruneck (Bozen)

Famiglia Cooperativa
Via Regina Elena
Caderzone (Trento)

Mario Masé
Via Nazionale
Strembo (Trento)

Theo Nigg
Piazza Karl Atz 3
Terlan (Bozen)

Famiglia Cooperativa
in Saone
Tione (Trento)

Vivaldelli
Via Ballino 29
Varone di Riva del Garda (Trento)

Cheeses
Caseificio Sociale
Cavalese (Trento)

Latteria Sociale
Lagundo (Bozen)

Caseificio Sociale
Via Fiamme Gialle 34
Predazzo (Trento)

Degust
Via Katerina Lanz 14
Rio in Pusteria (Bozen)

Latteria Sociale
Via castello I
San Candido (Bozen)

Mario Masé
Via Nazionale
Strembo (Trento)

VENETO

A *feast of colors with rice and vegetables*

A view of the walls and moat of Castelfranco Veneto, in the province of Treviso.

Everyone has seen photographs of the famous Carnival in Venice with people in magnificent costumes parading across Piazza San Marco and along the canals of this most beautiful and romantic city. And everyone recognizes the colorful diamond-patched costume of Harlequin, the famous Commedia dell'Arte character from Venice.

Like Harlequin's suit, the Venetian cuisine is also a patchwork of brilliant colors, from the red radicchio of Treviso and Verona to the green asparagus of Bassano del Grappa

and the fresh peas flavoring white risottos, from the warm brown tones of beans and chicken livers to the golden ones of polenta. The simple addition of cuttlefish ink turns the whiteness of rice into black. Is the table lacking yellow or orange? A purée of squash and a platter of biscuits made with yellow semolina flour and sultana raisins will take care of that.

Red radicchio of Verona and a bowl of *risotto ricco alla padovana.*

Along with the variety of colors, a variety of interpretations may be given to a particular dish. Every town has its own special way of cooking *baccalà* or salted cod: *alla vicentina* (Vicenza), *mantecato alla veneziana* (Venice) and *alla trevigiana* (Treviso). In any case, it really isn't salted cod, but rather *stoccafisso* or air-dried cod. Risottos are seasoned with the fennel or zucchini of Venice, the *luganega* sausage of Treviso, the tripe of Vicenza, the asparagus of Bassano del Grappa, or the chicken of Padua.

When it comes to meat, each locality is autonomous. Geese, chickens, and capons reign around Padua; kid and venison around Belluno. In Vicenza, they eat *polenta* and *osei* (small birds), in Verona horse meat is stewed

as *pastissada*, and in Venice a famous dish is *fegato di vitello alla sbrodega* (calf's liver and onions).

This individuality holds true for vegetables, too. At Treviso the fair of red radicchio is held in December, while the residents of Castelfranco Veneto celebrate their red-and-white-streaked radicchio the week before Christmas. Treviso is an extraordinarily captivating city with canals crossing narrow streets lined with medieval buildings. Among the many things to see is the Pinacoteca Luigi Bailo, which houses an impressive collection of paintings by Titian, Lotto, and Tiepolo.

For those who prefer nature to cities, the Veneto can offer the Pearl of the Dolomites, Cortina d'Ampezzo, where you can hike or ski in a landscape that includes some of the most spectacular peaks of the eastern Alps. And a plate of *cassunziei ampessani* (ravioli filled with ricotta cheese and beets and seasoned with butter, poppy seeds, and Parmesan cheese) will restore energy to any sports lover.

It is a good idea to visit Bassano del Grappa during April or May in order to participate in the Asparagus Exhibition and Contest. That is the ideal season to enjoy a visit to the Castle and Old Bridge, which was destroyed at least eight times in the last six centuries when the River Brenta flooded, and which the people of Bassano duly rebuilt in wood. Nearby Marostica flaunts its special product, cherries, in May and June. However, September is a better month for a visit, for every other year the famous game of chess is played on the chessboard in the piazza with local people, dressed in magnificent costumes, impersonating the chess pieces. To continue with the seasonal itinerary, a visit to Padua in autumn is not a bad idea. This city, famous for its art and university, welcomes guests in one of the most beautiful cafés of Italy, the nineteenth-century Caffè Pedrocchi, which is still the center of the city's intellectual life. After tea in one of its lovely rooms, the afternoon can be spent admiring Giotto's famous frescoes in the Cappella degli Scrovegni. The evening meal could include an excellent *pasta e fagioli* (pasta and beans) or a *risotto ricco alla padovana*, whose ingredients – fresh peas, veal, chicken livers, onion, and celery – attest to the richness of the dish.

Tagliatelle all'agordina
(Noodles with Dried Fruit and Nuts)

Preparation time
30 minutes

Cooking time
30 minutes

Difficulty
easy

Serves 6
- ¹/₄ cup sultana raisins
- 3 apples
- lemon juice
- 1 1-pound package dried tagliatelle (egg noodles)
- 6 tablespoons butter
- 1 cup shelled walnut halves, chopped
- 6 dried figs, chopped
- poppy seeds

Soft, aromatic white wine.
Recommended:
- Piave Verduzzo
- Cortese di Gavi

1 Soak the raisins in tepid water until plumped; drain. Peel, core, and slice the apples, and sprinkle with the lemon juice so they will not discolor.

2 Preheat the oven to 425°F. Butter a baking dish. Boil the *tagliatelle* in salted boiling water. When the noodles are *al dente*, drain them, place in a bowl, and toss with 3 tablespoons of the butter. In the prepared dish, make layers of the pasta and the fruits and nuts. Melt the remaining 3 tablespoons of butter. Cover the top layer with the poppy seeds and the melted butter. Bake for about 20 minutes. Serve immediately.

This unique dish is usually served on Christmas Eve in many of the towns in the Valle d'Agordo in the province of Belluno.

Baccalà mantecato

(Creamy Codfish)

Preparation time
20 minutes plus
resting time

Cooking time
30 minutes

Difficulty
easy

Serves 4
- 1 ¹/₂ pounds
  air-dried codfish,
  soaked
- about 1 cup extra
  virgin olive oil
- salt and pepper
- 1 fistful parsley
  leaves, chopped
- 1 clove garlic,
  chopped
- toasted slices of
  polenta (see recipe
  on page 50)

Dry white wine.
Recommended:
- Durello
- Colli del
  Trasimeno Bianco

1 Place the codfish in a large saucepan, cover it with cold water, and bring it slowly to a boil. Salt slightly, skim the surface, cover, and simmer for 20 minutes. Remove from the heat and leave the fish in the cooking liquid for another 20 minutes.

2 Drain and skin the fish, remove any bones, and flake it. Place it in a mortar. Using a pestle, pound the fish until it is smooth. Pour a thin stream of olive oil into the mortar, stirring energetically with a wooden spoon until the fish has absorbed the oil and the mixture is white and fluffy.

3 Season the fish mixture with salt and pepper. Stir in the parsley and garlic. Shape the *baccalà mantecato* into a mound, and serve surrounded by slices of hot toasted polenta.

Radicio in saor
(Marinated Radicchio)

Preparation time
20 minutes plus
resting time

Cooking time
20 minutes

Difficulty
easy

Serves 6
- 1 tablespoon sultana raisins
- 6 bunches radicchio of Treviso
- 8 tablespoons extra virgin olive oil
- 1 large onion, very thinly sliced
- salt and pepper
- 1 tablespoon pine nuts
- 2 cloves
- cinnamon
- grated zest of lemon
- ½ cup red wine vinegar
- 1 cup dry white wine
- 6 tablespoons mascarpone or ricotta cheese

*Sparkling wine.
Recommended:*
- Prosecco di Conegliano-Valdobbiadene
- Spumante di Franciacorta

1 Soak the raisins in lukewarm water until plumped; drain and reserve. Remove the outer leaves from the radicchio, taking care to keep the bunch intact. Cut each bunch lengthwise into quarters, and wash and dry. Place the radicchio quarters in a skillet with 4 tablespoons of the oil, salt, and pepper, and cook them covered, turning them, over high heat for 5 minutes or until they are wilted. Transfer them to a large serving platter.

2 In the skillet, heat the remaining 4 tablespoons of oil. Add the onions and a pinch of salt and sauté until the onions are wilted. Add the raisins, pine nuts, cloves, a pinch of cinnamon, and the lemon zest. Cook for a minute or two. Add the wine and vinegar and simmer for a few more minutes.

3 Pour the mixture over the radicchio and let marinate for 24 hours. Place the mascarpone in a bowl and stir it with a wooden spoon. Distribute the radicchio in six individual plates and top with the mascarpone.

Fagioli alla chioggiotta
(Beans, Chioggia Style)

Preparation time
20 minutes

Cooking time
50 minutes

Difficulty
easy

*Light red wine.
Recommended:*
- Merlot del Piave
- Morellino di Scansano

Serves 4
- 2 pounds fresh borlotti beans in shells
- 1 bay leaf
- 6 tablespoons extra virgin olive oil
- salt and pepper
- 1 onion, chopped
- 1 clove garlic, chopped
- ½ cup red wine vinegar
- ¾ pound tomatoes (about 3 medium), chopped

1 Shell the beans, place them into a pressure cooker with water to cover, the bay leaf, and 1 tablespoon of the oil. Cook for 18 minutes from the time it starts to steam. When the beans are cooked, add salt and mix. Drain, reserving the liquid, and set aside.

2 In a large skillet, heat 3 tablespoons of the oil. Add the onions and garlic and sauté until transparent. Mix in the drained beans. Add the vinegar and as soon as it is absorbed add the tomatoes together with a ladleful of the cooking liquid from the beans. Cook over medium heat for 10 minutes, mixing carefully with a wooden spoon.

3 Add the remaining 2 tablespoons oil, and season with salt and freshly ground pepper. Mix and serve the beans hot; they are also good at room temperature.

Fegato alla veneziana
(Liver, Venetian Style)

Preparation time
10 minutes

Cooking time
30 minutes

Difficulty
easy

Serves 4
- 2 tablespoons butter
- 4 tablespoons extra virgin olive oil
- 1 large onion, thinly sliced
- salt and pepper
- 1 pound calf's liver, cut into very thin strips
- 1 tablespoon chopped parsley

Light red wine.
Recommended:
- Cabernet di Lison Pramaggiore
- Cabernet Sauvignon di Grave del Friuli

1 In a nonstick pan, heat butter and olive oil. Add the onions and salt. Cover and cook over very low heat for about 25 minutes so that the onion softens without coloring.

2 Increase the heat to high and add the liver. Sauté quickly, stirring constantly. Remove from the heat, adjust the seasoning with salt and pepper, add the parsley, and serve.

This recipe is also called *fegato alla sbrodega*. It can be accompanied with bread fried in butter, mashed potatoes, or hot polenta.

Tortion
(Strudel)

Preparation time
30 minutes

Cooking time
30 minutes

Difficulty
medium

Serves 4 to 6
- $1/3$ cup sultana raisins
- white wine
- $1/2$ cup shelled almonds
- 6 shelled walnuts
- $1/4$ cup candied citron
- 1 tablespoon pine nuts
- 3 medium apples
- lemon juice
- 1 1-pound package frozen puff pastry, thawed
- 4 tablespoons sugar

Light sweet wine.
Recommended:
- Colli Euganei Moscato
- Vernaccia di Serrapetrona

1 Rinse the raisins and soak them in white wine until plumped, then drain. Drop the almonds in boiling water. After 3 minutes, drain them and skin them. Chop the raisins and almonds together with the walnuts, candied citron, and pine nuts. Peel and core the apples, slice them thinly, and sprinkle them with lemon juice so they do not discolor.

2 Preheat the oven to 425°F. Roll the puff pastry into a rectangle about $1/4$ inch thick. Dry the apples and distribute them uniformly over the pastry together with the other fruits and nuts, leaving a border of about $1/2$ inch all around. Sprinkle with 3 tablespoons of the sugar. Roll the puff pastry on itself so that it forms a roll. Press the edges together so that the filling does not fall out during baking.

3 Sprinkle a baking sheet with water and place the roll on it, curving it into the shape of a half moon. Brush it with water and sprinkle the top with the remaining tablespoon of sugar. Bake for about 30 minutes or until the *tortion* is golden brown in color. Serve sliced, either warm or at room temperature.

VENETO

SPECIALTIES

Antipasti (Appetizers)
Soppressa all'aceto balsamico, Sarde in saor.

First courses
Pasta e fasioi, Bigoli in salsa, Risi e bisi, Sopa coada, Risotto alla marinara, Risotto con i caparozzoli.

Entrées
Castraure fritte, Marsoni dell'Astico, Fegato alla veneziana, Baccalà alla vicentina, Poenta e s'ciosi, Faraona in salsa peverada, Torresani allo spiedo, Moleche fritte, Pastisada de caval.

Desserts
Baicoli, Crostoli, Ciosota, Pinza.

TYPICAL RESTAURANTS

Montanella
Via Costa 33, Arquà Petrarca
Tel. 0429/718200, Closed Tuesday evening
and Wednesday
Prices: Lire 40,000/60,000

Trattoria degli amici
Via Quirina 4, Arquà Polesine
Tel. 0425/91045-91187
Closed Wednesday
and in summer Saturday and Sunday at
noon
Prices: Lire 50,000

Aurora
Via Ebene 17, Asiago
Tel. 0424/462469, Closed Monday
Prices: Lire 50,000

Ca' Derton
Piazza D'Annunzio 11, Asolo
Tel. 0423/529648, Closed Monday
Prices: Lire 55,000

Aurora
Piazzetta San Severo, Bardolino
Tel. 045/7210038, Closed Monday
Prices: Lire 50,000

Melograno
Via Chiesa 35, Bassano del Grappa
Tel 0424/502593, Closed Monday
Prices: Lire 60,000

Osteria Penzo
Calle Larga Bersaglio 526, Chioggia
Tel. 041/400992, Closed Tuesday, and
in winter Monday evening
Prices: Lire 60,000

Ospitale
in Ospitale, Cortina d'Ampezzo
Tel. 0436/4585, Closed Monday
Prices: Lire 45,000/60,000

Pino
in Giare 2, Garda
Tel. 045/7255694, Closed Monday
Prices: Lire 20,000/30,000

Il Vecchio Marina
Via Roma Destra 120c, Jesolo
Tel. 0421/370645, Closed Monday
Prices: Lire 50,000/65,000

Il Porticciolo
Lungolago Marconi 22, Lazise

Risotto del bisato

Tel. 045/7580254, Closed Tuesday
Prices: Lire 60,000

L'Anfora
Via dei Soncin, Padua
Tel. 049/656629, Closed Sunday
and Monday at noon
Prices: Lire 40,000

San Pietro
Via San Pietro 95, Padua
Tel. 049/8760330, Closed Sunday
Prices: Lire 50,000/60,000

Combattente
San Benedetto, Strada Bergamini 60
Peschiera del Garda
Tel. 045/7550410, Closed Monday
Prices: Lire 50,000/60,000

Tavernetta Dante Dai trevisani
Corso del Popolo 212, Rovigo
Tel. 0425/26386, Closed Sunday
Prices: Lire 55,000

All'Antenna
Via Raga Alta 4, Schio
Tel. 0445/529812, Closed Tuesday
Prices: Lire 50,000/60,000

Beccherie
Piazza Ancillotto 11, Treviso
Tel. 0422/540871, Closed Sunday evening
and Monday
Prices: Lire 55,000

Toni del Spin
Via inferiore 7, Treviso
Tel. 0422/543829, Closed Sunday
and Monday at noon
Prices: Lire 45,000

Hostaria a le Bele
Via Maso 11, Valdagno
Tel. 0445/970270, Closed Monday
at noon and Tuesday at noon
Prices: Lire 55,000

Al Bacareto
San Marco-San Samuele 3447, Venice
Tel. 041/5289336, Closed Saturday
evening and Sunday
Prices: Lire 60,000

Alle Testiere
Castello, 5801-Calle del Mondo Novo,
Venice
Tel. 041/5227220, Closed Sunday
Prices: Lire 65,000

Antica Trattoria alla Maddalena
Mazzorbo 7c, Venice
Tel. 041/730151, Closed Thursday
Prices: Lire 30,000/45,000

Covo
Campiello della Pescaria, Castello 3968
Venice
Tel. 041/5223812, Closed Wednesday and
Thursday
Prices: Lire 50,000/110,000

Fiore
San Polo, Calle del Scaleter 2202, Venice
Tel. 041/721308, Closed Sunday and
Monday
Prices: Lire 110,000/120,000

Fried Cream

Alla Stueta
Via del Redentore 4b, Verona
Tel. 045/80322462, Closed Monday and
Tuesday at noon
Prices: Lire 50,000

Ciccarelli
Frazione Madonna di Dossobuono,
Verona
Tel. 045/953986, Closed Friday evening
and Saturday
Prices: Lire 40,000

Tre Marchetti
Vicolo Tre Marchetti 19B, Verona
Tel. 045/8030463, Closed Sunday
except July and August

WINES
White
Bianco di Custoza, Breganze, Cartizze,
Chardonnay, Colli di Conegliano, Colli
Euganei, Gambellara, Garganega,
Lessini Durello, Pinot bianco, Pinot
grigio, Recioto di Gambellara, Riesling
Italico, Sauvignon, Soave, Tocai,
Verduzzo, Vespaiolo di Breganze.

Red
Amarone, Bardolino, Breganze,
Cabernet, Cabernet Franc, Cabernet
Sauvignon, Colli di Conegliano, Colli
Euganei, Merlot, Pinot nero, Raboso del
Piave, Recioto, Refosco dal peduncolo
rosso, Valpolicella.

Dessert wine
Moscato, Torchiato di Fregona,
Torcolato, Vin Santo di Gambellara.

CHEESES
Asiago, Cansiglio, Comelico, Formaio
embriago, Morlacco, Pressato, Stracon.

SHOPPING FOR TYPICAL PRODUCTS
Wines
Enoteca del Soave
Piazza Salvo d'Acquisto 1, Monteforte
d'Alpone (Verona)

Enogamma
Via San Simone 32, Thiene (Vicenza)

Cantinone
Dorsoduro 992, Venice

Brigliadoro
Via S. Michele alla Porta 4, Verona

Cold Meats
Gastronomia Sgarbossa
Via Browning 141, Asolo (Vicenza)

Salumificio Pagliarin
in Villatora, Via XX Settembre 54
Saonara (Padua)

Salumificio Ballarin
Via Pordello 160, Treporti (Venice)

Cheeses
Caseificio Zanchetta
Via F. Filzi 1, Casale sul Sile
(Treviso)

Cooperativa Produttori Latte Schio
Via Vicenza 20, Schio (Vicenza)

Pandoro

Verona's traditional holiday specialty vies with the Milanese panettone as Italy's favorite cake for Christmas dinner.
Soft, fragrant, and delicate in taste, it can boast of ancient traditions and illustrious ancestors like the cake covered with flakes of pure gold that sparkled on the patrician tables of the Venetian Republic centuries ago.

Pandoro, or golden bread, made with egg yolks, sugar, butter, flour, and yeast, is traditionally served on Christmas Day. It probably originates from two different cakes: nadalin, *which is not very well known but still can be found, and* pan de oro. Nadalin *is a traditional Veronese cake prepared by mixing flour, sugar, butter, eggs, and yeast. The dough is left to rise for a few hours, and then placed in a mold and baked in the oven. It is served covered with vanilla sugar or toasted pine nuts.* Pan de oro, *on the other hand, was covered with shavings of pure gold and graced the tables of the aristocracy; obviously it no longer exists today.*
As for pandoro, its name also reflects the characteristic golden color conferred on it by egg yolks. Its shape, a conic trunk, is marked by wide ribs that give the cake, when seen from above, the shape of a star with eight points. The preparation of this cake is rather complicated, including three risings, between which different ingredients are added. First, an egg yolk is mixed with flour, sugar, and

BUYING PANDORO

Since pandoro is produced industrially and therefore available everywhere, it is best to play it safe and avoid unknown or very inexpensive brands.
As with all packaged foods, it is always a good idea to check the expiration date and make sure that the wrapping is intact.

yeast. After two hours of rising, additional egg yolks are added with more flour, sugar, and butter. After a second rising of two hours, more of the same ingredients are added, and after the third two-hour rising, cream is added, plus 3 ounces butter for every pound of dough. The pandoro is then placed in a mold and left to rise once again before being baked. Nowadays most pandoro is produced industrially, given the difficulty and time involved in making it.

CHARACTERISTICS
Pandoro is particularly soft, thanks to a lengthy preparation which guarantees the perfect homogeneity of its ingredients. It is fragrant, with a slight vanilla scent; and is pleasantly sweet to the taste.

SERVING SUGGESTIONS

Pandoro is particularly good combined with whipped cream, zabaglione, melted chocolate, or other sweet creams. It can also be filled with ice cream or with other fillings made with mascarpone or whipped cream.

Cut the pandoro into large cubes, pour hot zabaglione made with Moscato instead of Marsala over it, and serve immediately.

Cut the pandoro horizontally into slices. Spread some of the slices with custard cream and others with jam diluted with warm cream. Stack the slices and serve.

Pour melted chocolate mixed with a little cream over the pandoro, spread it with a spatula, and serve.

Slice off the top of the pandoro and dig out the center, cutting it into cubes. Soften some vanilla ice cream, mix it with pieces of canned pineapple, and some of the cubed pandoro from the center. Fill the shell with the ice cream mixture, replace the top, and refrigerate until serving time.

Slice off the top of the pandoro and dig out the center. Mix mascarpone with strained ricotta. Add some of the pandoro from the center along with pieces of candied fruit and semisweet chocolate. Fill the shell with the mixture, replace the top, and refrigerate until serving time.

Make a light custard sauce and pour it onto individual dessert plates. Place a slice of pandoro on top, cover it with whipped cream sprinkled with cocoa or cinnamon, and serve.

Whip some cream with a little sugar, and add chopped marrons glacés. Use this cream to fill the pandoro.

Place the pandoro in a medium hot oven in order to soften the butter present in the cake. When it is warm, remove it from the oven, sprinkle with powdered vanilla sugar, and serve.

THE RIGHT WINE

The perfect companion for pandoro is a semisweet, fruity white wine like a Recioto di Soave (also from the Veneto) or an Albana di Romagna.
A Moscato Passito di Pantelleria is also good, as is the esteemed Ramandolo dei Colli Orientali del Friuli.
It is best to avoid sparkling wines which, since they are fermented, do not go well with yeast-based cakes.

IN SEARCH OF PANDORO

Although pandoro is good to eat and can be served in a variety of ways, like panettone it is eaten almost exclusively during the Christmas holiday season. At that time, it can be purchased in supermarkets, or, for best quality, in a bakery.

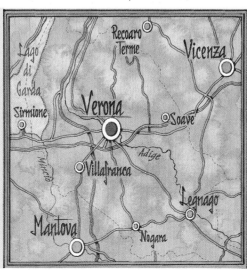

FRIULI-VENEZIA GIULIA

A simple, middle-European gastronomy

A detail of the mosaic floor in the Basilica of Aquileia.

To the north lie the Carnic Alps, where the rural simplicity of mountain tastes prefers robust, savory recipes based on polenta, beans, and pork. To the southeast is the province of Trieste, which has still not forgotten that it was once part of the Austro-Hungarian Empire and offers guests its own personal version of Hungarian goulash, Vienna sausages and sauerkraut, and boiled ham accompanied by Austrian horseradish sauce. The dual aspect of the rustic Friuli cuisine, which has also adopted culinary traditions from the countries on its borders, often produces unexpected and delicious surprises. Indeed, a simple order of potato dumplings may turn out to be filled with juicy plums, or coated with a mixture of cocoa, sugar, cinnamon, grated ricotta, and raisins. For those whose tastes do not run to combinations of the sweet and the salty, there is always a savory bowl of *jota*, the bean soup that originated in the Carnia and now symbolizes the entire region. Many versions exist: with or without pork, with barley as they make it in Trieste and Gorizia, or sometimes with chopped radicchio and celery.

While we are in the vein of simple fare, a healthy portion of polenta can always be found ready to accompany almost anything from salami to mountain cheese, from small birds to pork. Along the coast, it is sliced and

Cabbage leaves stuffed with meat and cooked in tomato sauce.

grilled and served with a *brodetto,* or fish chowder made with cuttlefish and peas. It comes as no surprise that one of the most popular Venetian dishes was adopted by Friuli, given that the latter was for a long time part of the Most Serene Republic of Venice. After a long walk through Udine, sample a tasty *polenta pasticciata* made with lamb, sausage, boiled ham, chicken, and fresh tomatoes. The traditional capital of Friuli has many treasures: the splendid Piazza della Libertà and the Loggia del Lionello, an elegant example of Venetian-Gothic architecture, the Renaissance arcade of San Giovanni, and the fifteenth-century column topped by the Lion of St. Mark.

From Udine it is not far to the Adriatic Sea. At Aquileia there are the ruins of what was one of the most important cities of the

Roman Empire. After seeing the magnificent mosaic floor of the Basilica, and visiting the Roman Forum, our itinerary continues to Trieste. Here, fish-lovers will find succulent seafood dishes. Any good menu is sure to include the classic *brodetto*, a fish soup made from sculpin, turbot, or mullet, and fresh tomatoes, which is usually accompanied by toasted slices of polenta; *capesante alla triestina* (scallops); sea dates; breaded and fried *sardoni*; and *grancevola alla triestina* (baked spider crabmeat).

If meat is preferred to fish, Trieste offers an opportunity to taste dishes based on Slavic recipes: goulash, first of all, and *rambasicci*, savory stuffed cabbage leaves filled with pork and beef and cooked with onions in oil and butter or in a tomato sauce. Because of its middle-European atmosphere, Trieste is unique among Italian cities. Any visit to the city starts from the the hill of San Giusto and the old town where the narrow winding streets lead to the cathedral and castle, and then continues down to the Piazza dell'Unità d'Italia on the seafront. Before heading off to Miramare Castle, which was built for Archduke Maximilian of Hapsburg, you can prepare yourself for the Austrian atmosphere with a Viennese-style cutlet accompanied by *patate in tecla*, potatoes that have been boiled, mashed, and then fried in salt pork together with finely sliced onions. Apart from potatoes, the region has little to offer in the way of vegetables which is understandable since Friuli has more rock than arable land. In any case, the artichokes and turnips that do grow there have a special taste and a sampling of *brovade* is definitely in order. For this dish, turnips are marinated in wine for at least a month, and are then cooked in pork broth with garlic, lard, and oil. In Trieste, artichokes are stuffed with bread, grated cheese, garlic, parsley, and oil.

Rich pastries filled with walnuts, almonds, pine nuts, raisins, and candied fruits reign in the realm of sweets. *Putizza* is eaten at Christmastime, *presnitz* at Easter, and during carnival the bakeries produce *fritole*, sweet pancakes made with flour, milk, eggs, raisins, cinnamon, lemon zest, and rum.

As evening falls one lingers at the table, surrounded by friends, sipping grappa. There are several types of grappa, including that of Refosco and Sauvignon and that of Picolit, not to mention the characteristic slivovitz, a plum brandy that is also produced in Austria and Slovenia.

Jota goriziana
(Bean and Barley Soup)

Preparation time
20 minutes plus
soaking time

Cooking time
2 hours

Difficulty
easy

Serves 6
- ¹/₂ pound dried
  borlotti beans
- 3 ¹/₂ ounces salt
  pork
- 1 onion, chopped
- 1 clove garlic,
  finely chopped
- 1 fistful parsley
  leaves, chopped
- 2 fresh sage leaves,
  chopped
- 4 tablespoons
  butter
- 5 ounces bacon,
  diced
- 6 cups meat broth
- 2 potatoes, diced
- 1 ¹/₂ cups
  sauerkraut, rinsed
- salt and pepper
- ¹/₂ pound pearl
  barley

Light red wine.
Recommended:
- Rosato di Latisana
- Sangiovese Rosato
  di Arborea

1 Cover the beans with lukewarm water and soak for 12 hours. Drain. In a mortar, pound the salt pork smooth and mix in the onions, garlic, parsley, and sage, continuing to pound it.

2 In a soup pot, melt the butter and sauté the salt pork mixture. Add the bacon and cook over low heat for 10 minutes or until the fat has melted. Add the beans and the broth and simmer for an hour.

3 Add the potatoes and sauerkraut to the pot. Season with salt and pepper, and cook over moderate heat for about 30 minutes. Lastly, add the pearl barley. After approximately 20 minutes, transfer the *jota* to a soup tureen and serve immediately.

Schinco de vedel

(Roast Veal Shank)

Preparation time
15 minutes

Cooking time
2 ¹/₂ hours

Difficulty
easy

Serves 4
- 1 3-pound veal shank
- ¹/₂ onion
- 3 tablespoons extra virgin olive oil
- salt and pepper
- 2 tablespoons butter
- 1 sprig fresh rosemary
- 2 leaves fresh sage
- 1 sprig fresh thyme
- 1 clove garlic
- 1 cup dry white wine
- broth

Light red wine.
Recommended:
- Aquileia Merlot
- Barbera dei Colli Tortonesi

1 Preheat the oven to 350°F. Trim the shank, wash and dry it, and rub it with the onion half. Place it in a roasting pan, drizzle with the oil, season with salt and pepper, and dot with the butter. Roast for about an hour.

2 Chop the rosemary, sage and thyme together with the garlic. Sprinkle this mixture on the veal shank, add the wine, and cook for another 1 ¹/₂ hours, basting from time to time with the cooking juices or some hot broth.

3 When the veal shank is nicely browned but not dry, transfer it to a warm serving platter and pour the cooking juices over it. Serve it with fried potatoes, or boiled potatoes that have been sliced and sautéed with chopped onions and salt pork.

Crafen di patate

(Stuffed Potato Fritters)

Preparation time
1 hour plus rising time

Cooking time
40 minutes

Difficulty
difficult

Serves 4 to 6
For the dough
- 1 pound white potatoes (about 5 medium)
- 1 tablespoon brewer's yeast
- 1 teaspoon sugar
- salt
- 1 to 2 tablespoons warm milk
- 3 tablespoons butter
- 2 eggs
- 1 ²/₃ cups white flour, sifted

For the filling
- 2 tablespoons extra virgin olive oil, plus additional for frying
- 1 clove garlic, crushed
- ¹/₂ pound mushrooms, thinly sliced
- 1 fisful parsley leaves, chopped
- salt and pepper

Rosé wine.
Recommended:
- Aquileia Rosato
- Castel del Monte Rosato

1 Wash the potatoes under cold water using a brush. Cover them with cold salted water, bring to a boil, and boil for 20 minutes or until they are tender. Drain and peel them, and while still warm purée them through a food mill using the disk with the smallest holes.

2 Dissolve the yeast in a bowl with the sugar, a pinch of salt, and the milk. Melt the butter but do not let it brown. Add the potatoes to the yeast mixture together with the melted butter, the eggs, and the flour. Work the dough until it becomes smooth and elastic. Shape it into a ball, cut a cross on the top, cover it, and let it rise.

3 In a frying pan, heat 2 tablespoons of the oil. Add the garlic and sauté until it turns golden; remove. Add the mushrooms and cook them over high heat. Shake the pan, stirring and tossing them until they become dry and crispy. Add the parsley, salt, and pepper. Stir once and remove from the heat.

4 Place the dough on a board and knead it rapidly. Roll it out with a rolling pin to a thickness of approximately ¹/₂ inch. Cut into disks 2 inches in diameter. Spread half of these with the mushroom mixture, and cover them with the remaining disks, sealing the edges so the filling cannot escape. Cover with a cloth and let rise for an hour.

5 Pour ¹/₂ inch oil into a skillet and fry a few *crafen* at a time, turning them with a slotted spoon when they are golden on one side. The heat should be high at first, and then moderate in order for the *crafen* to cook on the inside as well. When they are golden brown, dry them on absorbent paper, and serve them hot. *Crafen* can also be filled with a meat sauce, or pieces of any kind of cheese that melts.

Palacinche
(Crepes Filled with Jam)

Preparation time
20 minutes plus
resting time

Cooking time
30 minutes

Difficulty
medium

Makes 12 crepes
- 1 cup flour
- salt
- 1 cup milk
- 2 eggs
- 5 tablespoons
  butter, melted,
  plus extra for pan
- plum or apricot jam
- 3 tablespoons rum

Fortified wine or dessert wine.
Recommended:
- Picolit
- Sagrantino Passito
  di Montefalco

1 Sift the flour with a pinch of salt into a bowl. Pour the milk in slowly, mixing constantly so that no lumps form. Add the eggs one at a time, mixing well after each one, and 3 tablespoons of the melted butter. Cover and let rest for 1 hour.

2 Heat a little butter in a 5-inch frying pan. Remove any excess with a wad of paper towelling. Pour 2 tablespoons of batter into the pan. Tilt the pan so that the batter covers the bottom. Pour off any excess batter. When the crepe is cooked on one side, turn it over. Set it aside, and make eleven more, buttering the pan if necessary with the wad of paper towelling.

3 Preheat the oven to 425°F. Butter a baking dish lightly. Spread a thin layer of jam on each crepe and roll it up. Arrange the crepes side by side in the baking dish, sprinkle them with the remaining melted butter, pour the rum on top, and bake them for 5 minutes. Serve very hot.

FRIULI-VENEZIA GIULIA

SPECIALTIES

Antipasti (Appetizers)
Nervetti, Pancetta, Prosciutto di San Daniele, Sopressa friulana.

First courses
Cjarsons, Jota, Pistum.

Entrées
Boreto de rombo, Frico Musetto con la brovada, Pitina, Rambasici.

Desserts
Gnocchi di prugne, Gubana, Palacinke, Pinza.

TYPICAL RESTAURANTS

Antica Osteria La Molassa
in Ponte Molassa 1, Andreis (Pordenone)
Tel. 0427/76147, Closed Tuesday
Prices: Lire 45,000/50,000

Fritole istriane (Fritters, Istrian Style)

Trattoria al Parco
Via Stretta del Parco 1, Buttrio (Udine)
Tel. 0432/674025
Closed Tuesday evening and Wednesday
Prices: Lire 55,000

Trattoria da Giulietta
Via Pocivalla 16, Faedis (Udine)
Tel. 0432/711206, Closed Thursday
Prices: Lire 45,000

Trattoria alla Luna
Via Oberdan 13, Gorizia
Tel. 0481/530374, Closed Sunday evening and Monday
Prices: Lire 35,000/45,000

Vecia osteria del Moro
Via Castello 2, Pordenone
Tel. 0431/60201, Closed Wednesday
Prices: Lire 55,000

Antica Osteria al Ponte
Via Tagliamento 13
San Daniele del Friuli (Udine)
Tel 0432/954909, Closed Monday
Prices: Lire 50,000/60,000

Da Afro
Via Umberto I 14, Spilimbergo (Udine)
Tel. 0427/2264, Closed Tuesday
Prices: Lire 50,000

Buffet da Mario
Via Torrebianca 41, Triest
Tel. 040/639234, Closed Saturday and Sunday
Prices: Lire 30,000/60,000

Trattoria al Passeggio
Viale Volontari della Libertà 49, Udine
Tel. 0432/46216, Closed Saturday at noon and Sunday
Prices: Lire 50,000

Osteria alla Colonna
Via Gemona 98, Udine
Tel. 0432/510177
Closed Sunday
Prices: Lire 55,000

WINES

White
Chardonnay delle Grave del Friuli, Collio, Malvasia del Carso, Malvasia del Collio, Malvasia Istriana d'Isonzo, Pinot Bianco d'Isonzo, Pinot Bianco dei Colli Orientali del Friuli, Pinot Bianco del Collio, Pinot Bianco delle Grave del Friuli, Pinot Bianco di Aquileia, Pinot Bianco di Latisana, Pinot Grigio d'Isonzo, Pinot Grigio dei Colli Orientali del Friuli, Pinot Grigio del Collio, Pinot Grigio delle Grave del Friuli, Pinot Grigio di Latisana, Ribolla dei Colli Orientali del Friuli, Riesling Italico del Collio, Riesling Renano d'Isonzo, Riesling Renano delle Grave del Friuli, Riesling Renano di Aquileia, Riesling Renano dei Colli Orientali del Friuli, Sauvignon d'Isonzo. Sauvignon dei Colli Orientali del Friuli, Sauvignon del Collio, Sauvignon delle Grave del Friuli, Sauvignon di Aquileia, Tocai Friulano d'Isonzo, Tocai Friulano dei Colli Orientali del Friuli, Tocai Friulano del Collio, Tocai Friulano delle Grave del Friuli, Tocai Friulano di Aquileia, Tocai Friulano di Latisana, Traminer Aromatico

Zuppa di cren (Horseradish soup)

d'Isonzo, Traminer Aromatico delle Grave del Friuli, Traminer Aromatico di Aquileia, Traminer del Collio, Verduzzo dei Colli Orientali del Friuli, Verduzzo del Friuli Frizzante delle Grave del Friuli, Verduzzo di Ramandolo dei Colli Orientali del Friuli, Verduzzo Friulano d'Isonzo, Verduzzo Friulano delle Grave del Friuli, Verduzzo Friulano di Aquileia, Verduzzo Friulano di Latisana.

Rosé
Rosato delle Grave del Friuli.

Red
Cabernet d'Isonzo, Cabernet dei Colli Orientali del Friuli, Cabernet delle Grave del Friuli, Cabernet di Aquileia, Cabernet di Latisana, Cabernet Franc del Collio, Cabernet Franc delle Grave del Friuli, Cabernet Franc di Aquileia, Cabernet Sauvignon delle Grave del Friuli, Cabernet Sauvignon di Aquileia, Merlot d'Isonzo, Merlot

dei Colli Orientali del Friuli, Merlot del Collio, Merlot delle Grave del Friuli, Merlot di Aquileia, Merlot di Latisana, Pinot nero dei Colli Orientali del Friuli, Pinot Nero del Collio, Pinot nero delle Grave del Friuli, Refosco dal Peduncolo Rosso delle Grave del Friuli, Refosco dal Peduncolo Rosso di Aquileia, Refosco dei Colli Orientali del Friuli, Refosco di Latisana, Rosso del Carso, Terrano del Carso.

Dessert wine
Picolit dei Colli Orientali del Friuli.

CHEESES
Carnia, Frico Balcia, Liptauer, Montasio, Salato morbido, Scuete Frante, Strica, Tabor di Monrupino.

WHERE TO BUY TYPICAL PRODUCTS
Wines
Enoteca Quattro Vini
Corno di Rosazzo (Udine)

Enoteca Piazza
Via de Amicis 2, Maniago (Udine)

La Casa degli Spiriti
Via dei Torriani 15, Udine

Bere Bene
Viale Ippodromo 2, Trieste

Cold Meats
Azienda Agricola Le Fredis
Lanzacco (Udine)

Alimentari Mosetti
Via del Corso 27, Gorizia

Prosciuttificio Wolf
Via Volvia 88, Sauris (Udine)

Salumificio Lovison
Via Foscolo 18, Spilimbergo (Udine)

Cheeses
Latteria Sociale di Cividale
Corno di Rosazzo (Udine)

Azienda Zaro
*in Canebola, Via Farcadize
Faedis (Udine)*

Cooperativa Allevatori Valcanale
Via Pontebbana 19, Ugovizza (Udine)

Alimentari Mosetti
Via del Corso 27, Gorizia

Prosciutto di San Daniele

This is one of the best known and loved pork products both in Italy and abroad. By law, it can only be produced in a limited area, using selected pigs, and cured according to a special procedure.

This air-dried ham is known and loved both in Italy and abroad. By law, it can only be produced in a limited area, using selected pigs, and must be cured according to a special procedure. The DOC certification (name and origin controlled) limits the San Daniele production to hams that are prepared and cured within the city limits of San Daniele.

In addition to Friuli-Venezia Giulia, the pigs can also come from other Italian regions. They must weigh at least 160 kilograms (350 pounds) and be fed on special diets. Shortly after the pigs are born, the breeders brand them on the rear haunches so that they can be kept under close control. Once the hams arrive at the prosciutto factory, they undergo a careful inspection and receive a second stamp. The most important stages of the curing process are salting, pressing (which gives the hams their typical 'violin' shape), and aging (which, depending on the weight of the ham, lasts at least eleven months). The hams are then inspected for quality, at which time they receive DOC certification and are stamped again.

ANOTHER FAMOUS PROSCIUTTO

Another prosciutto famous for its quality is that from the Veneto Berico-Euganeo. It is

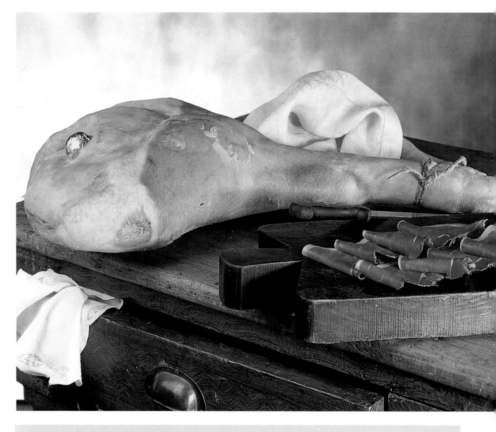

BUYING PROSCIUTTO

San Daniele prosciutto must be of a deep pink color with white fat. Avoid hams that are yellowish or too red in color.

The odor is strong and distinct, yet delicate, and has nothing in common with the odor of raw meat.

The ham has a fragrant and sweet, not salty, taste.

produced in a zone that includes fifteen communities, of which Montagnana is the most important. Once reserved only for the Doges and the patricians of Venice, it is still today a prosciutto of excellent quality. The pigs for these hams must have been born, raised, and slaughtered in the Veneto, or else in Lombardy, Emilia Romagna, Lazio, or Umbria.

The curing process is similar to that of San Daniele. After salting, the hams are pressed into their final shape, defined as semi-pressed. The aging of the hams can last anywhere from ten months to more than a year. Only perfect hams receive the Lion of St. Mark brand.

SERVING SUGGESTIONS

Thanks to its intense perfume and sweet, delicate flavor, San Daniele prosciutto has entered the kitchen, where it has been combined with meat and fish to create exquisite recipes.

Remove the fat from the slices of prosciutto. Thread 6 oysters onto a skewer and wind a slice of prosciutto between them like a ribbon. Prepare 1 or 2 skewers per person, and sauté them in butter in a skillet. Serve hot.

Scale, gut, and fillet some mullets. Place a slice of prosciutto between the two halves of each fillet. Arrange in a baking dish and bake at 325°F.

Wrap strips of lean and fat prosciutto around the edge of individual tournedos, and sauté or grill them.

Press slices of prosciutto onto thin slices of veal scaloppine so they stick. Sauté in a little butter with the prosciutto on the bottom first, then turn and cook on the other side. Serve hot with no additional salt.

Spread slices of prosciutto with foie gras paté, roll them up, and serve them with toast or crackers.

Slices of prosciutto should look wavy, not flattened, on the serving platter. Use a fork to place them individually on the platter. Accompany them with crisp white bread like montasù *veneto, or a soft*

white bread like ciopa. *If the prosciutto is very lean, it can be served with butter.*

STORING PROSCIUTTO

If the prosciutto has been bought sliced, keep it in its package without opening it in the least cold and dampest part of the refrigerator. Remove it a half hour before serving.
When buying vacuum-packed prosciutto, always check the expiration date, and keep it in the refrigerator.

THE RIGHT WINE

Choose a medium-bodied white like Pinot Grigio dell'Isonzo, Tocai del Piave, or Colli Euganei Bianco Superiore.

IN SEARCH OF PROSCIUTTO

San Daniele prosciutto can be found all around Udine. The prosciutto from the Prolongo factory, Via Trento e Trieste 115, in San Daniele is particularly noteworthy. As for the Berico-Euganeo area in the Veneto, the meat packers in and around Montagnana are very well-supplied.

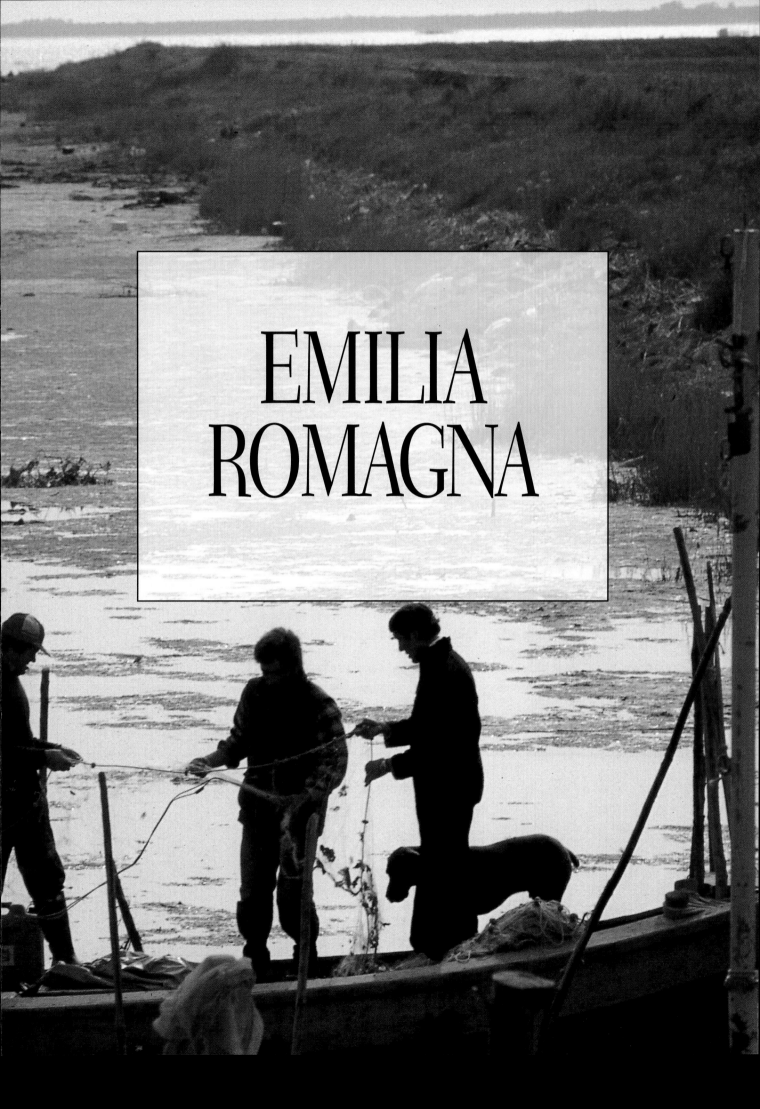

EMILIA
ROMAGNA

The gourmand's paradise

It has often been said that the way one cooks and eats is indicative of one's character. This is certainly true in Emilia Romagna. Its generous and opulent gastronomy is the fruit of the patient work of those who take pleasure in sitting down to a plate heaped high with their superb homemade pastas. The inhabitants of Emilia Romagna are a happy lot, pleasure-loving and playful, and they have produced a cuisine that would put the grumpiest of souls into a very good mood. If it were possible, the Emilians would roll out an enormous sheet of pasta made of flour and eggs and stuff it full of all their belongings, their houses, indeed, their cities, because the emblem of this region is stuffed pasta. There are infinite variations regarding the shapes and the names of the pasta dishes: *tortelli, tortelloni, tortellini, ravioli, cappelletti, anolini, gnocchi* … and all of them are stuffed.

Below: Making Parmigiano Reggiano cheese. Right: The baptistery and cathedral of Parma.

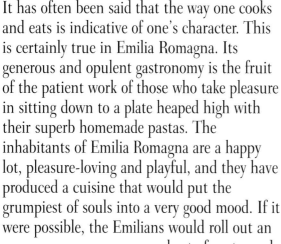

And the very same sheet of pasta, which must always be homemade, also produces *tagliatelle, cannelloni,* and *lasagne,* depending on how the pasta is cut and served. The stuffings can be *magro* (lean), in which case they are made with ricotta cheese and herbs, or *grasso* (fat), when they are made with different kinds of meat: beef, pork, or game; cooked or raw ham; even cheese and pumpkin. As for the seasonings, they are sinful: cream, meat sauces, broth, butter, and lots and lots of

Parmesan cheese. Emilia Romagna is also the home of Parmigiano Reggiano and Grana Padano, those cheeses par excellence that no Italian could ever do without. Whoever happens to pass through Emilia Romagna during the month of June would do well to stop at the Festival of the Rivoltoni that takes place at Granaglione in the province of Bologna, at which tortellini and ravioli filled with ricotta cheese and parsley and seasoned with melted butter or meat sauce and Parmesan cheese are offered to one and all free of charge. During the same month, there is the *Tortellata* of San Giovanni at Parma (June 23–24), when the restaurants offer a demonstration of their art in preparing the typical tortelli. However, Parma is not only renowned for its cuisine and the prosciutto it produces. It is also the home of the splendid frescoes of Correggio, the famous Renaissance artist who painted such masterpieces as the *Assumption of the Virgin* (in the dome of the Cathedral), the *Vision of St. John at Patmos* (in the dome of San Giovanni Evangelista), and the frescoes of the vaulted ceiling of the Camera di San Paolo, also known as the Camera del Correggio.

Even if pride of place goes to the pasta dishes in Emilia Romagna, the appetizers and main courses are not to be slighted. The latter are of fish or meat depending on whether one is in the Po River plain in Emilia, or between the Apennines and the Adriatic Sea in Romagna. Pork prevails over all meats and offers a variety of delicacies like *prosciutto* (Parma), *coppe, pancette, culatelli* (Bussetto in the province of Parma), *mortadelle* (Bologna), *salami da sugo* (Ferrara), *salami di Felino* (province of Parma). Famous nationwide among the main courses are the *cotechino* (pork sausage) and *zampone* (stuffed pig's feet), specialties from Modena in which different cuts of pork are minced and mixed with spices and stuffed into pig's feet. The same stuffing fills *cappello da prete*, whose shape resembles a priest's hat. These dishes are to be found on every Italian table during the Christmas and New Year holidays, and are usually accompanied by lentils or mashed potatoes.

A masterly use of the products of the sea distinguishes the cuisine of Romagna from that of Emilia. Its fish soups are among the tastiest in Italy. The expertise of the people of Romagna is evident in the way they have exploited their coasts. Rimini and Riccione are two of the country's most popular sea resorts, and on their crowded, lively beaches one can sample freshly grilled fish served with tomato sauce, or boiled fish served with a sauce of olive oil and lemon juice. The perfect time to be in Riccione is for the August 15 Feast of the Assumption of the Virgin when the *Sagra del Mare e del Pescatore* (Festival of the Sea and Fishermen) is held, since that is when the fishermen themselves offer the products of their nets.

Farther north along the Adriatic Coast is Ravenna, rich in history and art. In the fifth century, Ravenna was the capital of the Ostrogothic Kingdom of Theodoric during whose reign the Church of S. Apollinare Nuovo was built and decorated with precious mosaics. Equally famous and important is the sixth-century early Christian Basilica of S.Vitale which is also decorated with splendid Byzantine mosaics. From Ravenna, we move on to Ferrara, passing through the Valli di Comacchio, the biggest lagoon in Italy, where thousands of aquatic birds can be seen and a variety of local dishes based on eels can be sampled. Romagna is also famous for the *piadina*, a flat pancake-like bread that is filled with cheese, salami, or prosciutto, and eaten hot at any time of the day. And for those who want to eat their fill, at the Festival of the *Teggia* in Cattolica during the month of September *piadine* are offered to all the visitors together with salami and wine.

Detail of a Byzantine mosaic in the Basilica of San Vitale in Ravenna.

Typical products from Emilia. In the background, the Cathedral of Modena.

Erbazzone
(Spinach Pie)

Preparation time
30 minutes plus resting time

Cooking time
1 hour

Difficulty
medium

Serves 6
- 2 ⅓ cups flour
- salt
- ¾ cup lard
- 2 pounds spinach
- 3 tablespoons butter
- 1 fistful parsley leaves, chopped
- 2 cloves garlic, chopped
- ¾ cup grated Parmesan cheese
- 1 slice salt pork, chopped

Dry white wine.
Recommended:
- *Albana di Romagna*
- *Parrina*

1 Sift the flour onto a board, add a pinch of salt, dot with pieces of lard, and work with your fingers until the lard has completely absorbed all the flour. Shape the dough into a mound and make a well in the center. Pour in 4 tablespoons cold water, and knead, adding more water if necessary, until it becomes smooth and elastic. Shape the dough into a ball, wrap it in waxed paper, and let it rest in a cool place or in the refrigerator for 45 minutes.

2 In the meantime, wash the spinach and cook it with a pinch of salt and just the water clinging to the leaves. Drain, squeeze, and chop the spinach. Preheat the oven to 400°F.

3 Melt the butter in a frying pan and sauté the parsley and half of the garlic. Add the spinach, stirring it in the pan until it is dry.

4 Butter a round baking dish with low sides, about 10 inches in diameter. Roll the dough out into 2 disks, one larger than the other. Cover the bottom and sides of the dish with the larger disk.

5 Mix the grated Parmesan thoroughly with the spinach mixture and pour it into the crust. Level off the filling and cover it with the other disk. Fold the edges of the pastry towards the inside and crimp them down with a fork. Prick the surface and place the pie in the oven. Mix the salt pork with the remaining garlic. Take the pie out of the oven after 40 minutes and spread the mixture on the crust. Return to the oven for another 5 minutes.

Garganelli al ragù di piselli
(Egg Macaroni with Meat Sauce and Peas)

Preparation time
1 hour plus resting time

Cooking time
1 hour

Difficulty
medium

Serves 4 to 6
For the pasta
- 3 ¹/₄ cups flour
- 2 tablespoons grated Parmesan cheese
- 4 eggs
- nutmeg

For the sauce
- 2 ounces prosciutto
- 1 carrot
- 1 onion
- 1 clove garlic
- 1 fistful parsley leaves
- 3 tablespoons butter
- 2 tablespoons extra virgin olive oil
- 5 ounces ground veal
- 5 ounces chicken livers, chopped
- ¹/₂ cup dry white wine
- 1 10-ounce can Italian tomatoes
- ¹/₂ cup frozen peas
- salt and pepper
- grated Parmesan cheese to taste

Light red wine.
Recommended:
- Sangiovese di Romagna
- Chianti dei Colli Aretini

1 Sift the flour onto a board and mix in the cheese. Shape the mixture into a mound and make a well in the center. Break the eggs into the well, add a grinding of nutmeg, and work in the flour until the dough is smooth and compact. Make a ball, cover it with a cloth, and let it rest for about 15 minutes.

2 Roll the dough out into a sheet that is not too thin. Cut it into 2-inch squares.

3 Wrap each square diagonally around a small floured stick (a pencil will do) starting from one of the points, and run it over the 'comb' used for this pasta, pressing slightly with your fingers so that the pasta is ridged and the sides overlap. Slip the *garganelli* off the stick, line them up on the board, and let them dry.

4 Chop the prosciutto with the carrot, onion, garlic, and parsley. Heat the butter and oil and sauté this mixture for 15 minutes. Add the ground veal and chopped chicken livers and cook until browned. Add the wine and as soon as it evaporates add the tomatoes, peas, salt, and pepper. Cook over medium heat, covered, for about 30 minutes.

5 Boil the *garganelli* in abundant salted boiling water. Drain them after 6 or 7 minutes, when they are al dente. Sprinkle with grated Parmesan cheese and then add the sauce. Serve immediately.

The 'comb' is a small wooden instrument with threads on which the pasta is ridged.

Tagliatelle al prosciutto
(Egg Noodles with Prosciutto)

Preparation time
15 minutes

Cooking time
10 minutes

Difficulty
easy

Serves 6
- 7 ounces prosciutto, cut into $1/8$-inch slices
- $1/2$ onion
- 3 $1/2$ tablespoons butter
- $1/4$ cup dry white wine
- 1 1-pound package tagliatelle
- grated Parmesan cheese to taste
- salt and pepper

Light red wine.
Recommended:
- Sangiovese di Romagna
- Freisa di Chieri

1 Remove the fat from the prosciutto. Cut the fat into thin strips and chop it with the onion. Melt the butter in a small skillet. Add the onion-fat mixture and then the prosciutto. Sauté slightly; sprinkle with the wine and salt and pepper to taste. When the wine evaporates, remove from the heat and keep warm so that the prosciutto stays soft.

2 In the meantime, cook the *tagliatelle* in abundant salted boiling water. Drain when *al dente*, add the sauce and the grated Parmesan cheese and serve.

Totani al cartoccio
(Squid Baked in Foil)

Preparation time
30 minutes

Cooking time
30 minutes

Difficulty
easy

Serves 4
- 4 large squid (about 7 ounces each)
- 1 sprig rosemary
- 1 clove garlic
- 1 fistful parsley leaves
- 2 tablespoons bread crumbs
- salt and pepper
- 4 tablespoons extra virgin olive oil
- 8 orange or lemon slices
- 2 bay leaves

Dry white wine.
Recommended:
- Bianco di Scandiano
- Pinot Bianco

1 Preheat the oven to 425°F. Pull the tentacles from the body sac of the squid and empty the sacs, being careful not to tear them. Cut off and discard the eyes and discard the beak from the center of the tentacles.
Chop the tentacles with the rosemary, garlic, and parsley. Mix with the bread crumbs, salt, pepper, and olive oil. Fill the sacs with this mixture and sew the opening with white thread.

2 Grease 4 sheets of aluminum foil slightly. Place a squid on each sheet between 2 orange or lemon slices and $1/2$ bay leaf. Close the foil loosely since it will expand with steam, and prick the packets lightly with a needle.

3 Place the packets on a baking sheet or in a large baking dish, and bake for about 30 minutes. Transfer the closed packets to a serving platter and serve.

Cotechino in galera
(Pork Sausage Roll)

Preparation time
20 minutes

Cooking time
1 ½ hours

Difficulty
medium

Serves 4 to 6
- 1 1-pound cotechino (pork sausage)
- 1 1-pound slice of beef tenderloin, pounded thin
- 4 slices prosciutto
- 4 tablespoons extra virgin olive oil
- 1 small onion
- salt
- broth
- dry Lambrusco wine

Light red wine.
Recommended:
- Lambrusco Salamino di Santa Croce
- Colli Martani Sangiovese

1 Prick each end of the *cotechino* with a toothpick or a fork. Place the *cotechino* in an oval casserole, cover it with cold water, and cook slowly over low heat for 30 minutes. Drain the sausage and peel it carefully.

2 Cover the slice of beef with the prosciutto slices, and place the *cotechino* in the center. Roll it up and tie it with string like a roast.

3 Heat the oil in a Dutch oven and sauté the onion slightly. Add the meat and turn it so it browns on all sides, being careful not to prick it. Add salt and equal parts of broth and wine to cover the meat.

4 Cook over moderate heat, covered, for 1 hour. If necessary, before serving, reduce the sauce. Cut off the string, slice the meat thickly, and serve with the gravy.

Fragole all'aceto balsamico
(Strawberries with Balsamic Vinegar)

Preparation time
30 minutes plus
resting time

Difficulty
easy

Serves 4
- 1 pound
  strawberries or
  wild strawberries
- 3 tablespoons
  balsamic vinegar
  from Modena
- 1 tablespoon sugar

1 Place the strawberries into a colander. Spray cold water over the berries, drain, and dry with paper towelling.

2 Hull the berries, and if they are big, cut them. If you are using wild strawberries, leave them whole. Pour the balsamic vinegar over the berries and stir carefully. Let them sit for 15 minutes.

3 Just before serving, sprinkle the berries with the sugar, mix once, and spoon into individual dessert bowls.

EMILIA ROMAGNA

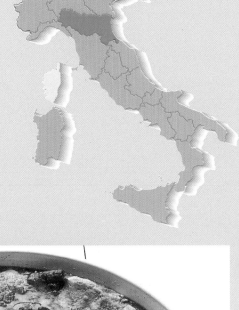

SPECIALTIES

Antipasti (Appetizers)
Prosciutto di Parma, Culatello.

First courses
Agnolini, Calzagatti, Cappellacci con la zucca, Cappelletti, Garganelli, Lasagne al forno, Passatelli, Pisarei e fasò, Strichetti, Strozzapreti, Tortellini.

Entrées
Coniglio alla cacciatora, Fegatelli in rete, Fritto misto, Guanciale di vitello, Salamina da sugo, Stracotto d'asino, Trippa alla parmigiana, Zampone.

Desserts
Bensone, Brazadela, Crema fritta, Pan Speziel, Panapapato, Spongata.

TYPICAL RESTAURANTS

Trattoria Boni
Via Saragozza 88, Bologna
Tel. 051/585060, Closed Saturday
Prices: Lire 45,000/55,000

Da Cesari
Via Carbonesi 8, Bologna
Tel. 051/237710, Closed Sunday
Prices: Lire 55,000/70,000

Franco Rossi
Via Goito 3, Bologna
Tel. 051/238818, Closed Sunday
Prices: Lire 100,000/120,000

Trattoria Campanini
Via Roncole Verdi 136, Busseto (Parma)
Tel. 0524/92569, Closed Tuesday
Prices: Lire 50,000/60,000

Trattoria da Faccini
in Sant'Antonio 10

Castell'Arquato (Piacenza)
Tel. 0523/896340 Closed Wednesday
Prices: Lire 60,000

Da Vasco e Giulia
Via Muratori 21, Comacchio (Ferrara)
Tel. 0533/81252, Closed Monday
Prices: Lire 60,000

Green Lasagne

La Pavona
Via Santa Lucia 45
Faenza (Ravenna)
Tel. 0546/31075, Closed Wednesday
Prices: Lire 40,000/55,000

Antica Trattoria Volano
Via Volano 20, Ferrara
Tel. 0532/761421, Closed Friday
Prices: Lire 40,000/60,000

E' Parlamintè
Via Mameli 33, Imola (Bologna)
Tel. 0542/30144, Closed Thursday
Prices: Lire 35,000/50,000

Osteria Giusti
Vicolo Squallore 46, Modena
Tel. 059/222533, Closed Sunday and Monday
Prices: Lire 70,000

Trattoria Antichi Sapori
Strada Montanara 318, Parma
Tel. 0521/648165, Closed Tuesday
Prices: Lire 45,000

Vecchia Osteria
Via Ferdinando di Borbone 125, Piacenza
Tel. 0523/504133, Closed Sunday evening and Monday
Prices: Lire 70,000

Ristorante Capannetti
Vicolo Capannetti 21, Ravenna
Tel. 0544/66681, Closed Sunday evening
and Monday
Prices: Lire 50,000/60,000

Cinque Pini
Via Martiri di Cervarolo 46c
Reggio Emilia
Tel. 0522/553663, Closed Wednesday
Prices: Lire 70,000/80,000

Hostaria da Ivan
Via Villa 73, Fontanelle di Roccabianca
(Parma)
Tel. 0521/870113, Closed Monday
and Tuesday
Prices: Lire 50,000/60,000

La Sangiovesa
Piazza Balacchi 14
Santarcangelo di Romagna (Forlì)
Tel. 0541/620710, Closed Monday
Prices: Lire 50,000

Trattoria Bolognese
Via Muratori 1, Vignola (Modena)
Tel. 059/771207, Closed Saturday
Prices: Lire 40,000/50,000

WINES
White
Albana di Romagna, Bianco del Bosco
Eliceo, Bianco di Scandiano, Malvasia
dei Colli di Parma, Monterosso Val
d'Arda, Montuni del Reno, Ortrugo,
Pagadebit, Pignoletto, Trebbianino Val
Trebbia, Trebbiano di Romagna, Val
Nure.

Red
Barbera, Bonarda, Cagnina di Romagna,
Fortana del Bosco Eliceo, Gutturnio,
Lambrusco di Sorbara, Lambrusco,

Rosa di Parma

Grasparossa di Castelvetro,
Lambrusco Reggiano, Lambrusco
Salamino di Santa Croce, Merlot
del Bosco Eliceo, Sangiovese
di Romagna.

Dessert wine
Malvasia dei Colli Piacentini.

CHEESES
Formaggio di Fossa, Furmaien,
Giuncata, Parmigiano Reggiano,
Rigatino, Squaquarone.

SHOPPING FOR TYPICAL PRODUCTS
Wines
Convivio Sapori d'Italia
Via Trento e Trieste 95
Carpi (Modena)

Bruno Valentini
Via Lisoni 6, Fornovo di Taro (Parma)

Cold meats
Gino Fereoli
Strada Parma 28
Pilastro di Langhirano (Parma)

Salumificio Dassena
in Spigarolo
Busseto (Parma)

Gogliardo Ranelli
in Santa Franca, Via Mogadiscio 79
Polesine Parmense (Parma)

Salumificio Bidinelli
Via Circondario 17, Correggio
(Reggio Emilia)

Pasquini e Brusiani
Via Tofane 38, Bologna

Salumeria Marchetti
Via Cortevecchia 35-37, Ferrara

Cheeses
Gastronomia Plinio e Paolo
Corso Isonzo 55, Ferrara

Adriano e Luisaetti
Via Sant'Eufemia 16, Modena

Casa del Formaggio
Via Bixio 108, Parma

Alpine
Via Cavour 41, Ravenna

Balducci
Via IV Novembre 7, Rimini

Zampone (stuffed pig's feet)

The Emilians are experts in the art of making sausages and salamis, and this specialty, in which pig's feet are stuffed with pork sausage, is one of their great achievements. The zampone requires a long cooking time, but happily today there are precooked products on the market which also keep for a long time.

These particular sausages are usually eaten during the winter holidays. They are traditionally served on New Year's Eve together with lentils since this dish is supposed to assure those who eat it good luck for the rest of the year. Zampone was invented in Modena in the early part of the sixteenth century when the city was overrun by the troops of Pope Julius II and the townspeople had to come up with ways to preserve their food supplies during the siege.

CHARACTERISTICS

Zampone is much more digestible nowadays than it used to be. It is made from equal proportions of meat from the shoulder of the pig, its fat, and rind. Once, half of the sausage was made of the rind, which made it difficult to digest. Apart from the change in proportions, its production has remained faithful to tradition.

Zampone is eaten during the coldest months of the year and especially, as mentioned above, during the winter holidays. The market demand and its short season used to create organizational difficulties that were not easy to resolve because the sausage was raw and would not keep for a long period after processing. However, this problem has been partially resolved by precooking, which allows for longer periods of preservation so that processing can start earlier in the year.

PRECOOKED ZAMPONE

Precooking offers some practical advantages: in the first place, the sausage does not have to be cooked for such a long time; and secondly, when the zampone is cooked for a short period there is no risk that its covering will be perforated. This explains why the precooked products are so popular. The first step of processing involves cutting off the pig's feet, which are then cleaned and refrigerated. The meat and fat are ground together, while the rind is chopped very finely separately. The ingredients are then mashed together with the seasonings in a mortar. A special machine refills the pig's feet. They are then scorched to remove any bristles, and perforated at the tips so that fat and gelatin can run off during the precooking process. As soon as they are cooked, the pig's feet are vacuum-packed and sterilized. Because they are packaged like this, they can be kept for months.

SERVING SUGGESTIONS

Zampone can be cooked in only one way, so any creativity has to be limited to the foods that accompany it: spinach, cabbages, artichokes, sauces, even tagliatelle!

In order to make sure that the casing does not tear, cover the zampone with cold water and soak it for at least 12 hours. Remove it from the water, make a deep incision at the hoof end so that the steam can escape, and then prick it with a toothpick.

Wrap the zampone up in a cloth and tie it firmly. In order to preserve its shape, tie it to a wooden spoon. Place it in a pot of cold unsalted water and bring it to a boil.

As soon as it starts to boil, lower the flame and let it simmer for at least 4 hours. Do not let it boil, since the casing might break.

When it is done, remove it from the heat and leave it in the cooking liquid. Then drain, remove the cloth, slice, and serve.

For precooked zampone, follow the cooking instructions on the package.

Serve sliced zampone with spinach dressed with oil and vinegar, and mostarda di Cremona.

After it is cooked, slice the zampone and simmer it for a few minutes with cooked Savoy cabbage.

Serve the zampone sliced on a bed of buttered tagliatelle.

Crumble the zampone with a fork and add it to a meat sauce for pappardelle or potato gnocchi.

Season boiled artichoke hearts with oil and lemon and serve them with sliced zampone.

IN SEARCH OF ZAMPONE

Zampone can be found in all the better shops throughout Italy.
In the province of Modena, the Salumeria Prostrati in Zocca has an excellent zampone.
At the Salumeria Fochetti Biondi in Sassuolo, you can find an unusual type of zampone called *sassolino*, which has a bacon-rind casing.

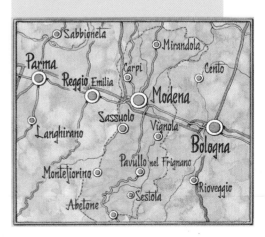

TUSCANY

Genuine country scents and tastes

The famous Piazza dei Miracoli in Pisa with the cathedral in the foreground and the Leaning Tower behind it.

Whoever visits Tuscany is struck most of all by its landscapes: passion and tradition are evident in the way the land is worked, the tidy farmhouses surrounded by green meadows, and hillsides covered with olive trees and vineyards.

What kind of cuisine could characterize a region that appreciates nature and knows how to exploit its rural traditions? The Tuscan gastronomy is rustic in character but at the same time refined; the cuisine tends to be simple, but is quick to make use of all the fragrances and flavors that nature can offer.

Tuscany is the realm of the grill and the skewer: the famous *bistecca alla fiorentina* must be grilled over a wood-burning fire, and with it vegetables from the garden, pork chops, and mushroom caps. And how are grilled foods seasoned? You only have to choose from the infinite variety of aromatic plants growing in the Tuscan

countryside: garlic, oregano, rosemary, basil, parsley, hot red pepper, sage, bay leaf, juniper berries, anise, tarragon. Add to this a generous dose of Tuscan olive oil and the dinner is served! It is a meal based on quality because simplicity and genuineness are what is expected from country cooking, not complicated, rich, colorful creations.

Soups and *minestrone* ('big soup') play leading roles in this rustic tradition: pasta and chickpeas, rice and beans, black cabbage soup, onion soup, *pappa al pomodoro* (bread and tomato soup), *zuppa di magro* (soup for fast-days), and potato soup. Then there are tasty hams from pigs or wild boar, aromatic salamis, *soppressate* (a flattened salami), and tiny sausages flavored with ginger and served as an antipasto together with olives and a flask of Chianti, one of Italy's most famous wines.

Just as the Tuscan landscape numbers among its cities veritable treasure troves of art (Florence, first and foremost, followed by Pisa, Lucca, Siena, and countless others), the Tuscan cuisine displays its gastronomic masterpieces.

In Arezzo, an ancient Etruscan town, you can feast your eyes on *La Leggenda della Croce* cycle of frescoes by Piero della Francesca in the Church of San Francesco, and feast your stomach on an exquisite pheasant made with cream and truffles, from

A plate of *cacciucco alla livornese* (Leghorn's famous fish soup).

a fourteenth-century recipe. Or choose a crayfish soufflé, so delicate that it is often served as a first course at important dinners.

The specialties of the coastal cities of Tuscany are based on fish. *Cacciucco alla livornese* (the renowned fish soup of Leghorn) presents the perfumes and flavors of the sea to every palate.

To the south is the Maremma and its protected nature reserves: the lagoon of Orbetello, the Monti dell'Uccellina, Lake Burano, the Grosseto scrubland. The Grossetto area is noted for its excellent turtle soup and *uccelletti alla maremmana* (small birds flavored with garlic and anchovies and served with olives and dried wild cherries). At the Festival of Eels at Orbetello, held every year in June, marinated and smoked eels are offered to the visitors. That is a good time to taste another Tuscan specialty: le *cieche*, tiny, newly born and still blind eels that are fished at the mouths of the Arno River at Pisa and the Ombrone River at Grosseto as they are about to return to the rivers. They are usually cooked in olive oil and seasoned with garlic and sage leaves, but they can also be turned

into a pie when mixed with eggs, grated dry bread, Parmesan cheese, and lemon juice. There are many other fairs and festivals. If you are near Lucca on August 15, go to Camigliano where the *Sagra del Minestrone* is held and an entire meal is offered to those present: minestrone, codfish, and boiled beans Lucca style, together with the local wine. And while you are there, take a walk through the streets of Lucca and visit its splendid Romanesque churches.

Before leaving Tuscany, do not forget to sample its desserts and cakes. First of all, the *panforte di Siena*, a fruitcake that dates back to the thirteenth century, made of candied fruits, almonds, walnuts, orange peel, cinnamon and other spices. Panforte is not the only glory of Siena, that lovely city that is built on a human scale and remains truly steeped in its history. The ideal time to be there is on July 2 or August 16 when the seventeen *contrade* (quarters) of the city compete in the famous *corsa del Palio*, a horse race that takes place in the picturesque Piazza del Campo.

Lastly, wherever you happen to eat a Tuscan meal, don't forget to finish it off with a glass of vin santo (sweet wine) and *cantuccini* (or *biscottini di Prato*), those delicious dry cookies filled with slivered almonds.

Panforte (fruitcake) and *ricciarelli* (almond cookies), typical sweets from Siena. The famous Piazza del Campo is in the background.

Flag-wavers at the Palio of Siena, which takes place in the Piazza del Campo twice every year.

Crostini campagnoli
(Crostini with Nuts and Olives)

Preparation time
20 minutes

Difficulty
easy

Serves 4
- 20 large black oil-cured olives, pitted
- 15 walnut halves
- 1 sliver garlic
- grated zest of 1 lemon
- salt
- extra virgin olive oil
- 4 slices stale Tuscan bread

Rosé wine.
Recommended:
- Rosato di Bolgheri
- Schiava dell'Alto Adige

1 Pit the olives in the following way: press the flat blade of a knife across them so that the pits pop out, or else squeeze the olives between your fingers.
Pound the olives in a mortar together with the walnuts, garlic, and lemon zest.

2 Transfer the mixture to a bowl, season with salt, and add just enough olive oil to make a creamy paste, mixing with a wooden spoon.

3 Toast the bread slices, spread the mixture on them, and serve immediately.

Zuppa garmugia
(Meat and Vegetable Soup)

Preparation time
30 minutes

Cooking time
50 minutes

Difficulty
easy

Serves 4
- 3 tablespoons extra virgin olive oil
- 2 slices bacon, cut into thin strips
- 1 small leek, sliced
- 1 onion, thinly sliced
- 3 $\frac{1}{2}$ ounces ground beef
- 2 artichokes, trimmed and thinly sliced
- $\frac{1}{2}$ cup shelled fava beans
- $\frac{1}{2}$ cup shelled peas
- 4 cups hot chicken or beef broth
- 2 dozen asparagus tips
- toasted bread slices (optional)

Light red wine.
Recommended:
- Rosso di Bolgheri
- Merlot

1 In a soup pot, heat the oil. Add the bacon, leeks, and onions and sauté until browned. Add and brown the ground beef, and then add the artichokes, fava beans, and peas. Pour the hot broth into the pot and cook the soup over medium heat, covered, for 20 minutes.

2 Add the asparagus tips and cook until tender. Serve the soup with toasted bread, if desired.

Cacciucco
(Fish Soup)

Preparation time
1 hour

Cooking time
1 hour

Difficulty
medium

Serves 6
- 10 tablespoons extra virgin olive oil
- 4 cloves garlic
- 1 small hot red pepper
- 1 ½ pounds mixed octopus and squid, cleaned and cut up
- 1 cup red wine
- ½ onion, chopped
- 1 stalk celery, chopped
- 1 carrot, chopped
- 1 pound mullet
- 1 pound plum tomatoes
- salt
- 1 pound mixed dogfish and monkfish, sliced
- 1 pound mixed langoustines and shrimp
- 12 mussels
- 1 fistful parsley leaves, chopped
- 6 slices country bread

Light red wine. Recommended:
- Elba Rosso
- Ischia Rosso

1 In a large earthenware pot, heat 5 tablespoons of the oil and sauté 2 whole garlic cloves and the red pepper. Remove the garlic and add the octopus. Cook over low heat for about 20 minutes. Add the squid and continue to cook, adding a little wine.

2 In another pan, heat the remaining 5 tablespoons oil and sauté the onions, celery, carrots, and 1 clove chopped garlic. Add the mullet. Add the tomatoes and 2 ladlefuls of water. Salt and cook for 20 minutes. Pour into the earthenware pot.

3 Bring the liquid to a boil and add the sliced fish and the shellfish, and at the very last minute the mussels and parsley. Taste and adjust the salt, remove the hot pepper and, if necessary, add additional boiling water.

4 In the meantime, toast the bread and rub it with a peeled, slightly crushed garlic clove. Place a slice of bread in each soup plate or individual earthenware bowl. Spoon the fish and broth into the bowls.

Pollo in galera
(Stewed Chicken)

Preparation time
20 minutes

Cooking time
2 hours

Difficulty
easy

Serves 6
- 1 3-pound free-range chicken
- 1 ½ pounds small white onions
- ½ cup vinegar
- 12 cloves
- salt and pepper
- 3 tablespoons extra virgin olive oil
- 6 thin slices stale country bread

*Light red wine.
Recommended:*

- Chianti delle Colline Pisane
- Sangiovese dei Colli Pesaresi

1 Rinse the chicken under cold water and dry thoroughly. Place it in a heavy-bottomed pot. Peel the onions, rinse them, and arrange them around the chicken. Add the vinegar, cloves, salt, and pepper. Pour the oil over the chicken and add enough water to cover it.

2 Seal the pot with aluminum foil, and cover it with the lid. Simmer over low heat for 2 hours.

Toast the slices of bread and arrange them on a warm serving platter. Uncover the chicken and remove it and the onions to the serving platter. Reduce the gravy if necessary and pour it over the chicken.

A free-range chicken is better for this recipe because it keeps its shape and stays tender and flavorful.

Bensone garfagnino
(Candied Fruit Cake)

Preparation time
30 minutes

Cooking time
30 minutes

Difficulty
medium

Serves 4 to 6
- ²/₃ cup raisins
- 1 ¹/₂ cups sugar
- ³/₄ cup butter
- 4 eggs
- 2 ¹/₂ cups flour
- ¹/₂ cup potato flour
- 3 teaspoons baking powder
- salt
- grated zest of 1 lemon
- grated zest of 1 orange
- 1¹/₂ cup mixed candied fruit, chopped
- milk (as needed)

Light sweet wine.
Recommended:
- Lunigiana Bianco Amabile
- Oltrepò Pavese Moscato

1 Preheat the oven to 425°F. Butter and flour a 10-inch cake pan with high sides. Cover the raisins with warm water and soak. Beat the sugar and butter together in a mixing bowl. When the mixture is fluffy, add the eggs one at a time, beating well after each addition.

2 Sift both flours with the baking powder and a pinch of salt. Drain the raisins, dry them, and flour them. Add the flour mixture to the wet ingredients a spoonful at a time, mixing constantly. Then add the lemon and orange zests, the raisins, and the candied fruit. The batter should be creamy. If necessary, add a little milk. Pour into the cake pan and bake for 30 minutes. Test it with a toothpick to make sure that it is done. If the toothpick comes out dry, it is ready. Unmold and cool before serving.

Castagnaccio
(Chestnut Flour Cake)

Preparation time
10 minutes

Cooking time
45 minutes

Difficulty
easy

Serves 6 to 8
- 4 cups chestnut flour
- ¹/₂ teaspoon salt
- 4 to 5 tablespoons olive oil
- ¹/₄ cup pine nuts
- ¹/₄ cup sultana raisins, soaked and drained
- 1 teaspoon rosemary

Strong dessert wine.
Recommended:
- Vin Santo Bianco Pisano di San Torpé
- Moscato di Siracusa

1 Preheat the oven to 425°F. Oil a 12-inch tart pan with low sides.

2 Sift the flour into a bowl, add the salt, and slowly add about 2 cups water, stirring constantly with a spoon. Add 3 tablespoons of the oil. The batter should be fairly liquid and smooth.

3 Pour the batter into the pie plate; it should be less than one inch high. Sprinkle the pine nuts, raisins, and rosemary on the surface. Pour a tablespoon or two of oil over it. Bake for 45 minutes or until the top is brown and cracked. Let it cool in the pie plate. Slice and serve.

TUSCANY

SPECIALTIES

Antipasti (Appetizers)
Crostini con fegatini, Finocchiona, Insalata di farro, Lardo di Colonnata, Panzanella, Sbriciolona.

First courses
Acquacotta, Cacciucco. Garmugia, Minestra di farro, Pappa al pomodoro, Pappardelle sulla lepre, Pici, Ribollita, Zuppa di cavolo nero.

Entrées
Baccalà alla livornese, Cinghiale alla maremmana, Costata alla fiorentina, Peposo, Scottiglia, Tagliata di manzo, Trippa alla fiorentina.

Desserts
Brigidini, Buccellato, Cantuccini, Castagnaccio, Panforte.

TYPICAL RESTAURANTS

Il vignaccio
Via di Santa Lucia 26, Camaiore (Lucca)
Tel. 0584/914200, Closed Wednesday
Prices: Lire 60,000

Venanzio
in Colonnata
Piazza Palestro 3, Carrara
Tel. 0585/758062, Closed Thursday
Prices: Lire 70,000

Da Tonino
Piazza Garibaldi, Cortona (Arezzo)
Tel. 0575/630500, Closed Tuesday
Prices: Lire 60,000/70,000

Ristorante Barca
Via Guerrazzi 60, Portoferraio
(Leghorn)
Tel. 0565/918036, Closed Wednesday
Prices: Lire 60,000

Trattoria La Panzanella
Via dei Cappuccini 10, Empoli
Tel. 0571/922182, Closed Sunday
Prices: Lire 45,000

Coco Lezzone
Via del Parioncino 26 r, Florence
Tel. 055/287178, Closed Sunday
Prices: Lire 60,000/70,000

Trattoria Acquacotta
Via dei Pilastri 51 r, Florence
Tel. 055/242907, Closed Tuesday evening
and Wednesday
Prices: Lire 50,000

Trattoria Baldini
Via il Prato 96 r, Florence
Tel. 055/287663, Closed Saturday
and Sunday
Prices: Lire 50,000

Il Canto del Gallo
Via Mazzini 29, Grosseto
Tel. 0564/414589, Closed Sunday
Prices: Lire 45,000/60,000

Ristorante Il Tartufo
Via Oberdan 70, Leghorn
Tel. 0586/884735, Closed Monday
Prices: Lire 40,000/55,000

Trattoria Buatino
Via Borgo Giannotti 508, Lucca
Tel. 0583/343207, Closed Sunday
Prices: Lire 30,000/45,000

Lorenzo
Via Carducci 61
Forte dei Marmi (Lucca)
Tel. 0584/84030, Closed Monday
Prices: Lire 120,000

Cacciucco di ceci (Chickpea soup)

Guinea fowl baked in paper

Da Riccà
Lungomare di Ponente
Marina di Massa (Massa)
Tel. 0585/241070, Closed Wednesday
Prices: Lire 90,000

Pieve di San Sigismondo
in Poggio alle Mura 222
Montalcino (Siena)
Tel. 0577/866026, Closed Tuesday
Prices: Lire 45,000

Da Bussé
Piazza Dumo 31, Pontremoli
(Massa Carrara)
Tel. 0187/831371, Closed Friday
Prices: Lire 45,000

Dorandò
Vicolo dell'Oro 2, San Gimignano
(Siena)
Tel. 0577/941862, Closed Monday
Prices: Lire 80,000

Ristorante Castelvecchio
Via Castelvecchio 65, Siena
Tel. 0577/49586, Closed Tuesday
Prices: Lire 40,000/50,000

Trattoria da Vadò
Borgo San Lazzaro 9, Volterra (Pisa)
Tel. 0588/86477, Closed Wednesday
Prices: Lire 40,000

WINES

White
Bianco della Valdinievole, Bianco delle Colline Lucchesi, Bianco di Pitigliano, Bianco Vergine della Valdichiana, Bolgheri, Candia dei Colli Apuani, Elba, Montecarlo, Monteregio, Montescudaio, Parrina, Pomino, Val d'Arbia, Vernaccia di San Gimignano.

Rosé
Barco Reale, Carmignano rosato, Val di Cornia rosato.

Red
Brunello di Montalcino, Carmignano, Chianti, Elba, Montecarlo, Monteregio, Montescudaio, Morellino di Scansano, Parrina, Pomino, Rosso di Montalcino, Rosso di Montepulciano, Sassicaia, Val di Cornia rosso, Vino Nobile di Montepulciano.

Dessert wine
Moscadello di Montalcino, Vin Santo.

CHEESES
Caciotta, Marzolino del Chianti, Pecorino Toscano, Raviggiolo, Ricotta.

SHOPPING FOR TYPICAL PRODUCTS
Wines
Enoteca Dionisio
Via Vittorio Emanuele 187
Camaiore (Lucca)

Enoteca Lenzi
Piazza Orsini 18
Castiglione della Pescaia (Grosseto)

Sauro e Assunta
Piazza della Sala, Pistoia

Casa del Caffè
Via San Matteo, San Gimignano (Siena)

Cold Meats
Salumeria Marini
Via A. Selva 313, Ferruccia (Pistoia)

Macelleria Gonnelli
Via Tasso 77, Reggello (Florence)

Dario Cecchini
in Panzano, Via XX Luglio 11
Greve (Florence)

Cheeses
Da Lando
Via Vittorio Emanuele 41
Camaiore (Lucca)

La Cacioteca
Via Fillungo 242, Lucca

Bottega dei Portici
Piazza Garibaldi 3
Palazzuolo sul Senio (Florence)

Angella
Via Garibaldi 2
Pontremoli (Massa Carra)

Finocchiona (salami with fennel seeds)

This salami is typical of the Chianti zone between Florence and Siena, which is even more famous in Italy and abroad for its wine. Although it originated in Chianti, finocchiona is now produced throughout the region.

CHARACTERISTICS

Finocchiona is a large salami that can be as much as eight inches in diameter. Only pork from very lean pigs is used to prepare it. The meat, which must not be at all fibrous, used to come only from the belly of the pig, but now meat from the shoulder and leg is also used. Fifty percent of the mixture is composed of firm, good-quality fat that comes from the jowls or stomach of the pig. The ingredients, which are not too finely ground, are seasoned with wild fennel seeds, just enough garlic to flavor the mixture, salt and pepper, and some red Chianti wine. The salami is aged from five months to a year, depending on the size, given that the larger the salami, the longer it takes to dry. It is only during the aging process that the salami acquires its taste and odor, so a fresh young salami will have neither the smooth, mellow taste of the aged product, nor its firm consistency.

STORING FINOCCHIONA

When buying a piece of finocchiona, cover the cut part with plastic wrap and hang it in a cool dry place, preferably a cellar. When buying already sliced finocchiona, keep it sealed in its original

package on the bottom shelf of the refrigerator; once the package has been opened, it should be consumed as soon as possible.

BUYING FINOCCHIONA

• Make sure that the salami is compact, homogeneous, and tender, all of which indicate proper aging. It should be neither soft nor hard to the touch.
• It should be dark red in color, not bright red or brown.
• It should have the distinct odor of fennel, while that of the garlic should be imperceptible.
• It should be sweet to the taste, mellow, and full-bodied; the taste should complement its odor.

SERVING SUGGESTIONS

Finocchiona often crumbles when sliced. This happens to be one of the characteristics of this salami, which is also called sbriciolona, *or 'crumbler'. It is therefore advisable not to slice it too thinly.*

Finocchiona is an essential part of any Tuscan antipasto and should be accompanied by the region's typical salt-free bread. It can also enhance the flavor of a variety of other preparations.

When cutting it, let the slices fall directly onto slices of bread, preferably the salt-free variety.

One very tasty way of serving finocchiona, although it is rather rich, is to crumble it up and mix it with butter and mascarpone. Spread this mixture on toasted country bread.

Cut some thick slices of the salami, crumble them up and, without cooking them, add them to a risotto of leeks.

Slice finocchiona thin and serve it garnished with grilled eggplant slices seasoned with garlic and oil.

Crumble it up and add it to focaccia dough, which should then be baked using less oil.

To make a savory vegetable pie: cook spinach with crumbled finocchiona, fill

a pastry crust with this mixture, and bake it.

Blanch a head of romaine lettuce and drain it. Cut it into four quarters, and sauté these quickly in a skillet. Serve them with slices of finocchiona.

Blanch and dry some romaine lettuce leaves. Cover each with some fresh cheese, pieces of pâté, and julienned strips of finocchiona. Roll up each leaf and serve. Tender leaves of Savoy cabbage can be substituted for the lettuce.

Prepare a salad with diced celery and thinly sliced white mushrooms. Season it with a little salt, extra virgin olive oil, and pieces of finocchiona.

THE RIGHT WINE
It is not necessary to serve a wine with the salami, given its intense aroma and taste. However, if you choose to do so, a good Parrina Bianco goes well with it.

IN SEARCH OF FINOCCHIONA

Until just a few years ago there used to be a food fair dedicated to finocchiona in the small town of Bivigliano, north of Florence, during the month of October. Nowadays, this salami can usually be found at the gastronomic stands of the numerous festivals and country fairs held throughout the region, especially during the summer months. Not far from Bivigliano on the road that goes from Borgo San Lorenzo to Pontassieve is the Ruffino winery (famous for its Chianti), and nearby at the Macelleria Giancarlo Perigli you can find an exceptional finocchiona.

THE
MARCHES

Simple ingredients, original dishes

In order to understand the origin of the Marches cuisine, take a look at a map of the region: the Apennine mountain range gives way to green hills and these in turn roll down to the coastline of the Adriatic Sea. There are thickly wooded oak groves, and ancient walled towns inhabited by hospitable people who are attached to their traditions, and continue to make agriculture one of the chief economic resources of the region, producing wheat, corn, tomatoes, cauliflower, wine, and olives.

With the wheat they make flour and with the flour they make pasta, which is one of the principal dishes of the Marches. The Macerata specialty of *vincisgrassi* is that town's own personal interpretation of the better-known Emilian lasagne. The origins of *vincisgrassi* have long been disputed. Some maintain that the name comes from that of Prince Windischgrötz, the commander of the Austrian expeditionary force in the war against Napoleon Bonaparte in 1799. It seems that some anonymous cook served him lasagne seasoned with the local black truffles,

ham, cream, and cheese every day. Others maintain that the recipe was already known at the beginning of the 1700s, and that it was a very popular dish since in those days the local people found truffles as easily as if they were potatoes, and so even the humblest peasant's table was graced by that priceless tuber. Things have changed since then unfortunately. In the trattorias of the Marches, ground meat, brains, and sweetbreads have taken the place of truffles in the *vincisgrassi*. However, this delicious dish is still a joy to the palate! It can be preceded by an antipasto of *olive all'ascolana*, the local giant green olives that are filled with ground meat, breaded, and fried. Actually, stuffed olives should be eaten in Ascoli Piceno, for it was that city that invented them. But first, a visit is in order to the fruit and vegetable market held in the larger cloister of the Church of San Francesco in Piazza del Popolo. The church is built of travertine and its warm color is the salient feature of the buildings in the old part of the city. If you happen to be there in

The Church of San Vittore at Genga in the province of Ancona.

the beginning of the summer, do visit the fair held at Acquasanta Terme on June 26 so you can taste the smoked ham, *lonza*, *ciausculo* (a creamy salami that is spread on bread), and of course the famous stuffed olives. But let's get back to the first courses. Besides *vincisgrassi*, another specialty of the Marches is *polenta*. Indeed, it is so characteristic of the region that the local people refer to themselves ironically as *marchigià magna pulenda* (polenta-eaters of the Marches).

It can be eaten in many ways, but the most original is perhaps the soft version which is poured onto a huge wooden board, and seasoned with a meat sauce, with everyone at the table eating from this common dish. How can we not talk about *porchetta*? Although today it is considered a specialty of Lazio and Sardinia, this way of roasting a whole pig was invented in the Marches. You may even come across one being roasted. This takes place outdoors, after the pig has been duly stuffed with wild fennel, rosemary, and garlic. Those who are not worried about their figures and have good digestion can venture forth on long gastronomic walks sampling what the region has to offer. On the first Sunday of May, the *Sagra della Porchetta* is held at Monterado in the province of Ancona. The promontory of Conero, that rocky Apennine cliff that drops into the Adriatic, is a good place for a constitutional. Today the Conero is a regional park where it is often possible to catch sight of storks and honey buzzards.

And now that we are at the sea, it is time to discuss the *brodetto marchigiano*, the wonderfully rich and filling fish soup of the Marches. There are many recipes for it but there are only three variations: with tomato, without tomato, with saffron. What is important is the quantity and quality of the fish. Some superstitiously say that it must include at least thirteen kinds of fish!

If meat is preferred to fish, then head inland where they make spitted quail, partridges, or squab, game, free-range casserole-cooked chickens, or chickens stuffed with olives. And afterwards, some pecorino cheese and a glass of Verdicchio di Jesi. The great originality of the Marches cuisine is to be found in the desserts, which are often made with ingredients that seem to be more suitable for savory dishes. In Ascoli Piceno, they make *calcioni* (a sweet cheese ravioli) with pecorino cheese, and in Ancona, *frustenga*, a sweet polenta mixed with dried figs, walnuts, and raisins.

Above: Palazzo del Popolo in Ascoli Piceno.
Left: Grilled spitted quails on a bed of bay leaves.

125

Ciavarro
(Grain, Bean, and Pork Rind Soup)

Preparation time
20 minutes

Cooking time
3 hours

Diffficulty
easy

Serves 4
- 3 cups dried beans (assortment of chickpeas, white beans, lentils, and corn)
- 1/2 pound pork rind
- 1 cup chopped plum tomatoes
- salt and pepper
- extra virgin olive oil

Light red wine.
Recommended:
- Rosso Conero
- Barbera dei Colli Tortonesi

1 Soak the chickpeas in lukewarm water for 24 hours; soak the other beans for 12 hours.

2 Wash and dry the pork rind and cut it into bite-sized pieces.

3 Drain the chickpeas. Place them in a soup pot (not aluminum) with the pork rind. Cover with enough water to come up 3-inches above the chickpeas and simmer over low heat for about 3 hours. After the first hour, add the white beans and corn and 30 minutes after that, the lentils and tomatoes. Add extra boiling water if the soup thickens too much.

4 Thirty minutes before serving, add salt and pepper to taste. The soup should be thick. Serve with a drizzle of oil and fresh black pepper.

Tonno briaco
(Tuna Steaks with Marsala)

Preparation time
20 minutes

Cooking time
30 minutes

Difficulty
medium

Serves 4
- 9 tablespoons extra virgin olive oil
- 1 medium onion, thinly sliced
- 1 fistful parsley leaves, chopped
- 1 bay leaf
- 4 tuna steaks (about 7 ounces each)
- salt and pepper
- $1/2$ cup dry Marsala wine
- 4 slices country bread
- 4 salted anchovies, rinsed and boned (or 8 fillets)
- 1 tablespoon capers
- 1 tablespoon lemon juice

Dry white wine. Recommended:
- Verdicchio di Matelica
- San Severo Bianco

1 In a large skillet, heat 4 tablespoons of the oil and sauté the onions, parsley, and bay leaf. Add the tuna steaks and brown them. Add very little salt, pepper, and the Marsala wine. Cook each side over high heat for 10 minutes.

2 In the meantime, fry the bread slices in 2 tablespoons of the oil, drain them, and arrange on a warm serving platter.

3 As soon as the tuna steaks are cooked, remove them from the skillet, reserving the juices. Place the tuna on the bread slices and keep warm.

4 Sauté the anchovies in the remaining 3 tablespoons oil, mashing them with a fork. Add the cooking juices from the tuna, the capers, and the lemon juice. Taste and correct for salt. Bring the mixture just to a boil and then pour it over the fish and serve.

Marsala wine is one of the most prized fortified wines in Italy. Its name comes from the Sicilian city where it was first produced. It has a heady bouquet and a warm, full-bodied flavor. Some Marsala wines have a slightly bitter almond taste.

Lu cuticusu
(Aromatic Fava Bean Salad)

Preparation time
30 minutes

Cooking time
15 minutes

Difficulty
easy

Serves 4
- 6 pounds unshelled fava beans
- 3 salted anchovies, rinsed and boned
- 2 cloves garlic
- 1 teaspoon fresh marjoram leaves
- 5 tablespoons extra virgin olive oil
- 1 tablespoon white wine vinegar
- salt

Rosé wine.
Recommended:
- Rosato Collameno
- Rosato di Arborea

1 Shell the fava beans and cook them in boiling salted water until the skin is wrinkled but they still taste 'fresh', about 8 minutes.

2 Chop the anchovy fillets with the garlic and the washed and dried marjoram leaves. Drain the fava beans, transfer them to a salad bowl, and toss them with the oil, the vinegar, and the chopped mixture. Season with salt and serve immediately.

Cuticusu, which means 'tickle' in Macerata, indicates the appetizing quality of this dish.

Scarafolata

(Sweet Fritters)

Preparation time
30 minutes

Cooking time
30 minutes

Difficulty
medium

Serves 8
- 4 eggs
- 4 tablespoons sugar
- 4 cups flour
- 1 tablespoon baking powder
- salt
- $1/2$ cup milk
- $1/4$ cup olive oil
- $1/4$ cup Mistrà or other anisette
- grated zest of 1 lemon
- vegetable oil for frying
- confectioner's sugar

Light dessert wine.
Recommended:
- Vernaccia di Serrapetrona
- Moscato di Sardegna

1 In a mixing bowl, beat the eggs with the sugar. Sift the flour into the bowl together with the baking powder and a pinch of salt. Mix well, adding the milk, olive oil, anisette, and lemon zest. The batter should be smooth and very creamy.

2 Heat 1 inch oil in a skillet and when it is hot but not smoking, add the batter by the tablespoon. Move the skillet in a clockwise direction so the fritters can roll around in the hot oil. When they are golden and puffed, remove them with a slotted spoon and drain on absorbent paper. When all the fritters have been cooked, transfer them to a serving platter and sprinkle them with confectioner's sugar.

Mistrà (anisette) is a liqueur made by macerating aniseeds in alcohol.

THE MARCHES

Spelt with zucchini blossoms

SPECIALTIES

Antipasti (Appetizers)
Alici con cipolle, Bruschetta, Ciavuscolo, Fricandò di verdure, Lonzino, Olive all'ascolana, Tortino di verdure.

First courses
Brodetto di pesce, Ciavarro, Frascarelli, Pinciarelli, Polenta alla spianatoia, Vincisgrassi.

Entrées
Coniglio in gaggiotto, Coniglio in porchetta, Fricò alla cacciatora, Fritto misto all'ascolana, Frittura di paranza, Piccione in casseruola, Pollo in potacchio, Porchetta allo spiedo, Stoccafisso all'anconetana.

Desserts
Calcioni, Ciambellone, Frustenga.

TYPICAL RESTAURANTS
Trattoria La Cantineta
Via Gramsci, Ancona
Tel. 071/201107, Closed Sunday
Prices: Lire 40,000/50,000

Strabacco
Via Oberdan 2, Ancona
Tel. 071/54213, Closed Monday
Prices: Lire 50,000/60,000

Ristorante Incontri
Via Fortezza Pia 3, Ascoli Piceno
Tel. 0736/252227, Closed Tuesday
Prices: Lire 45,000

Osteria dell'Arte
Vicolo dell'Arco della Luna 7
Camerino (Macerata)
Tel. 0737/633558, Closed Friday
Prices: Lire 50,000

Al Pesce Azzurro
Viale Adriatico 48
Fano (Pesaro)
Tel. 0721/803165, Closed Monday
Prices: Lire 20,000

Hotel Astoria
Viale Vittorio Veneto 8
Fermo (Ascoli Piceno)
Tel 0734/228601
Prices: Lire 40,000/60,000

Osteria della Miseria
Via Mandorli 2
Gabicce (Pesaro)
Tel. 0541/958308, Closed Monday
Prices: Lire 35,000/45,000

Hostaria Santa Lucia
Via Marche 2b
Jesi (Ancona)
Tel. 0731/64409, Closed Monday
Prices: Lire 70,000

Osteria dei Fiori
Via L. Rossi 61, Macerata
Tel. 073 260142, Closed Sunday
Prices: Lire 35,000/50,000

Il Bragozzo
Strada delle Marche 154
Pesaro
Tel. 0721/391472, Closed Monday
Prices: Lire 50,000

Il Cantuccio di Leo
Via Perfetti 18, Pesaro
Tel. 0721/68088, Closed Wednesday
Prices: Lire 70,000/80,000

Vanda
in Castel Cavallino
Via Mari 6, Urbino (Pesaro)
Tel. 0722/349117, Closed Wednesday
Prices: Lire 50,000/60,000

WINES
White
Bianchello del Metauro, Falerio dei Colli
Ascolani, Verdicchio di Jesi, Verdicchio
di Matelica.

Red
Lacrima di Morro d'Alba, Rosso Conero,
Rosso Piceno, Sangiovese.

Dessert wine
Vernaccia di Serrapetrona.

CHEESES
Casciotta di Serrapetrona, Formaggio
di Tufo, Giuncata, Pecorino, Slattato.

SHOPPING FOR TYPICAL PRODUCTS
Wines
Enoteca Anconavini
Via D. Chiesa 19, Ancona

Enoteca Mercurio
Galleria del Commercio 3, Macerata

Enoteca Vino Vip
Viale Verdi 78, Pesaro

Cold Meats
Salumeria Bilei
Via Cialdini 5-7, Fabriano (Ancona)

Norcineria Altonera
Via Roma, Castel Sant'Angelo
(Macerata)

Vissana Salumiardi
Corso Cesare Battisti 57
Visso (Macerata)

Salumi Passamonti
Via Leopardi 12, Monte Vidon Combatte
(Ascoli Piceno)

Cheeses
Gastronomia Marinelli
Via Rodi 15, Ancona

Casa del Formaggio
Piazza Kennedy 10-11, Ancona

Cooperativa Agricola del Petrano
Strada del Monte Paganuccio
Cagli (Pesaro)

Piccola Bontà
Via Montebello 62
San Benedetto del Tronto (Ascoli Piceno)

Rib lamb chops with rosemary

UMBRIA

The region of simplicity and harmony

A panoramic view of Assisi.

Assisi, and Città di Castello are reflected in the Umbrian gastronomy.

In spite of its costliness, in no other region is the prized black truffle used as it is in Umbria. The black truffles of Norcia and Spoleto are pounded with a pestle in the mortar with oil, anchovies, and garlic to make sauces for spaghetti, or grated abundantly onto simple omelettes.

At Cerreto di Spoleto, in the province of Perugia, the black truffle is the king of a local market held every Thursday from November to March. Of course, music lovers prefer to go to Spoleto, which has served as the stage for the Festival of Two Worlds during June and July for some forty years.

What type of cuisine could characterize the region that was the birthplace of Saint Francis of Assisi, that has a landscape dotted with medieval villages permeated by a truly spiritual atmosphere and small towns that are masterpieces of tranquility and sobriety? In a landscape rich in woods, rivers, cliffs, and hills marked by vineyards and olive groves, the Umbrians have created a simple, solid cuisine that respects their origins. As in Tuscany, grilled and spitted meats are sovereign. The roasts are memorable in this meat-raising region where the pigs are fed acorns. All kinds of game is hunted – woodchuck, partridge, pheasant, quail, wild pigeons, and hare – but nature is always respected. And everything is seasoned simply with a genuine pale green olive oil, one of the finest in Italy. The harmony and lightness of cities like Perugia, Gubbio,

Right: Risotto with black truffles from Norcia.

134

And the city really does become a stage where opera, music, theater, and dance are performed in every nook and cranny.

The places to visit in Umbria are infinite. On the Lazio border, Orvieto boasts one of the most significant creations of Italian architecture in its cathedral, which also possesses Luca Signorelli's famous fresco of *The End of the World.* Another glory of the city is the wine it produces. Orvieto wine, either dry or semisweet, is an excellent accompaniment for the caciotta and pecorino cheeses that the Umbrian shepherds continue to produce to delight the palates of one and all.

Then there is Perugia, with its National Gallery of Umbria, which houses such masterpieces as Duccio di Boninsegna's *Madonna and Child,* Beato Angelico's huge polyptych, and Perugino's *Adoration of the Magi.* Perugia has gastronomic masterpieces as well, like *palombacci alla perugina* (wild pigeons wrapped in slices of raw ham) and meat soup. Apropos of meat, Perugian beef is famed for its excellence.

A compulsory stop for any visitor who decides to go to Umbria is Assisi. One of the typical dishes there is *cipollata,* in which the simple, almost humble onion manages to express the spiritual atmosphere of the town. Assisi is also famous for its *rocciata,* a cake made with dried fruits and softened with wine.

Umbria may not be a region that excels in its pasta courses; however, the originality of its antipasti makes up for this. Probably the most interesting is *mezzafegato,* a felicitous combination of pig's liver, orange peel, pine nuts, raisins, and sugar. Then there is the garlicky and peppery *capocollo, budelluci* (pig's intestine aromatized with wild fennel and then smoked and cooked on a spit or grill), and *castaldo tartufato,* a cheese made from cow's and sheep's milk and pebbled with white truffles.

Lastly, before leaving Umbria, a sampling of some of the regional sweets and a glass of good vin santo is recommended: the *pinoccate perugine,* a candy made of wafers, candied orange peel, and pine nuts, are served at Christmastime; at carnival instead there is *cicerchiata,* a ring cake covered with sugar and colored sprinkles. Equally famous and based on ancient recipes are the *pan pepato* from Spoleto and Foligno and the *pan nociato* from Todi.

Zuppa alla todina
(Chestnut and Chickpea Soup)

Preparation time
30 minutes plus soaking time

Cooking time
1 ½ hours

Difficulty
easy

Serves 6
- 1 cup dried chickpeas
- 9 ounces chestnuts in shells
- 3 tablespoons extra virgin olive oil, plus more for garnish
- 1 fistful parsley leaves, chopped
- 1 clove garlic chopped
- 1 cup tomato purée
- salt and pepper
- 6 slices country bread, toasted

Light red wine.
Recommended:
- Colli Martani Sangiovese
- Chianti di Montalbano

1 Soak the chickpeas in lukewarm water for 24 hours. Drain them, reserving the cooking liquid, and rinse. To save time, cook them in a pressure cooker with 6 cups water for 30 minutes from the time it steams.
When they are cooked, add salt, and let them sit for 10 minutes, then drain, reserving the liquid.

2 Make a slit in the chestnut shells with a sharp knife. Place the chestnuts in a 450°F oven for about 20 minutes. Peel them carefully and chop them.

3 In a Dutch oven heat 3 tablespoons oil and sauté the parsley and garlic. Stir in the chestnuts, the tomato purée, and after a minute or two, the drained chickpeas. Mix well, then add the chickpea cooking liquid, salt, and pepper. Simmer for 30 minutes.

4 Place a slice of toasted bread in each soup plate, add the soup, and garnish with a drizzle of oil.

Quaglie nel pane
(Wrapped Quails)

Preparation time
30 minutes

Cooking time
30 minutes

Difficulty
medium

Serves 8
- 8 quails
- salt and pepper
- 8 fresh sage leaves
- 3 tablespoons butter
- $1/2$ cup dry white wine
- 2 pounds bread dough, already risen (see recipe on page 176)
- 8 slices bacon, rolled thin
- olive oil

Light red wine. Recommended:
- Colli del Trasimeno Rosso
- Franciacorta Rosso

1 Wash and dry the quails inside and out. Place a pinch of salt and a sage leaf inside each. Tie them with white thread.

2 Preheat the oven to 450°F. In a skillet, melt the butter until it bubbles. Add the quail and sauté until browned. Season with salt and pepper. Pour the wine over the quail and evaporate it over high heat. Remove from the heat.

3 Knead the dough briefly, divide it into 8 pieces, and roll out each piece with your palms. Remove the thread from the quails, wrap each in a piece of bacon, and place it on the dough. Moisten with cooking juices and then seal inside the dough.

4 Place the quail on an oiled baking sheet and bake for 20 minutes. When the bread is golden, remove from the oven and serve.

Cipollata

(Braised Onions, Prunes, and Raisins)

Preparation time
15 minutes plus
soaking time

Cooking time
30 minutes

Difficulty
easy

Serves 4
- ¼ cup sultana
  raisins
- 1 cup prunes
- 1 ½ pounds
  onions (about 5
  medium), sliced
  ¼-inch thick
- 4 tablespoons extra
  virgin olive oil
- salt
- 5 cloves
- 1 fistful parsley
  leaves, chopped
- 1 to 2 sprigs
  marjoram, leaves
  chopped
- ½ teaspoon
  cinnamon

Light red wine.
Recommended:
- Colli Altotiberini
  Rosso
- Cesanese del Piglio

1 Soak the raisins and prunes separately in lukewarm water. Boil the onions for about 10 minutes in abundant water. Drain and dry the raisins and prunes; pit the prunes and chop them.

2 In a large skillet, heat the oil. Drain the onions and add them to the skillet. Add salt and cover the skillet. Cook over low heat for 10 minutes. Add the cloves, raisins, prunes, parsley, and marjoram leaves. Cook for another 10 minutes, mixing from time to time. Add a tablespoon of boiling water if the mixture becomes too dry.

3 Sprinkle with cinnamon and serve.

Crostoni ubriachi
(Crostini with Chocolate Cream and Almonds)

Preparation time
30 minutes plus
resting time

Cooking time
15 minutes

Difficulty
easy

Serves 6
- 3 ½ ounces bittersweet chocolate
- ½ cup fresh brewed coffee
- ½ cup rum
- ½ cup alchermes (or use amaro, or a liqueur of choice)
- 6 slices stale country bread
- ¾ cup almonds

1 Break half the chocolate into pieces and melt them over very low heat. Remove from the heat and stir in the coffee, 5 tablespoons of the rum, and 5 tablespoons of the alchermes. Dip the bread slices into this mixture and remove them when they are moist but not mushy. Arrange them on a serving platter. If they are too big, cut them in half.

2 Preheat the oven to 350°F. Drop the almonds into boiling water for not more than 3 minutes, drain them, and skin them. Place them on a baking sheet and toast them in the oven until golden.

Chop them and place them in a bowl. Grate the remaining chocolate and add it to the almonds with the liqueurs.

3 Spread this mixture on the bread slices and set them aside for 15 minutes before serving.

Alchermes is a dark red liqueur made by macerating cinnamon, abelmosk, and carnations in alcohol. To this mixture is added rose water, extract of jasmine, and an infusion of rice, sugar, and cochineal for coloring.

UMBRIA

SPECIALTIES

Antipasti (Appetizers)
Brustengo, Budellucci, Capocollo, Crescia, Crostoni, Mazzafegato, Pizzola ternana, Torta al testo.

First courses
Ciriole, Imbrecciata, Risotto con gli strigoli, Manfrigoli, Pappardelle al cinghiale, Rigatoni alla norcina, Stringozzi, Zuppa di cicerchie.

Entrées
Beccaccia al crostone, Cipollata, Lumache alla folignate, Palombacci alla ghiotta, Piccione ripieno, Tegamaccio.

Desserts
Brustengolo, Cicerchiata, Crescionda, Maccheroni dolci, Mostaccioli, Pan nociato, Pan pepato, Pinoccata, Rocciata, Tozzetti.

TYPICAL RESTAURANTS

Piazzetta dell'Erba
Via S. Gabriele dell'Addolorata 15 b
Assisi (Perugia)
Tel. 075/815352, Closed Monday
Prices: Lire 30,000/40,000

Buca di San Francesco
Via Brizi 1, Assisi (Perugia),
Closed Monday
Prices: Lire 70,000

Il Bersaglio
Via V. E. Orlando 14
Città di Castello (Perugia)
Tel. 075/8555534, Closed Wednesday
Prices: Lire 45,000/60,000

Villa Roncalli
Via Roma 25, Foligno (Perugia)
Tel. 0742/391091, Closed Monday
Prices: Lire 80,000/90,000

Taverna del Lupo
Via Ansidei 6, Foligno (Perugia)
Tel. 075/9274368, Closed Monday
Prices: Lire 80,000

Trattoria da Sara
Strada Calvese 55-57, Narni (Terni)
Tel. 0744/796138, Closed Wednesday
Prices: Lire 45,000/60,000

Cantina della Villa
in Colle di Nocera 141
Nocera Umbra (Perugia)
Tel. 0742/810666, Closed Wednesday
Prices: Lire 40,000

Hotel Grotta Azzurra
Via Alfieri 12, Norcia (Perugia)
Tel. 0743/816513
Prices: Lire 75,000

Ristorante I Sette Consoli
Piazza Sant'Angelo 1a, Orvieto
Tel. 0763/343911, Closed Wednesday
Prices: Lire 50,000/60,000

La volpe e l'uva
Vi Ripa Corsica 1, Orvieto
Tel. 0763/341612, Closed Monday and Tuesday
Prices: Lire 30,000/40,000

Pan nociato todino (Nut bread from Todi)

Aladino
Via delle Prome 11, Perugia
Tel. 075/5720938, Closed Monday
Prices: Lire 70,000

Cesarino
Via della Gabbia 13, Perugia
Tel. 075/5736277, Closed Wednesday
Prices: Lire 40,000

Trattoria Pecchiarda
Vicolo San Giovanni 1, Spoleto
Tel. 0743/221009, Closed Thursday
Prices: Lire 40,000

Trattoria Carlino
Via Piemonte 1, Terni
Tel. 0744/420163, Closed Monday
Prices: Lire 45,000

La Mulinella
Ponte Naia 29, Todi (Perugia)
Tel. 075/8944779, Closed Wednesday
Prices: Lire 35,000

Taverna del Pescatore
in Pigge, Staatsstraße Flaminia Vecchia
139 km, Trevi (Perugia)
Tel. 0742/780920, Closed Wednesday
Prices: Lire 50,000/60,000

WINES
White
Grechetto, Malvasia, Orvieto, Torgiano, Trebbiano.

Red
Montefalco, Sagrantino di Montefalco, Sangiovese, Torgiano.

Dessert wine
Sagrantino di Montefalco liquoroso.

Purée of fava beans with *bruschetta* (toasted bread)

CHEESES
Pecorino, Caciotta al tartufo, Scamorza.

SHOPPING FOR TYPICAL PRODUCTS
Wines
Cantina Foresi
Piazza Duomo 2, Orvieto

Enoteca Vivo Vino
Corso Vecchio 201, Terni

Accademia dei Convivanti
Via San Bonaventura 11, Todi

Cold Meats
Salumificio Elli Giulietti
Corso Cavour 13, Città di Castello (Perugia)

Ansuini
Via Anicia 105, Norcia (Perugia)

Salumeria Olivieri
Via Mazzini 66, Foligno (Perugia)

Cheeses
Gastronomia Carraro
Corso Cavour 101, Orvieto

Fattoria L'Arco
Cordigliano 19, Todi

Caciotte cheeses

The delicate-tasting cheeses called caciotte are produced for the most part in central Italy, where they are made according to traditional methods. The only differences among the cheeses have to do with the kind of milk used to make them and the local methods of production.

Although they are classified under the same generic name, some cheeses vary in taste and aroma according to their region or even their province of origin. For example, caciotte are always to be found among the local products in the markets of the central Italian regions. They have an ancient origin. In fact, the Italian word cacio comes from the Latin caseus, while the more recent formaggio ('cheese' in current Italian) has its origin in formaticum. The name refers to the small rounds of cheese whose weight ranges between one and two kilograms (about two to four pounds). These may be made of milk from sheep, goats, cows, water buffalo, or a mixture of these. Some cheeses are colored on the outside with tomato, others are pressed between walnut leaves, and still others are aromatized with truffles or hot pepper.

Apart from these local differences, a typical caciotta is produced from sheep's milk in a standard way. The milk is heated to 96.8°F, often before pasteurization, at which time it receives a culture of selected lactic acid bacteria. It is then curdled with calf's or lamb's rennet. The curd is broken up into

BUYING CACIOTTE

• Caciotta has a cylindrical shape with slightly convex sides and it weighs from 2 to 4 ½ pounds.
• It has a thin, smooth or slightly wrinkled crust that is either white or straw yellow in color.
• The cheese has a soft texture, and it is compact in consistency.
• It has the sweet, delicate taste of milk, and a pleasant aroma.

walnut-sized lumps and the whey is removed. The remaining curd is placed in molds which are salted in a saline solution, and then aged for 20 to 30 days. A pleasant bland cheese is thus obtained, especially bland when made with calf's rennet. It lacks the sharpness that characterizes some of the stronger cheeses, but it maintains all the originality of an age-old production.

PRODUCTION OF CACIOTTE

In order better to understand this cheese, it might be worth knowing more about the different local productions, starting with that of Tuscany. The Maremma zone produces the greatest amount of caciotte. There the cheese is made principally with cow's milk and acquires a particularly sweet flavor. The pecorino senese, produced entirely from sheep's milk, is often treated with tomato on the surface, which gives it its distinct reddish-orange coloring. In Umbria, for some decades now, the cheese, made from cow's milk, is prepared by adding grated black truffles to the curd. Other varieties are aromatized with onion or herbs. The prized fresh caciottina made from water buffalo milk in Lazio weighs about half a pound, while the caciotta from the neighboring Agro Romano is a yellow cheese with a greenish cast that is due to a particular kind of forage. Some caciotte from Campania contain flakes of hot pepper.

SERVING SUGGESTIONS

The caciotte on the market vary depending upon how long they are aged, and therefore they lend themselves to different uses in the kitchen. They go well with crisp vegetables, in stuffings, and as seasonings because of their mild flavor. And to exalt their flavor, try serving them with a fine honey.

Cut fresh caciotta into cubes and mix these with fresh tomatoes that have been marinated with salt, basil, and extra virgin olive oil, and season pasta with this sauce.

Serve fresh young caciotta with a seasonal salad or zucchini dressed with oil.

Use medium-aged caciotte in fillings for ravioli.

Cube fresh caciotta and mix it with chopped celery, sliced raw mushrooms, and a shaved truffle, and dress it with oil and lemon juice.

The more savory caciotte, especially those from sheep's milk, can be served as a main course with boiled rice, buttered carrots, or a leek fondue.

Serve sharp-tasting caciotte with a thin veil of truffled honey.

Serve thin slices of a well-aged caciotta with a salad of thinly sliced raw artichokes dressed with oil, lemon juice, and salt.

Serve the younger caciotte, especially the sweet-tasting ones made from cow's milk, with white bread; serve medium-aged caciotte with country bread, and well-aged varieties with whole-wheat breads.

THE RIGHT WINE
Light white wines go best with the younger cheeses: a Lugana, a Ribolla, or a Gavi. For the stronger-tasting cheeses, full-bodied whites are recommended, like a Tocai del Collio, a Vernaccia di San Gimignano, or a Greco di Tufo.

IN SEARCH OF CACIOTTE

Along the state or provincial roads of central Italy, you will find cheese-makers and shops selling local cheeses that usually never leave their area of production.

Quality products can be found at the following: La Parrina, Via Aurelia km. 146, at Albinia, near Orbetello (province of Grosseto); Giacomo Vitto, Via della Repubblica 45, in Amelia (province of Terni).

LAZIO

Savory peasant fare

One would expect a rich, high-sounding cuisine from a region like Lazio, one that is reminiscent of the banquets of Imperial Rome or the ostentation of the papal courts. But it is nothing like that. The gastronomy of Lazio is the most plebian of the entire peninsula. It is a gastronomy of pastoral rather than agricultural tradition, a cuisine that is not particularly refined but that is savory and creative. One eats well and relatively inexpensively in a Roman trattoria. As a matter of fact, there is a popular saying that goes: 'the more you spend, the worse you eat!' It is a cuisine that seasons with pork fat. Food is fried with lard, not oil; pasta is seasoned with *guanciale* (bacon from the jowls of the pig), and beans are flavored with pork rind. Rome is the kingdom of *supplì* (rice croquettes filled with meat sauce), and *panzerotti* (similar to ravioli) filled with ham and cheese, both of which are fried. They are eaten as an antipasto, but are even better as a tasty snack to be consumed while visiting the ancient monuments and palaces that fill the Eternal City.

Among the typical regional pasta dishes that have become popular throughout the country are *spaghetti alla carbonara* (made with guanciale, eggs, Parmesan cheese, and black pepper), *penne all'arrabbiata* (with tomato sauce and lots of hot red pepper), and lastly, *bucatini all'amatriciana* (with tomato sauce, *guanciale*, hot red pepper, and pecorino cheese). This last dish really is from the Abruzzo because Amatrice, the town where its name originates, was once part of the province of L'Aquila in Abruzzo, but today is in the Lazio province of Rieti. If you would like to taste a first course that is rarely found in any trattoria outside of Rome, then order *pagliata con rigatoni*. The *pagliata* corresponds to the duodenum part of the intestine, most often of veal, and its taste comes from the chyme, a particular substance which is found there. Those with refined palates may turn up their noses, but if they make the effort, they will discover a great delicacy!

The best among the entrées are *abbacchio*, succulent milk-fed baby lamb, wild boar, and suckling pig, while beef and veal are less popular. Another typical plebian dish, one that

Above: Typical products of Lazio with Piazza Navona in the background. Below: *Bucatini all'amatriciana.*

might follow the pagliata, is *coda alla vaccinara* (oxtail simmered with tomatoes, onions, carrots, and celery).

Visitors who have already been to Rome and wish to see something of the surrounding area should strike out for the Castelli Romani (the hills lying to the southeast), where it is traditional for the Romans to spend their Sundays in October. Especially worth a visit are Frascati (and its famous Villa Lancellotti and Villa Aldobrandini), Grottaferrata, Nemi, Ariccia (the *Sagra della Porchetta* is held here on the first Sunday of September), Albano, and Castel Gandolfo, the summer residence of the Pope. Be sure to go to one of the typical wine cellars that abound in the area for a sampling of the famous *porchetta* (roast suckling pig on a spit) and the local white wines: the classic Frascati, the Marino, the Velletri, the Colli Albani.

From Castel Gandolfo head north toward Viterbo, the home of the thirteenth-century Palazzo Papale, the ancient residence of the popes, and from there to Tuscania and Tarquinia in the land of the Etruscans. You can even try an Etruscan dish, the *minestra tuscia*, a delicate vegetable and semolina soup served with grated Parmesan cheese and a glass of white wine.

Here, a vegetarian meal is easy, since the Lazio countryside is known for its vegetables and ways to cook them. First and foremost are the artichokes which are prepared *alla giudia* (Jewish style), fried in olive oil, or *alla romana*, filled with garlic, parsley, and wild mint. A well-known salad vegetable in Lazio that is unknown elsewhere are *puntarelle*, the sprouts of a variety of chicory in season in February and March.

The pastoral tradition of Lazio has produced many excellent cheeses: the classic *pecorino romano*, buffalo mozzarella, and the creamy ricotta cheese that is used in all sorts of recipes, including vegetable pies, pastas, cakes, and tarts.

Detail of a fresco in Tarquinia, an ancient Etruscan city.

Stairs of the Palazzo Papale in Viterbo.

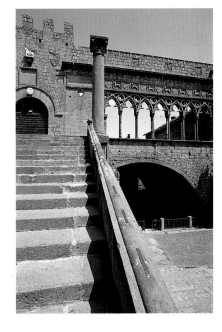

Supplì al telefono
(Stuffed Rice Croquettes)

Preparation time
30 minutes plus
cooling time

Cooking time
20 minutes

Difficulty
medium

Serves 8 to 10
- 3 tablespoons butter
- 1 small onion, sliced
- 1 ½ cups arborio rice
- 4 cups meat broth
- 3 eggs
- freshly grated nutmeg
- salt and pepper
- ¼ cup grated Parmesan cheese
- 1 fistful parsley leaves, chopped
- 5 ounces mozzarella cheese, diced small
- flour
- bread crumbs

Dry white wine.
Recommended:
- Cerveteri Bianco
- Gambellara

1 In a large saucepan, melt the butter and sauté the onion. Add the rice and stir until it is toasted. Add the boiling broth by the ladleful, making sure that each one is absorbed before adding the next one. Remove the rice from the heat when it is *al dente*. After a few minutes, mix in 1 of the eggs and a grating of nutmeg. Pour the mixture onto a large platter and let it cool.

2 Beat 1 egg with salt and pepper and add the Parmesan, the parsley, and the mozzarella.

3 Flatten a tablespoonful of the rice mixture in the palm of your hand, and place a teaspoonful of the cheese filling in the center. Enclose the filling by closing your hand; the *supplì* should have an elongated shape.

4 Beat the remaining egg in a soup plate with a pinch of salt. Dip the *supplì* in flour first, then in the egg, and lastly in the bread crumbs.

5 Heat 1 inch of lard or oil in a skillet and fry the *supplì* over moderate heat so the cheese will have time to melt. Remove them when they are golden brown, and drain them on paper towels. Serve immediately.

Spaghetti alla carbonara
(Spaghetti with Bacon and Egg Sauce)

Preparation time
10 minutes

Cooking time
20 minutes

Difficulty
easy

Serves 4
- 4 eggs
- salt and pepper
- 4 tablespoons grated pecorino or 5 tablespoons grated Parmesan cheese
- 3/4 pound spaghetti (or bucatini or penne)
- 1 tablespoon extra virgin olive oil
- 3 1/2 ounces *guanciale* or lean bacon, cut into strips or cubes

Dry white wine. Recommended:
- Frascati
- Pinot Grigio dell'Isonzo

1 In a large bowl, beat the eggs with a pinch of salt, a generous grinding of black pepper, and 2 tablespoons of the grated cheese.

2 Boil the pasta in abundant boiling water, salting it less than usual. At the same time, heat the oil in a skillet and brown the guanciale or bacon, stirring it often so that the fat melts and the meat becomes crisp.

3 Give the eggs another beating. Drain the pasta, pour it into the bowl with the eggs, and mix it rapidly. Then pour the mixture into the skillet and mix until it is well blended and the eggs have become creamy. Serve with the remaining cheese and another grinding of black pepper. (An alternate method is to pour the freshly drained pasta into the skillet with the bacon, and then into the bowl with the egg-cheese mixture.)

This recipe is typical of Roman cuisine. Some say it originated during the American occupation in World War II; others that it was created by the charcoal sellers in the Lazio hills.

Baccalà in agrodolce alla romana
(Sweet-and-Sour Salt Cod)

Preparation time
20 minutes

Cooking time
1 hour

Difficulty
easy

Serves 6
- 12 prunes, pitted
- 1 tablespoon sultana raisins
- 1 apple
- juice and grated zest of 1 lemon
- 2 pounds soaked salt cod
- 10 tablespoons extra virgin olive oil
- flour
- 1 onion, chopped
- 1 clove garlic, chopped
- 1 fistful parsley leaves, chopped
- 1/2 cup dry white wine
- 2 tablespoons vinegar
- 1 1-pound can chopped tomatoes
- 1 tablespoon pine nuts
- 1 small fresh chile pepper, seeded and finely minced
- 1 tablespoon sugar
- salt

Dry white wine.
Recommended:
- Colli Albani
- Montecarlo Bianco

1 Soak the prunes and the raisins in lukewarm water. Peel and core the apple, slice it, and sprinkle it with the lemon juice. Rinse the cod, remove the bones, cut it into pieces, and pat dry.

2 Heat 6 tablespoons of the oil in a skillet. Flour the pieces of cod, and then fry them for 4 minutes on each side. When they are golden brown, remove them and set aside. Add the remaining 4 tablespoons oil to the skillet and sauté the onions, garlic, and parsley. Add the wine and vinegar and boil over high heat until reduced by two-thirds. Add the tomatoes. Bring the mixture to a boil and add the apple slices, the drained prunes and raisins, the pine nuts, and the lemon zest. Mix well and simmer for about 15 minutes.

3 Add the pieces of cod, hot pepper, sugar, and salt. Cook over moderate heat, shaking the pan occasionally so that the fish absorbs the sauce. Transfer to a serving platter, and serve.

Uccelletti finti di campagna
(Beef and Ham Roulades)

Preparation time
30 minutes

Cooking time
30 minutes

Difficulty
easy

Serves 4
- 1 pound boneless beef tenderloin
- 4 thin slices raw ham
- 8 sage leaves
- salt and pepper
- 2 slices country bread, quartered
- 2 ounces salt pork, cut into 8 pieces
- melted lard or extra virgin olive oil

Light red wine.
Recommended:
- Cesanese del Piglio Secco
- Latisana Merlot

1 Slice the beef into two steaks with the knife held parallel to the cutting surface. Pound each steak to about ¼ inch thick. Cut the meat into four 2 ½-inch squares. Cover each with a piece of ham and a sage leaf, and roll it up. Salt and pepper the rolls.

2 On each of 4 skewers, alternate a piece of bread, a piece of salt pork, a roulade, a sage leaf, a piece of salt pork, and a piece of bread. When all the skewers are ready, brush them with melted lard.

3 Preheat the oven to 350°F. Grease a baking sheet and arrange the skewers on it. Bake them for about 30 minutes, turning them so they brown on all sides. Transfer to a warm platter and serve.

Carciofi alla romana
(Artichokes, Roman Style)

Preparation time
20 minutes

Cooking time
30 minutes

Difficulty
medium

Serves 4
- 8 artichokes
- juice of 1 lemon
- 1 clove garlic, chopped
- 3 tablespoons chopped parsley
- 3 tablespoons chopped mint leaves
- salt
- extra virgin olive oil

Dry white wine.
Recommended:
- Montecompatri Colonna
- Pinot Grigio

1 Remove the outer leaves of the artichokes, trim the stem to 1 inch, and slice one third off the tops. Remove the hairy chokes. Place the artichokes in water and lemon juice so they do not discolor. Chop the garlic and add to the chopped herbs.

2 Open the leaves of the artichokes gently, fill the centers with the chopped herbs, and then close the leaves. Arrange the artichokes in a casserole, stems up. Add salt and 2 parts water to 1 part olive oil, leaving the stems above the surface. Cover and cook over medium heat for 30 minutes.

Roman artichokes are thornless and have purple leaves with dark green veins. The *cimaroli* are young, tender artichokes.

Crostata di ricotta
(Ricotta Cheese Tart)

Preparation time
40 minutes plus resting time

Cooking time
40 minutes

Difficulty
medium

Serves 6 to 8
For the dough
- 2 ¹/₂ cups flour
- ³/₄ cup butter, softened and cut into pieces
- ³/₄ cup sugar
- salt
- 1 egg
- 2 egg yolks
- grated zest of ¹/₂ lemon

For the filling
- 4 tablespoons sultana raisins
- 1 ¹/₂ pounds ricotta cheese
- 1 ¹/₄ cups sugar
- 1 egg
- 3 egg yolks
- grated zest of ¹/₂ lemon and ¹/₂ orange
- ¹/₂ teaspoon cinnamon
- 3 tablespoons pine nuts
- 2 tablespoons candied orange and lemon peel, chopped
- rum
- 1 egg, beaten
- powdered sugar

Light white wine.
Recommended:
- Aleatico di Gradoli
- Moscato dell'Oltrepò Pavese

1 Sift the flour onto a board, and add the butter. Work the two ingredients together until they form crumbly pellets. Shape into a mound, make a well in the center, and add the sugar, a pinch of salt, the egg and the yolks, and the grated lemon zest. Work the ingredients together rapidly and shape into a ball. Cover with plastic wrap and place in the refrigerator for 30 minutes.

2 Soak the raisins in lukewarm water. Pass the ricotta cheese through a food mill using the disk with the smallest holes. Mix it with the sugar, egg, egg yolks, lemon and orange zests, cinnamon, pine nuts, drained and dried raisins, and a dash of rum.

3 Preheat the oven to 350°F. Butter and flour a 10-inch pie plate. Roll out two-thirds of the dough on a floured board and place it in the pie plate. Add the cheese mixture, and level it out. Roll out the remaining dough, and cut it into strips. Place these over the filling in a lattice pattern.
Crimp the edges with the prongs of a fork. Brush the dough with the beaten egg, and bake for about 40 minutes until the crust is golden.

4 Remove the tart from the oven, and let it cool. Transfer it to a serving plate, and sprinkle it with powdered sugar.

153

LAZIO

Rigatoni with *pagliata*

SPECIALTIES

Antipasti (Appetizers)
Bruschetta, Fave e pecorino, Panzerotti, Supplì di riso, Carciofi alla giudìa.

First courses
Bazzofia, Bucatini all'amatriciana, Farricello, Minestra tuscia, Pasta con l'arzilla e broccoli, Pasta e ceci, Penne all'arrabbiata, Pezzata, Rigatoni alla gricia, Rigatoni con la pajata, Riso e rigaglie, Sagne, Spaghetti alla carbonara, Stracciatella alla romana, Tonnarelli cacio e pepe.

Entrées
Abbacchio a scottadito, Abbuot, Baccalà alla romana, Coda alla vaccinara, Fritto di cervella, Garofolato, Spuntature di maiale, Stracotto di bufala, Pollo alla ciociara, Saltimbocca alla romana, Trippa alla romana.

Desserts
Ciambelletti di magro, Maritozzi, Romanella, Torta di ricotta.

TYPICAL RESTAURANTS

Da Gianfranco
Via Burbon del Monte 39
Acquapendente
Tel. 0763/717042, Closed Monday
Prices: Lire 50,000

La Vecchia Osteria
Via Gramsci 103, Anzio
Tel. 06/9846100, Closed Tuesday
Prices: Lire 60,000

La Giaretta
Via Ferretti 108, Civita Castellana
Tel. 0761/53398, Closed Monday
Prices: Lire 50,000

L'Angoletto
Via Guglielmotti 2, Civitavecchia
Tel. 0766/32825, Closed Monday
Prices: Lire 60,000

Zarazà
Via Regina Margherita 21, Frascati
Tel. 06/9422053, Closed Monday
Prices: Lire 60,000

Hostaria Tittino
Vicolo Cipresso 2-4, Frosinone
Tel 0775/251227, Closed Sunday
Prices: Lire 60,000

La Briciola di Adriana
Via Gabriele d'Annunzio 12, Grottaferrata
Tel. 06/9459338, Closed Sunday evening
and Monday
Prices: Lire 65,000

La Locanda del Bere
Via Foro Appio 64, Latina
Tel. 0773/258620-618620, Closed Sunday
Prices: Lire 50,000

Ristorante degli Angeli
Località Madonna degli Angeli 1
Magliano Sabina
Tel. 0744/91377-91892, Closed Sunday
evening and Monday
Prices: Lire 60,000

Punta Incenso
Località Forna, Via Cala Caparra, Ponza
Tel. 0771/808517, Closed Tuesday,
except in summer
Prices: Lire 60,000

Bistrot
Piazza San Rufo 25, Rieti
Tel. 0746/498798, Closed Sunday evening
and Monday at noon
Prices: Lire 50,000

Pecora Nera
Via del Terminillo 33, Rieti
Tel. 0746/497669, Closed Sunday
Prices: Lire 50,000

Ponte della Ranocchia
Umgehung Appia 29, Ecke Via Tola 58,
Rome
Tel. 06/7856712, Closed Sunday
Prices: Lire 55,000

Da Vittorio
Via Mario Musco 29-31, Rome
Tel. 06/5408272-5414165, Closed
Saturday evening and Sunday
Prices: Lire 55,000

Fauro
Via Fauro 44, Rome
Tel. 06/8083301, Closed Sunday
Prices: Lire 55,000

Dito e luna
Via dei Sabelli 51, Rome
Tel. 06/4940726, Closed Sunday
Prices: Lire 60,000

Tram Tram
Via dei Reti 44-46, Rome
Tel. 06/490416, Closed Monday
Prices: Lire 55,000

Uno e Bino
Via degli Equi 58, Rome
Tel. 06/4460702, Closed Monday
Prices: Lire 60,000

Zampagna
Via Ostiense 179, Rome
Tel. 06/5742306, Closed Sunday
Prices: Lire 40,000

Lobster tails

La Torre
Via della Torre 5, Viterbo
Tel. 07626467
Closed Sunday
Prices: Lire 60,000

WINES
White
Bianco Capena, Cerveteri, Colli Albani,
Colli Lanuvini, Cori, Est! Est! Est!,
Frascati, Genazzano Greco di
Vignanello, Marino, Montecompatri
Colonna, Trebbiano di Aprilia, Velletri,
Vignanello, Zagarolo.

Red
Aleatico di Gradoli, Cerveteri, Cesanese
del Piglio, Cesanese di Affile, Cesanese
di Olevano Romano, Cori, Genazzano,
Velletri, Vignanello.

Dessert wine
Aleatico di Gradoli liquoroso.

CHEESES
Cacioricotta, Caciotta, Marzoline,
Mozzarella di bufala, Pecorino, Ricotta,
Scacione.

SHOPPING FOR TYPICAL PRODUCTS
Wines
Enoteca Del Gatto
Via XX Settembre 21, Anzio

Enoteca Izzi
Corso Claudio 14, Fondi (Latina)

Enoteca del Porto
Via del Porto 2, Terracina

Cold Meats
Salumeria Cencioni
Via Cairoli 18, Viterbo

Cheeses
Salumeria Cencioni
Via Cairoli 18, Viterbo

Pecorino Romano cheese

Produced from October to June, primarily in the provinces of Rome, Frosinone, Cagliari, and Grossetto, Italy's oldest cheese is highly prized throughout the rest of the world. At the beginning of the twentieth century, there was a veritable boom in the exportation of this cheese, particularly to North America, where it is referred to as Romano cheese.

ORIGIN

Pecorino was probably first made from sheep's milk, since these animals were the first to be raised by prehistoric man. The descendants of Adam and Eve, Abel and later Abraham, are often depicted in biblical illustrations with their herds of sheep. In those days, sheep's milk was drunk to enrich their meager diets; today it is almost exclusively turned into cheese.

CHARACTERISTICS

The repertoire of pecorino cheeses includes a dozen varieties, and pecorino Romano is considered a classic among these. By law, cheeses bearing this name must be made exclusively from sheep's milk. The milk is curdled with lamb's rennet, and then the cheeses are salted for a period of three months, during which time they are periodically washed with a saline solution and perforated to facilitate the penetration of the salt. Rounds of pecorino Romano can weigh from about eighteen to forty-four pounds. They have a hard crust that can be either smooth and light-colored or covered by a thin black rind. The cheese is either white or straw-colored.

BUYING AND STORING PECORINO

• Do not buy pecorino that has been cut from rounds that have protuberances, since these are caused by the proliferation of germs that produce gases which can alter even the external appearance of the cheese.

• Make sure that the cheese does not look greenish or reddish in color since this is indicative of substandard storage.

• The cheese should have a strong, pungent odor and, thanks to the salting process, be savory to the taste and rather sharp depending on how long it has been aged.

• Do not buy pieces of pecorino weighing more than two pounds unless you are going to eat them fairly soon. Vacuum-pack leftover cheese if you have a machine to do so, or wrap it in plastic wrap or aluminum foil, and keep it on the bottom shelf of the refrigerator.

• Keep the portion of cheese that you will use frequently, wrapped in a cloth or in plastic wrap, in the dampest part of the refrigerator or in the vegetable bin.

• Never freeze pecorino since it crumbles very easily once it has been frozen and thawed.

SERVING SUGGESTIONS

Pecorino Romano is an extremely versatile cheese. When aged from three to eight months, it is an excellent table cheese. It can be served whole from a cheese board, or in chunks on a bed of lettuce. Thanks to its sharp taste, it is usually served grated on pasta dishes and vegetables.

Serve grated pecorino cheese on pasta dishes that are typical of central Italy like spaghetti all'amatriciana or spaghetti alla carbonara, or on spaghetti that has been seasoned simply with black pepper.

Serve it with raw fava beans, and a glass of new wine.

Using the large holes of a grater, grate a piece of pecorino that has not been aged very long. Add it to some sautéed onions in a saucepan, and mix well so that the cheese melts. Remove it from the heat and add an egg yolk to the mixture, stirring it until it becomes creamy. Serve this sauce with short pasta or gnocchi.

Grate the cheese using the large holes of a grater, and add it to fillings for regional dishes like timbales and baked pastas.

Sprinkle abundant pecorino on vegetables to be gratinéed, like peppers and eggplant.

Serve thin slices of pecorino on cooked vegetables like turnip tops and dandelion greens, or on raw ones like arugula, watercress, or radishes.

MISTAKES TO AVOID

Pecorino Romano should not be served with carpaccio or meat salads, pastas with meat sauces, or with any kind of fish, nor should it be used in stuffings for cuttlefish, squid, or other mollusks, or in shellfish gratins.

THE RIGHT WINE

Accompany younger pecorino cheeses with full-bodied whites like Torgiano or Vernaccia di San Gimignano.
Aged pecorino goes better with medium-old reds like Donnaz, Montepulciano d'Abruzzo, and Cesanese del Piglio.

IN SEARCH OF PECORINO

The DOC (controlled origin) pecorino Romano is only produced in Lazio, Sardinia, and in the province of Grosseto (Tuscany). This is the oldest Italian pecorino cheese, a descendant of that of the ancient Latins. Although the zone of production is extensive, it was originally confined to the Agro Romano, the countryside around Rome. Nowadays, most pecorino Romano is produced in Sardinia. In the Roman countryside, where this cheese first came to light, you will be able to find it in any of the local trattorias. In the springtime it is served with baby fava beans. Artisan-produced cheeses often have a covering of black ashes, or one that is tinged red with tomato sauce. In the past, this color was obtained by covering the cheese with the blood of a sheep.

ABRUZZO AND MOLISE

An attachment to tradition and hot pepper

If it were necessary to choose an image to symbolize these two regions, *la chitarra* (guitar) would be the most obvious. Not the musical instrument, however, but rather that ancient rectangular wooden frame with steel strings stretched across it which is used to make the famous *maccheroni alla chitarra*. A sheet of pasta dough (made with durum wheat and eggs) is placed on the wires, and then a rolling pin is passed over it so that square noodles are formed, as thick as they are wide. Traditionally, they are served with a succulent meat sauce made with lamb and peppers or with the classic *amatriciana* sauce.

La chitarra is symbolic not only because it has produced one of the most typical dishes of this area, but also because it is indicative of the continuation of ancient customs, and of the safeguarding of local traditions which have resisted modernization. If anything, the gastronomy of Abruzzo and Molise is authentic, genuine,

and uncorrupted by a need to satisfy palates that are different from those that have always inhabited these regions. In this way, by knowing the local specialties, one can also know the local traditions. However, take warning not to be burned by the hot red pepper which, not by chance, is called *diavolillo*, invoking the devil, and which is an indispensable ingredient in many local dishes. One cannot really say that Abruzzo and Molise cooks know the meaning of the word 'moderation.' They take cooking seriously, in the sense that guests are sacred and should be very well treated. In Abruzzo, the tradition still exists of the *panarda*, a dinner of at least thirty courses, each and every one of which must be tasted so as not to offend the cooks who have dedicated so much time and energy to such an undertaking.

What is most striking in these regions is the variety. On the coast, fish prevail: red mullets, shellfish, 'blue' fish (like anchovies, sardines, and mackerel), and all those fish used in preparing magnificent fish soups (or *brodetti,* as they are called in Abruzzo), that is, sculpin, ray, octopus, John Dory, and lobster. Inland, beef is overshadowed by lamb, kid, and rabbit dishes, which are accompanied by tasty vegetables. Among these

Right: Grilled red mullets.
Above: A view of Castel di Sangro, in the province of L'Aquila.

160

are cardoons and the tender white celery from L'Aquila, which is served with oil and hot red pepper as an antipasto, and is omnipresent in the region's soups and stews. L'Aquila is a good departure point for an unusual itinerary that leads to Sulmona, famous for its sugar-coated almonds, then along the valley of the Aternum River, dotted with churches and medieval castles,

to the Piana di Navelli, the plateau where saffron has grown since it was brought here by a Dominican friar in the fourteenth century. The flowers of the purple autumn crocus produce this spice that originated in the Middle East. Patient hands delicately separate the brilliant red stigmas from the corollas, and place them to dry on top of sieves near the warmth of the fireplace. It takes about 200,000 flowers to make one kilogram (2.2 pounds) of saffron. No wonder it costs so much! Curiously, traditional Abruzzi cuisine does not use this priceless spice.

From the Piana di Navelli, after a detour to Rocca Calascio to visit the solitary

church of Santa Maria della Pietà and a stunning castle, we will head to Molise. Very few tourists visit Molise, which makes it all the more fascinating. A real Molisan dinner will start with slices of smoked ham and *mulette* (the local version of the better-known *capocollo* salami) followed by the typical thistle soup or a plate of pasta seasoned with a lamb ragù or a sauce of tomatoes and hot red pepper. The main course might be baby lamb roasted with garlic, oil, and rosemary, covered with beaten eggs and grated pecorino cheese. All this abundance can be digested by exploring the ancient Roman ruins of Saepinum, one of the most extraordinary archeological sites of central Italy.

From the mountains we can strike out for the Adriatic, where the menus include flavorful seafood salads, grilled or fried fish, spaghetti with mussels or clams, seafood risottos, and delicious fish soups. Seafood lovers can go to the Sagra del Pesce, which is held in the medieval part of Termoli on the last Sunday in August.

Lastly, before leaving Abruzzo and Molise, have a sip of Centerbe, a highly alcoholic liqueur whose name means 'a hundred herbs', and which is very much in keeping with the absence of half measures so typical of this area.

Archeological excavations at Saepinum in the province of Campobasso.

Left: A view of Casteldelmonte in the province of L'Aquila.

Cardo in brodo alla chietina
(Cardoon Soup)

Preparation time
40 minutes

Cooking time
30 minutes

Difficulty
medium

Serves 6
- 1 3-pound cardoon
- juice of 2 lemons
- 1 tablespoon flour
- 6 cups chicken broth
- ¾ pound ground pork
- 7 eggs
- ¾ cup grated pecorino cheese
- ¾ cup grated Parmesan cheese
- 3 chicken livers, chopped

Light red wine.
Recommended:
- Marsicano Rosso
- Rosso dei Colli Euganei

1 Remove the tough outer stalks from the cardoon, cut the remaining stalks into inch-long pieces, remove the filaments, and place the pieces in water with the juice of 1 lemon. Place the flour in a soup pot and whisk in 2 cups cold water and the juice of 1 lemon. Bring to a boil. Add salt and the cardoons and simmer for 20 minutes. Drain the cardoons, refresh in cold water, drain again, and return to the pot.

2 In a large saucepan, bring the broth to a boil. Mash the ground pork with 2 eggs and the pecorino cheese, add salt, and shape into tiny meatballs. Simmer them in the broth for 5 minutes. Beat the remaining eggs with the Parmesan. Pour the mixture onto the cardoons and mix until they are well coated. Add the broth and meatballs and the chicken livers. Simmer briefly and serve.

Cozze ripiene
(Stuffed Mussels)

Preparation time
30 minutes

Cooking time
10 minutes

Difficulty
easy

Serves 4
- 2 pounds mussels
- 1 fistful parsley leaves
- 2 cloves garlic
- hot red pepper
- 3 tablespoons bread crumbs
- 2 tablespoons grated pecorino cheese
- 1 tablespoon extra virgin olive oil

Rosé wine.
Recommended:
- Biferno Rosato
- Alto Adige Schiava Rosato

1 Place the mussels in a bowl of cold water and separate them from one another. Cut off the tufts and scrub the shells under cold running water by scraping them against one another or with a brush.

2 Place the mussels in a frying pan over high heat until they open. Throw away the empty shell halves, and leave the mussels on their halves, but detach them. Place them in a shallow baking dish.

3 Preheat the oven to 425°F. Wash and dry the parsley and chop it with the garlic and the hot pepper. Transfer to a bowl and mix with the bread crumbs, pecorino cheese, and olive oil. Cover each mussel with the breadcrumb mixture, and bake them for about 10 minutes or until a light crust has formed. Transfer to a warm platter and serve.

Scrippelle 'im busse
(Crepes in Broth)

Preparation time
10 minutes

Cooking time
20 minutes

Difficulty
medium

Serves 4
- ³/₄ cup flour
- 1 egg
- ¹/₂ cup milk, combined with ¹/₂ cup water
- salt
- 1 tablespoon chopped parsley
- nutmeg
- 4 cups chicken or beef broth
- olive oil for greasing pan
- ¹/₂ cup grated pecorino or Parmesan cheese

Dry white wine. Recommended:
- Trebbiano d'Abruzzo
- Trentino Riesling Renano

1 Sift the flour into a mixing bowl. Beat the egg slightly and add it to the flour, mixing well so that it is not lumpy. Add the milk and water slowly with a pinch of salt, the parsley and a grind of nutmeg. Let the batter rest and, in the meantime, bring the broth to a boil.

2 Just before making the crepes, stir the batter. It should be liquid; if not, add more milk. Lightly oil a small frying pan and when the oil is hot add two tablespoons of the batter. Cook the crepe on both sides and set it aside. Repeat with the remaining batter.

3 When all the crepes have been prepared, sprinkle them with half of the grated cheese and fold them in half twice. Place them in individual soup plates, sprinkle them with the remaining cheese, and then ladle the boiling broth over them.

Cover each bowl with a plate and let sit for a minute or two before serving.

Spiedini di mare
(Seafood Skewers)

Preparation time
30 minutes plus
marinating time

Cooking time
10 minutes

Difficulty
easy

Serves 4
- ¾ pound small squid
- ¾ pound small cuttlefish
- 1 ½ pounds large shrimp
- 1 clove garlic
- 10 tablespoons dry white wine
- 6 tablespoons extra virgin olive oil
- salt and pepper
- parsley sprigs

Dry white wine.
Recommended:
- Biferno Bianco
- Bianco del Vesuvio

1 Remove the .tentacles from the squid and cuttlefish. Remove and discard the beak from the tentacles. Discard the heads and the contents of the body sacs. Rinse the tentacles and sacs under cold water and dry them. Detach the heads from the shrimp and peel them.

2 Peel the garlic clove and cut it in half lengthwise. Place the garlic in a mixing bowl and add the wine, olive oil, a pinch of salt, and a grind of pepper. Beat with a fork until well blended. Add the cuttlefish, squid, and shrimp and mix until evenly coated. Cover and marinate for 30 minutes.

3 Thread the cuttlefish, squid, and shrimp on 8 wooden skewers, alternating them, and return them to the marinade. Heat an iron grill, and when it is very hot, cook the skewers on it, for about 10 minutes. Turn them frequently brushing them with parsley sprigs dipped in the marinade. Transfer the skewers to a warm platter and serve.

Brasciole
(Meat Roulades)

Preparation time
30 minutes

Cooking time
30 minutes

Difficulty
medium

Serves 4
- 4 eggs
- 2 tablespoons grated pecorino cheese
- salt and pepper
- 4 3½-ounce slices veal
- extra virgin olive oil
- 7 ounces scamorza cheese
- 1 onion
- 1 fistful parsley leaves
- 3 ½ ounces bacon or ham fat
- 4 slices raw ham
- 8 Swiss chard leaves, washed and dried
- 1 cup dry white wine

Light red wine.
Recommended:
- Pentro di Isernia Rosso
- Roero

1 Beat the eggs with the pecorino cheese, salt and pepper in a mixing bowl. In a frying pan that is the same size as the veal slices, heat 1 teaspoon oil and make an open-faced omelette. Repeat the operation three more times. Slice the scamorza cheese thinly. Chop the onion, parsley, and bacon.

2 Pound the veal slices delicately with a meat pounder, taking care not to tear them. On each one place 1 omelette, 1 slice raw ham, 1 or 2 Swiss chard leaves, and some thin slices of the scamorza cheese.

3 Roll the veal slices up and tie them with kitchen string to make roulades.

4 Heat 3 tablespoons oil in a skillet. Add the chopped onion, parsley, and bacon and sauté until the onion is golden. Add the roulades, season them with salt and pepper, cover, and cook over moderate heat for about 10 minutes until a knife inserted into the center of a roulade reveals pink, opaque meat. Add a little wine from time to time. Serve immediately.

Torta di mandorle
(Almond Cake)

Preparation time
30 minutes plus
resting time

Cooking time
30 minutes

Difficulty
medium

Serves 4 to 6
- ³/₄ cup almonds
- 4 eggs
- ³/₄ cup sugar
- ¹/₂ cup flour, sifted
- 3 tablespoons bread crumbs
- grated zest of 1 lemon
- 1 teaspoon cinnamon
- salt
- powdered sugar

Light sweet wine.
Recommended:
- Moscato del Molise
- Oltrepò Pavese Moscato

1 Preheat the oven to 350°F. Butter and flour an 8-inch cake pan. Cover the almonds with boiling water for not more than 3 minutes, drain them, and wrap them in a rough dish towel. Press gently with the palms of your hands and rub to remove the skins. Open the towel and use your fingers to remove any skins that remain attached. Spread the almonds in a baking dish and place them in the oven for about 10 minutes, turning them once with a spatula. When they are dry and slightly toasted, remove them from the oven and chop them.

2 Separate the eggs, putting the whites and the yolks in two different bowls. Add the sugar to the yolks and beat until foamy. Add the chopped almonds, flour, bread crumbs, lemon zest, and cinnamon and mix well.

3 Beat the whites with a pinch of salt until soft peaks form. Fold into the almond batter. Pour the batter into the prepared pan, level it, and bake for about 30 minutes until a knife inserted in the center comes out clean. Transfer the cake to a platter and let it cool. Sift powdered sugar over the cake, and serve.

ABRUZZO AND MOLISE

Polenta maritata from Molise

SPECIALTIES

Antipasti (Appetizers)
Friselle, Muletta, Scapece di Vasto.

First courses
Cavatelli con gli scampi, Maccheroni alla chitarra, Scrippelle, Spaghetti allo scoglio, Tacconi, Taccozze, Zuppa di ortiche.

Entrées
Agnello a cacio e uova, Agnello all'arrabbiata, Agnello sotto la coppa, Arrosticini, Brodetto di pesce, Fegatini di agnello, Lepre alla teramana, Mazzarelle teramane, Scamorza allo spiedo, Torcinelli alla brace.

Desserts
Bocconotti, Ferratelle, Pizza dolce, Tarallucci.

TYPICAL RESTAURANTS
Gambero
Viale Marconi 1, Alba Adriatica
Tel. 0861/712728, Closed Monday
Prices: Lire 60,000

Al Caminetto
Via degli Alpini 95, Carsoli
Tel. 0863/995105, Closed Monday
Prices: Lire 60,000

Primavera
Viale Benedetto Croce 69, Chieti
Tel. 0871/560157, Closed Sunday
Prices: Lire 40,000/50,000

Bandiera
Contrada Pastini 32, Civitella Casanova
Tel. 085/845219-845789, Closed Wednesday
Prices: Lire 60,000

Locanda della Tradizione Abruzzese
Via Piane, Corropoli
Tel. 0861/810129, Closed Wednesday
Prices: Lire 30,000/40,000

Osteria del Moro
Lungomare Spalato 74, Giulianova
Tel 085/8004973, Closed Wednesday
Prices: Lire 50,000

Osteria dello Stracciavoce
Via Trieste 159, Giulianova
Tel. 085/8005326, Closed Monday
Prices: Lire 50,000

Villa Majella
Via Sette Dolori 30, Guardiagrele
Tel. 0871/809362, Closed Monday
Prices: Lire 50,000

Il Mandrone
Frazione San Pietro, Isola del Gran Sasso d'Italia
Tel. 0861/976152, Closed Wednesday
Prices: Lire 50,000

Osteria Antiche Mura
Via XXV Aprile 2, L'Aquila
Tel. 0862/62422, Closed Sunday
Prices: Lire 35,000/45,000

Trattoria del Giaguaro
Piazza Santa Maria Paganica 4, L'Aquila
Tel. 0862/28249, Closed Monday evening and Tuesday
Prices: Lire 50,000

Bilancia
Contrada Palazzo 10, Loreto Aprutino
Tel. 085/8289321, Closed Monday
Prices: Lire 50,000

Cantina Aragonese
Corso Matteotti 88, Ortona
Tel. 085/9063217, Closed Sunday evening and Monday
Prices: Lire 60,000

Cantina di Jozz
Via delle Caserme 61, Pescara
Tel. 085/28513, Closed Monday
Prices: Lire 50,000

Fattoria Fernando
Via Aremogna 13, Pescara
Tel. 085/28513, Closed Monday
Prices: Lire 50,000

Murena
Lungomare Matteotti 1-3, Pescara
Tel. 085/378246, Closed Sunday
Prices: Lire 60,000

Plistia
Via Principe di Napoli 28, Pescasseroli
Tel. 0863/910732, Closed Monday
Prices: Lire 40,000/50,000

Pizza rustica from Teramo

Antica Taverna
Via Fannini 3, Pizzoferrato
Tel. 0872/946255
Prices: Lire 30,000

Giocondo
Via del Suffragio 2, Rivisondoli
Tel. 0864/69123, Closed Tuesday
Prices: Lire 40,000

La Cabina
Via Aufinate 1, San Pio delle Camere
Tel. 0862/93567, Closed Monday
Prices: Lire 60,000

Clemente
Vico del Vecchio 11, Sulmona
Tel. 0864/52284, Closed Thursday
Prices: Lire 40,000

Antico Cantinone
Via Ciotti 5, Teramo
Tel. 0861/248863, Closed Sunday
Prices: Lire 40,000

Sotto le Stelle
Via Nazario Sauro 50, Teramo
Tel. 0861/247126, Closed Sunday
Prices: Lire 50,000

Sosta
Via Regina Margherita 34, Torano Nuovo
Tel. 0861/82085, Closed Tuesday
Prices: Lire 50,000

Hostaria del Pavone
Via Barbarotta 15-17, Vasto
Tel. 0873/60227, Closed Tuesday
Prices: Lire 50,000/65,000

Da Casciano
Viale Marconi 29, Agnone
Tel. 0865/77511, Closed Tuesday
Prices: Lire 35,000

Antica Trattoria del Riccio
Via Sannio 7
Cantalupo nel Sannio
Tel. 0865/814246

Adriano
Via Napoli 14, Carovilli
Tel. 0865/838688, Closed Tuesday
Prices: Lire 35,000

Emilio
Via Spensieri 21, Ferrazzano
Tel. 0874/416576, Closed Tuesday
Prices: Lire 45,000/60,000

Tana dell'Orso
in Colle dell'Orso, Frosolone
Tel. 0874/890785, Closed Tuesday
Prices: Lire 45,000

Ribo
Contrada Malecoste, Guglionesi
Tel. 0875/680655, Closed Monday
Prices: Lire 40,000/50,000

Taverna Maresca
Corso marcelli 186, Isernia
Tel. 0865/3976, Closed Sunday
Prices: Lire 40,000

WINES
White
Biferno, Pentro di Isernia, Trebbiano
d'Abruzzo.

Red
Biferno, Cerasuolo d'Abruzzo,
Montepulciano d'Abruzzo, Pentro di
Isernia.

CHEESES
Burrino, Caciocavallo, Caciofiore aquilano,
Cacioricotta, Cambese, Incanestrato,
Marcetto, Mozzarella, Pampanella, Pecorino,
Scamorza molisana, Scamorza passita.

SHOPPING FOR TYPICAL PRODUCTS
Wines
Azienda Agricola Di Majo
Contrada Ramitello 4, Campomarino (CB)

Enoteca Visaggio
Via De Cesaris 44, Pescara

Cold Meats
Salumi Giuliani
Via Patini 21, L'Aquila

Alimentari Aquilino
Piazza Roma 11, Anversa degli Abruzzi
(L'Aquila)

Macelleria Cavaliere
Prato del Toro 1, Castel del Giudice
(Isernia)

Cheeses
Antonio Puisone
Via San Bartolomeo 31, Bojano
(Campobasso)

Caseificio Petronio
Via San Donato 56, Castel del Monte
(L'Aquila)

Salumeria Antonio
Via Nazario Sauro 120, Giulianova
(Teramo)

Scamorza cheese

Scamorza originates in southern Italy as a fresh cheese that is sold after five or six days of ripening. It is also available in a smoked version throughout Italy, where it is appreciated for both its flavor and its versatility in the kitchen.

Scamorza is a thread-forming cheese that is produced from cow's milk or from a mixture of milks. It can be placed halfway between the more savory, drier caciocavallo and the delicate, creamier mozzarella. Its texture is similar to that of many of the southern cheeses, such as provolone.

There are more hypotheses regarding the origin of this cheese than there are historical sources. It seems that it was first made by chance, or rather, by mistake. Some maintain that during the preparation of some provolone, or caciocavallo, the curd turned out to be too acid. In an attempt to rectify it, the curd was treated with water that was hotter than usual and so scamorza was created. This seems to be a logical explanation since the method used to produce scamorza in Molise is the same as that used for making caciocavallo, the only difference being the use of hotter water during the thread-forming stage of the cheese.

Unlike caciocavallo, scamorza does not require a long aging period, nor does it keep for a long time. Scamorza is produced in the summer. Italians prefer to eat fresh cheeses in the summer and set aged cheeses aside for the colder months.

CHARACTERISTICS

Scamorza is produced from fresh milk that has been heated slightly. With the addition of calf's rennet the milk curdles, and the curds are then treated with very hot water so that they form a thread. During this stage the cheese assumes its characteristic flask-like shape. It is then immersed in a saline solution for a few hours, after which it is removed and left to ripen for a few days. Scamorza can also be smoked. Originally, smoking the cheese kept mold from forming on the outside. The cheeses were strung in such a way as to form a knob on the top. However, the heat produced during the smoking process caused the cheese to drip from the thin neck-like part. For this reason,

BUYING SCAMORZA

The scamorza should have the following characteristics:
• a thin, alabaster-white crust;
• a smooth, milky-white texture;
• a delicate milky aroma, vaguely reminiscent of straw;
• a mild, buttery taste.
The smoked variety should have the following characteristics:
• the crust is brown in color, and may tend toward gray;
• the interior is of a white or pale straw color;
• it is smoky in aroma and taste.

today's smoked cheeses have a particular shape, rounder and neckless, since they are tied around the middle instead.

SERVING SUGGESTIONS

Scamorza is used more or less like mozzarella in the kitchen. Because it melts so well it is often used in pasta dishes, vegetable pies, and timbales.

STORING SCAMORZA

Cheese that has not been cut open may be hung in a cool place. However, it should be eaten relatively fresh since keeping it for too long will alter its taste.

The consistency of the cheese is indicative of its freshness. A very soft cheese has more water and should be eaten within a short time. If it is firm but not dry, it can be kept for a few days. Cheese produced industrially can usually be kept for a longer period.

Opened cheese should not be kept for long. It should be kept in the refrigerator, wrapped in plastic wrap or in a cloth.

Substitute scamorza (also the smoked variety) for mozzarella when making pizzas and calzone.

Serve potato gnocchi with butter, pieces of smoked scamorza, and Prague ham cut into matchsticks.

Either boil or bake whole potatoes. Cut them in half and scoop out a little of the flesh. Fill the halves with cubes of scamorza and Emmenthal cheese, and bake them until the cheese melts.

Cut the scamorza into thin slices and use these for melanzane alla parmigiana. Slice it and use it as in mozzarella in carrozza.

Line a pie plate with puff pastry. Cut the scamorza into cubes and distribute these on the pastry together with bacon slices. Cover with a mixture of egg yolks and heavy cream, and bake at 425°F for 20 minutes.

Bread and grill thick slices of scamorza.

Make layers of thinly sliced scamorza and vegetables such as eggplant, peppers, potatoes, onions, and zucchini in a baking dish. Bake and serve when the cheese melts.

Serve scamorza at room temperature with slices of fresh country bread.

THE RIGHT WINE

Serve scamorza cheese with light white wines like Martina Franca or Falerio dei Colli Ascolani. For the smoked variety, a dry aromatic white like Sylvaner dell'Alto Adige is suitable.

IN SEARCH OF SCAMORZA

Scamorza originates in the Abruzzo, Molise and Basilicata. However, it is available throughout Italy, and many of the industrially produced cheeses are of excellent quality. There are shepherds in Molise who make their own cheeses daily. Among these are Mario Antenucci in Agnone (province of Isernia), and Marco Santilli in Montenero Valcocchiara (province of Isernia).

APULIA

Pastoral and seafaring traditions

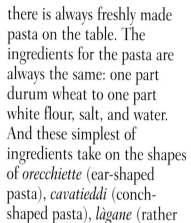

The first image that comes to mind when one thinks of Apulia is the bunch of red tomatoes the size of cherries hanging in every kitchen in the region. Time may have passed, and rural centers may have lost their populations to big urban agglomerates, but the Apulians continue to love the simplicity and genuineness of country cooking. They only need to pick tomatoes off the vine, season them with their own olive oil, and arrange them on *frisedde* (dried rings of bread that have been softened with a bit of water) and they have a meal.

The pastoral tradition continues through a variety of focaccias and pizzas which can be eaten at any time during the day or, even better, on the occasion of an outing to the country, in the shade of an olive tree. The pizzas can be filled with mozzarella and tomatoes, or onions, olives, capers, and anchovies, or ricotta cheese and raw ham. When, on the other hand, the Apulians sit down to a dinner at home or in a trattoria,

there is always freshly made pasta on the table. The ingredients for the pasta are always the same: one part durum wheat to one part white flour, salt, and water. And these simplest of ingredients take on the shapes of *orecchiette* (ear-shaped pasta), *cavatieddi* (conch-shaped pasta), *làgane* (rather like lasagna), *lanache* (similar to noodles) and so on. Pasta traditionally is cooked with the vegetable that will season it: turnip tops, cauliflower, chicory, arugula.

Tomatoes, oil, pasta, vegetables … from a rural Apulia to a seafaring Apulia. Taranto triumphs with its seafood dishes for obvious reasons. The city lies between a bay (Mar Grande) and a coastal lagoon (Mar Piccolo) and its waters abound in fish that can satisfy the most refined of palates: dentex, octopus and squid, spiny lobsters, inkfish, and gilthead, not to speak of mussels, which are raised in the Mar Piccolo where they reach gigantic proportions. Because of this abundance of fish, Taranto is famed for its fish soups, which are prepared with shellfish, grouper, sculpin, red mullets, crayfish, and cuttlefish. A dinner of these delicacies from the sea can be finished off with a visit to the National Archeological Museum and its superb collection of ancient Greek artifacts, among which is the bronze statue of Zeus.

Another place renowned for its fish soups is Fasano in the province of Brindisi. In August,

A salad of leeks, onions, and wild onions.

numerous gastronomic fairs are held featuring local specialties like spaghetti with shellfish, red mullet, and tempting fish fries.

For those who are interested in investigating the medieval, the first stop to make is at Bari on the Adriatic coast for a visit to the Cathedral and the Basilica of San Nicola, which was finished in the year 1000 when Saint Nicholas's remains were brought to Italy. However, it might be a good idea to stop off at Alberobello on the way to Bari in order to see the extraordinary landscape of *trulli*, the traditional round peasant houses with their conical roofs. At the end of December, at the 'Christmas at the *Trulli*' festival, visitors are offered *orecchiette* with meat sauce, thrushes in wine sauce, and a sampling of the local wines, Rosatello della Selva and Bianco di Coccolicchio. One of Bari's most famous specialties is *tiella di riso e cozze*: a dish composed of layers of onions, tomatoes, potatoes, rice, and mussels, all of which is doused with olive oil and baked.

The real medieval jewel of Apulia is, however, Castel Del Monte, which in itself is an excuse for making a trip to this region. Immersed in

its spectacular solitude high above Andria, this octagonal castle built by Frederick II of Swabia continues to be the subject of passionate studies regarding its real function, and fascinating theories that attribute to it important symbolic aspects.

After returning to the Adriatic coast for a visit to Trani's magnificent cathedral, one can then head north toward the promontory of Gargano, an environmental paradise dotted with picturesque villages like Vieste and Peschici. The Festival of Oranges, held at Rodi Garganico during the month of May, offers not only oranges, but also tangerines, lemons, figs, and carobs for purchase, and seafood and dairy specialties for tasting.

Before this cultural-gastronomic itinerary comes to an end with the usual desserts, mention must be made of the *lampascioni*. These wild onions that grow everywhere in Italy, but above all in Apulia, are served in a variety of ways: boiled, roasted, in a sweet-and-sour sauce, or with other foods.

And lastly, the desserts: *carteddate natalizie* (shell-shaped honey pastries made at Christmas), marvelous cream puffs filled with black cherry jam and custard cream, *scarcedda pasquale* (an Easter cake), plus an infinite variety of almond cookies.

The characteristic *trulli* of Alberobello.

Crater, fifth century A.D., the National Archeological Museum of Taranto.

Scalcione

(Leek Pie)

Preparation time
30 minutes plus
rising time

Cooking time
30 minutes

Difficulty
easy

Serves 4
*For the bread
dough*
• 4 teaspoons
  brewer's yeast
• 4 cups flour
• salt
For the filling
• ¼ cup sultana
  raisins
• 3 tablespoons extra
  virgin olive oil
• 1 pound leeks,
  trimmed, washed,
  and thinly sliced
• 4 salted anchovies,
  rinsed and boned,
  or 8 fillets
• 2 tablespoons
  salted capers, rinsed
• 3 ½ ounces
  (½ cup) oil-cured
  black olives, pitted

*Light red wine.
Recommended:*
• San Severo Bianco
• Piave Verduzzo

1 Dissolve the yeast in 2 tablespoons lukewarm water. Sift the flour onto a board, shape it into a mound and add a pinch of salt. Make a well in the center and pour in a little lukewarm water. Work the dough with your hands. Add the dissolved yeast and continue to work the dough until it is smooth and elastic. Shape it into a ball and cut it across the top. Place it in an oiled bowl and cover it with a cloth. Let it rise for about one hour, or until it has doubled in volume.

2 Soak the raisins in lukewarm water.

3 In a frying pan, heat the oil and sauté the leeks for 2 minutes. Remove the pan from the heat and add the anchovies, mashing them with a fork. Add the capers and olives, return the pan to the heat, and cook until leeks are soft, about 2 minutes.

4 Heat the oven to 425°F. Oil a 12-inch pie plate. Divide the dough into two pieces, one slightly larger than the other. Place the larger piece in the pie plate, pressing it with your palms and fingers so that it covers the bottom and sides. Pour the leek mixture onto the dough and cover it with the drained raisins. Roll the remaining piece of dough into a disk and cover the filling. Seal the edges and prick the top with a fork. Bake for about 20 minutes. Serve the scalcione hot directly from the pie plate.

Orecchiette con le polpette

(Ear-Shaped Pasta with Meatballs)

Preparation time
30 minutes

Cooking time
30 minutes

Difficulty
medium

Serves 4
- 1 slice stale bread
- ¹/₂ cup milk
- ³/₄ pound ground veal and pork
- 1 egg
- 6 tablespoons grated pecorino cheese
- 1 fistful parsley leaves, chopped
- 1 clove garlic, minced
- ¹/₂ cup extra virgin olive oil
- ¹/₂ onion, sliced
- ¹/₂ cup dry white wine
- 2 cups tomato purée
- salt and pepper
- ³/₄ pound orecchiette
- 20 fresh basil leaves

Light red wine.
Recommended:
- Rosso di Cerignola
- Sangiovese di Romagna

1 Soak the bread in the milk and squeeze out the excess liquid. Mix the ground meat in a bowl with the egg, 3 tablespoons of the grated cheese, parsley, garlic, and bread. Shape the mixture into meatballs the size of walnuts.

2 Heat the oil in a skillet and fry the meatballs, shaking the pan so that they brown uniformly. Add the onion, salt, and pepper. When the onion is transparent, add the wine and cook over high heat until the wine has evaporated. Add the tomato purée and cook over moderate heat for 20 minutes. Taste and season with salt and pepper.

3 Boil the pasta in abundant salted water. Chop the basil leaves coarsely and add them to the sauce. Drain the pasta when it is al dente and add it to the sauce. Transfer to a serving bowl, cover with the remaining grated cheese, and serve.

On the Murge plateau they serve this dish with tender stalks of raw celery.

177

Tiella di riso e cozze
(Rice and Mussels)

Preparation time
40 minutes

Cooking time
35 minutes

Difficulty
medium

Serves 4
- 1 ½ pounds mussels
- ½ pound onions (2 medium), thinly sliced
- 1 fistful parsley leaves
- 2 cloves garlic
- 1 pound cherry tomatoes (about 20), chopped
- 1 pound potatoes (about 3 medium), peeled and thinly sliced
- salt and pepper
- extra virgin olive oil
- ½ cup grated pecorino cheese
- ½ cup rice

Soft, aromatic white wine.
Recommended:
- Lizzano Bianco
- Tocai Italico di Lison Pramaggiore

1 Clean and scrape the mussels and place them in a dry pot over medium heat just until the shells begin to open. Pry open the shells (discarding any mussels that are still shut) and remove the meat. Strain and reserve the mussel liquid in the pot. Chop the parsley and garlic together.

2 Preheat the oven to 425°F. Make layers in an earthenware casserole in this order: half of the tomatoes, the onions, half of the parsley and garlic, salt, a drizzle of olive oil, half of the potatoes, the remaining tomatoes, the mussels, the grated cheese, the remaining parsley and garlic, the rice, the remaining potatoes, salt and pepper, and a drizzle of olive oil. Add water to the mussel liquid to make 1 cup, and pour into the casserole. Bake for 35 minutes, or until rice is tender.

When working with mussels, discard any that are cracked or punctured before cooking. After cooking discard any unopened mussels.

Zuppa ai frutti di mare

(Shellfish Soup)

Preparation time
30 minutes

Cooking time
15 minutes

Difficulty
easy

Serves 4
- 2 pounds mussels
- 2 pounds clams and razor clams
- ½ cup extra virgin olive oil
- 1 clove garlic, thinly sliced
- 1 onion, thinly sliced
- 1 ½ cups chopped tomatoes
- 1 fistful basil leaves, chopped
- salt and pepper
- 1 fistful parsley leaves, chopped
- toasted slices of bread

Dry white wine.
Recommended:
- Martina Franca
- Cinque Terre

1 Scrape the mussels under cold running water and rinse the other shellfish.

2 In a large saucepan, heat the oil. Add the garlic and onion and sauté until softened. Add the tomatoes, basil, a pinch of salt, and a grinding of black pepper. Bring the soup to a boil and cook until slightly reduced. Add the shellfish. Cover and cook over high heat until the shells have opened.

Add the parsley and mix well. Remove from the heat after a few minutes, and serve with the toasted bread.

Langoustines and shrimp can also be added to this soup.

179

Caponata estiva
(Mixed Summer Vegetables)

Preparation time
40 minutes

Cooking time
45 minutes

Difficulty
easy

Serves 6
- 1 pound eggplant
- ¾ pound sweet peppers (about 3 medium)
- ¾ pound potatoes (about 2 medium)
- 10 ounces zucchini (about 2 medium)
- 2 medium onions
- 2 cloves garlic
- 5 ounces green beans
- extra virgin olive oil
- 2 cups tomato purée
- salt and pepper
- flour
- vegetable oil for frying
- fresh basil leaves

Light red wine.
Recommended:
- San Severo Rosso
- Rosso del Vesuvio

1 Remove the stem and slice the eggplant, horizontally into ½-inch circles. Place the slices in a colander, sprinkle them with salt and let them drain. Remove the stem, seeds and inner filaments from the peppers, and cut them into squares. Peel the potatoes, cut off the ends of the zucchini and the green beans, and slice all these vegetables. Slice the onion and the garlic thin.

2 In a frying pan, heat 7 tablespoons oil and sauté the onion and garlic until softened but not browned. Add the peppers and green beans and cook over moderate heat for 5 minutes. Then add the potatoes and zucchini and cook for about 15 minutes more, stirring. Add the tomato purée, salt and pepper, and cook for 30 minutes.

3 Rinse the eggplant and dry it. Flour the slices and fry them in 1-inch of hot oil until tender. Drain and add them to the other vegetables. Tear the basil leaves with your fingers and add them. Stir once more, season with salt and pepper to taste, and serve.

Scarcedda
(Easter Cake)

Preparation time
30 minutes

Cooking time
30 minutes

Difficulty
medium

Serves 6 to 8
- 4 cups flour
- salt
- 1 ½ teaspoons baking powder
- ½ cup sugar
- 2 egg yolks
- ⅓ cup plus 2 tablespoons olive oil
- 2 eggs, one washed and dried

Light dessert wine.
Recommended:
- Moscato di Trani
- Moscato dell'Oltrepò Pavese

1 Preheat the oven to 425°F, and oil a baking sheet. Sift the flour with a pinch of salt and the baking powder. Mix in the sugar and shape the mixture into a mound. Make a well in the center. Add the egg yolks and the oil, and work the mixture together until it is smooth and homogeneous.

2 Pull off an egg-sized piece of dough and set it aside. Divide the remaining dough into three equal parts. Make three thin ropes of the same length. Braid them together, form a ring, and connect the ends. Place the clean egg at the junction point of the loaf, and fix it with two strips of dough made from the piece that was set aside.

3 Beat the remaining egg and brush it onto the surface of the braid but not on the whole egg. Place the scarcedda on the baking sheet and bake it for 30 minutes until golden. Let it cool completely on a rack before serving.

The *scarcedda* is traditionally served during the Easter holidays. More eggs can be placed on the top depending on the size of the cake.

APULIA

SPECIALTIES

Antipasti (Appetizers)
Impepata di cozze, Peperonata, Scamorza al forno.

First courses
Capunti, Cavatelli con senapelli, Ciceri e tria, Fricelli, Orecchiette con le cime di rapa, Purea di fave con cicoria, Sagna penta, Spaghetti ai frutti di mare, Tiella di riso e cozze.

Entrées
Cazzmarr, Cozze arraganate, Gnumeredde, Paranzella, Pecora in pignata, Tordi al vincotto, Turcinieddi alla brace, Zuppa di pesce.

Desserts
Bocconotti, Carteddate, Quaresimali, Scarcedda, Sporcamuss, Taralli glassati.

TYPICAL RESTAURANTS
Antichi Sapori
Piazza Sant'Isidoro 9, Andria
Tel. 0883/569529, Closed Monday
Prices: Lire 30,000

Taverna Verde
Largo Adua 19, Bari
Tel. 080/5540870, Closed Sunday
Prices: Lire 35,000/45,000

Terranima
Via Putignani 213-215, Bari
Tel. 080/5219725, Closed Sunday
Prices: Lire 50,000

Pantagruele
Via Salita di Pipalta 1-3, Brindisi
Tel. 0831/560605, Closed Sunday evening and Monday
Prices: Lire 60,000

Già sotto l'Arco
Corso Vittorio Emanuele 71, Carovigno
Tel. 0831/996286, Closed Monday
Prices: Lire 30,000/40,000

Fontanina
Strada Provinciale per Alberobello, Castellana Grotte
Tel. 080/406810, Closed Monday
Prices: Lire 60,000

Cibus
Via Chianche di Scarano 7, Ceglie Messapica
Tel. 0831/388980, Closed Tuesday
Prices: Lire 35,000

Capriccio
Via della Libertà 71, Cisternino
Tel. 080/9542553, Closed Wednesday
Prices: Lire 50,000

Mulino
Via Castel del Monte 135, Corato
Tel. 080/8723925, Closed Monday
Prices: Lire 60,000

Da Pompeo
Vico al Piano 14, Foggia
Tel. 0881/724640, Closed Sunday
Prices: Lire 60,000

Osteria di Salvatore Cucco
Piazza Pellicciari 4, Gravina in Puglia
Tel. 080/3261872, Closed Sunday evening and Monday
Prices: Lire 40,000

Centro Storico
Via Eroi de Dogali 6, Locorotondo
Tel. 080/9315473, Closed Wednesday
Prices: Lire 25,000/40,000

Coppola Rossa
Via dei Celestini 13, Manfredonia
Tel. 0884/582522
Closed Sunday evening and Monday
Prices: Lire 60,000

Il Baracchio
Corso Roma 38, Manfredonia
Tel. 0884/583874
Closed Thursday
Prices: Lire 40,000/50,000

Ritrovo degli Amici
Corso Messapia 8, Martina Franca
Tel. 080/4839249
Closed Sunday evening and Monday
Prices: Lire 35,000/50,000

Apulian *zeppole*

Van Westerhout
Via De Amicis 3-5, Mola di Bari
Tel. 080/47466989
Closed Tuesday
Prices: Lire 65,000

Bistrot
Corso Dante 33, Molfetta
Tel. 080/3975812
Closed Wednesday
Prices: Lire 35,000/45,000

Antica Locanda
Via Spirito Santo 49, Noci
Tel. 080/4972460
Closed Sunday evening and
Tuesday
Prices: Lire 55,000

Peppe Zullo
Via Piano del Paradiso, Orsara di Puglia
Tel. 0881/964763
Prices: Lire 50,000

Osteria del Tempo Perso
Via Tanzarella 47, Ostuni
Tel. 0831/303320
Closed Monday
Prices: Lire 50,000

Cantinone
Via San Lorenzo 1, Putignano
Tel. 080/4913378, Closed Wednesday
Prices: Lire 55,000

Ristor
Via Alberto Mario 38, Ruvo di Puglia
Tel. 080/813736, Closed Monday
Prices: Lire 40,000/50,000

Bruna
Via Risorgimento 8, San Donato di Lecce
Tel. 0832/658207, Closed Monday
Prices: Lire 55,000

Mussels with garlic and oil

Federiciano da Miki
Via Chiesa Madre 10, Vico del Gargano
Tel. 0884/994879, Closed Wednesday
Prices: Lire 60,000

WINES
White
Castel del Monte, Gioia del Colle, Gravina, Leverano, Lizzano, Locorotondo, Martina, Franca, Ostuni, San Severo.

Red
Alezio, Brindisi, Cacc'e Mitte, Castel del Monte, Copertino, Gioia del Colle, Leverano, Lizzano, Malvasia Nera, Matino, Nardò, Orta Nova, Ottavianello di Ostuni, Primitivo di Gioia del Colle, Primitivo di Manduria, Rosso Barletta, Rosso Canosa, Rosso di Cerignola, Salice Salentino, San Severo, Squinzano.

Dessert wine
Aleatico di Gioia del Colle, Aleatico di Puglia, Moscato di Trani, Primitivo di Manduri liquoroso.

CHEESES
Burrata, Caciocavallo, Cacioricotta, Caciotta, Canestrato, Giumeata, Marzotica, Mozzarella, Pecorino, Primosale, Provolone, Ricotta Schianta, Scamorza.

SHOPPING FOR TYPICAL PRODUCTS
Wines
La Stalla del Nonno
Via XXIV Maggio 26-28
Palo del Colle (Bari)

Maiellaro
Piazza Garibaldi 50, Polignano a Mare

Cold Meats
Michele Trivisano
Via Castagneto 28, Orsara (Foggia)

Salumificio Martino
Via Paolotti 8, Martina Franca (Taranto)

Cheeses
Caseificio Notarnicola
Via Cielo Alto, Alberobello

Cooperativa Caseificio Pugliese
Statale 98, Corato (Bari)

Masi
Corso Mazzini 195, Ostuni (Brindisi)

Olives

Olives are the fruit of the olive tree, a tree of ancient Asiatic origin which is now cultivated in all the Mediterranean countries. Eating olives are green or black in color depending on how ripe they are at the time of picking. Olives are processed differently depending on how they will be used and preserved.

Italy is dedicated to the cultivation of olives. Indeed, all its regions except for the mountainous ones produce olives. The zone of cultivation extends between the 30° and 45° parallels, which includes the entire Mediterranean area from North Africa to the Po Valley. A particularly mild climate in some localities north of this zone makes the cultivation of olives possible, for example, along Lake Garda. As long as the winters are not too cold, the tree will grow. In the period between December and February, the tree, albeit in its vegetative phase, cannot endure more than a few hours of temperatures that are below 20°F. An olive tree can live for centuries in a favorable climate, alternating years of greater and lesser production.

VARIETIES OF OLIVES

The many varieties of olives existing in Italy are divided into those that are eaten and those that are used for making olive oil. The immature olive, when it is picked at the end of the summer, has a green color and firm flesh. The mature olive, that is the winter one, is purplish in color with a softer flesh. Olives are not eaten fresh because of

BUYING OLIVES

There is a remarkable variety of olives on the market from which to choose. Green olives:
• have undergone treatment with lime and caustic soda in which case they have a particularly sweet taste;
• have been soaked in pure water, and then in brine: they are available all over central Italy and are more or less light in color;
• have been put in a very salty brine and then in water, followed by a milder brine: these are so light in color as to be called 'white';
• have been put in brine, then lightly pounded, and left to ferment in an aromatic solution of herbs, garlic or hot pepper: these are referred to as 'pickled.'

Black olives:
• have been put in water, then salted, put back in water, and lastly in brine: they have a puplish color and a pleasantly bitter taste;
• have been put in water, then left to dry or oven-dried: they are black in color and have a wrinkled skin;
• have been treated with lime and caustic soda, then put in brine: they are large and black in color;
• have been treated with lime and caustic soda, or fermented in brine, and then mixed with herbs or other aromatic ingredients, such as orange peel, and lastly seasoned with olive oil: they are usually black in color and are referred to as 'aromatized.'

their strong bitter taste. Methods for preserving olives go back thousands of years since these fleshy drupes have always been a source of food and energy for mankind. In Roman times, olives were left to soften in a mixture of ashes and water; today they are treated with caustic soda and lime and then carefully washed. Greek olives, which do not undergo this treatment, have a stronger taste. They are simply salted and put in a brine where lactic acid fermentation refines their taste. During this process, a substance develops which inhibits the growth of microorganisms that could alter the product.

SERVING SUGGESTIONS

Olives are recommended as a flavorful addition to many different preparations such as pâtés, mousses, pasta sauces, and salad plates.

Keep loose olives in their liquid in a covered container in the refrigerator. They will keep for weeks in this way. Check periodically that they do not start to wrinkle or become moldy. Olives packed in jars should be refrigerated once the jar has been opened and also checked periodically for mold.

Fry oven-dried olives, cover them with dried hot pepper, and serve.

Pit purplish-black olives, grind them in a meat-grinder or blender, adding wild fennel or other herbs, and serve this pâté with toasted squares of bread.

Cover a tablespoon of black olive paste with heavy cream in a small saucepan, and cook over low heat. Use this sauce with tagliolini *(thin egg noodles).*

Make a salad with black and green olives, a thinly sliced red Tropea onion (soak it in cold water so it will not be so strong), fresh tomatoes, raw celery, and cubes of cheese.

Blend a can of tuna fish with its oil and some melted butter. Add pitted green olives cut in longitudinal strips to this cream, and serve it as a spread with toasted squares of bread, or as a sauce for linguine *or similar pasta.*

Serve olives with cubed cheeses, anchovies, capers, tuna fish in oil, and peppers or any other vegetables that have been preserved in oil.

Choose a crispy-crusted soft bread, rolls, or French bread to go with them.

THE RIGHT WINE

Even though they are usually served with wine as an aperitif, the 'bitter' taste of some olives does not lend itself to wines. 'Sweet' olives are preferable for an aperitif and go well with whites like Cialla Bianco, Orvieto, or Vermentino Ligure.

IN SEARCH OF OLIVES

Good-quality olives can be found in many of the open-air markets throughout Italy. Often the oil mills themselves sell their own preserved olives.

In Apulia, the farms along the provincial road between Brindisi and Ostuni sell their local products. One, the Masseria Asciano in Contrada Lardagnano Nuovo at Ostuni, has three types of olive oils and olives prepared and preserved in different ways. The zone around Foggia is famous for its olives, which are similar to the large green Greek ones.

CAMPANIA

The art of pasta and pizza

Right: A view of
Atrani on the
Amalfi Coast.
Below: Skewers of
shellfish.

If the cuisine of Campania were to be
represented by a painting, it would be
a colorful, sunny landscape filled with people
relaxing. But such a picture could not convey
the salty odor of the sea, nor the voices of
women cooking, and the warmth of those in
the kitchen who have no secrets to keep, but
only recipes to share to give life more zest.

It is in Naples that the Italian dish par
excellence was created: pizza. And it is in
Campania that the art of making pasta in a
thousand different shapes was refined, each
served with the simplest yet most delicious

water buffalo at Battipaglia, and the flour
and water have been kneaded with a touch of
local cheer.

Those who know pizza and are interested
in cultural aspects of gastronomy cannot miss
the Antica Pizzeria della Regina d'Italia Brandi
in Naples. This is where the renowned Pizza
Margherita was invented and named after
Margherita of Savoy, Queen of Italy from 1878
to 1900.

A more relaxing itinerary than that of the
lively and hectic Neapolitan scene will take
you along the Amalfi Coast to Positano, where
a Pizza Fair is held every June. If you continue
along the spectacular Amalfi Drive, which is
literally cut out of the rock that drops
dramatically into the sea, you can visit Amalfi,
Atrani, and Ravello. There, magnificent dishes
await you: fish fried and marinated in vinegar,
garlic, onion, and bay leaf; salads of octopus
dressed with oil, lemon, garlic, and parsley; sea
bass, lobsters, and on and on. Any luncheon
or dinner can only end happily with a small
babà al limoncello, a delicate sweet cake bathed
in a lemon liqueur.

seasoning of all, tomato sauce. In short,
the dishes that have always characterized
the Italian cuisine were created in this region,
which is all the more reason that they should
be tasted on the spot.

The tomatoes have ripened in the sun at
San Marzano, the mozzarella comes from the

From the Gulf of Salerno you can return

to the Bay of Naples and ferry over to the exclusively elegant island of Ischia, which is closely related to Vesuvius in that it is also volcanic in nature. In any one of its restaurants, romantically situated on the tiny bays surrounding the island, you can taste such typical dishes as pasta and beans made in the Ischian way (with three or four different kinds of pasta); *spaghetti alla puttanesca* (with tomatoes, black olives, anchovies, capers, garlic, and hot red pepper), and spaghetti with mussels. For those who prefer meat, there is rabbit Ischia-style (with tomato, basil, and rosemary), or *pollo alla diavola* (chicken cooked in the dry white wine of the island).

On returning to Naples, a visit to the archeological excavations at Pompeii and Herculaneum will increase your appetite for the famous *sartù*, a timbale of rice seasoned with mushrooms, peas, sausage, breaded and fried meatballs, mozzarella and Parmesan

Figures from a Neapolitan nativity scene.

cheeses. Otherwise, you can opt for the simple *strangolapreti alla napoletana* (which literally means 'priest strangler' and is a pasta made with durum wheat and potatoes) served with a beef or pork sauce typical of the region.

Besides its wonderful churches and museums, Naples is particularly famous for its extraordinary nativity scenes that have graced many a church. If you want to purchase some of these original figures, you will find an enormous selection in Via San Gregorio Armeno during the weeks before Christmas. And since it is nearby, visit the unique cloister of Santa Chiara, exquisitely decorated in majolica.

And finally, before leaving the region, sample its pastry masterpieces: the *pastiera*, a tart filled with ricotta cheese and candied fruit usually made at Easter time; the *struffoli*, pastry balls flavored with orange or lemon and dipped in honey; and the *zeppole di San Giuseppe*, fritters traditionally eaten on St. Joseph's Day.

The typical Neapolitan Easter cake, the *pastiera*.

Pizza Margherita

Preparation time
20 minutes

Cooking time
20 minutes

Difficulty
easy

Serves 4
- 1 pound bread dough, already risen (see recipe on page 176)
- 1 14 $^1/_2$-ounce can chopped tomatoes
- salt
- $^1/_2$ pound fresh mozzarella, thinly sliced
- 10 basil leaves, torn
- 1 tablespoon grated Parmesan or Romano cheese
- 2 tablespoons extra virgin olive oil

Dry white wine.
Recommended:
- Ischia Bianco
- Trebbiano di Romagna

1 Preheat the oven to 450°F. Oil an 11-inch pie plate. Knead the dough rapidly, shape it into a ball, and place it in the pie plate, stretching it out with your hands and fingers so that it is higher around the edge.

2 Pour the chopped tomatoes with their juices onto the dough, mashing them with a fork. Salt slightly. Arrange the mozzarella, basil, and grated cheese on the tomatoes. Drizzle the olive oil over the top. Bake for about 20 minutes, and serve immediately.

Pizza Margherita was invented by the pizza-maker Raffaele Esposito in 1889 on the occasion of the visit to Naples of Queen Margherita of Savoy.

Vermicellini con alici fresche

(Thin Spaghetti with Fresh Anchovies)

Preparation time
20 minutes

Cooking time
20 minutes

Difficulty
medium

Serves 4
- 1 pound fresh anchovies
- 6 tablespoons extra virgin olive oil
- 1 ½ cups chopped tomatoes
- salt and pepper
- 2 heaping tablespoons bread crumbs
- 2 tablespoons chopped parsley
- ¾ pound vermicellini
- 1 clove garlic, sliced

Dry white wine. Recommended:
- Capri Bianco
- Vermentino di Gallura

1 Detach the heads from the anchovies, open them along the belly, and remove the center bone and tail. Clean them under cold water and pat dry with paper towels.

2 In a skillet, heat 5 tablespoons olive oil. Sauté the garlic, removing it before it browns. Add the anchovies and cook over medium heat for 3 minutes. Stir in the tomatoes, and season with salt and pepper. Cook over high heat for about 10 minutes, until the anchovies are in pieces.

3 Heat the remaining tablespoon of olive oil in a skillet and brown the bread crumbs in it. Add them to the sauce together with the parsley. In the meantime, boil the pasta in abundant salted water. Drain it when it is al dente and mix it with the sauce in a serving platter. Serve immediately.

Calamari ripieni alla campana
(Stuffed Squid)

Preparation time
40 minutes

Cooking time
1 hour 10 minutes

Difficulty
medium

Serves 4
- 2 tablespoons sultana raisins
- 2 cloves garlic
- 1 stalk celery
- 6 basil leaves
- 4 tablespoons extra virgin olive oil
- 2 cups chopped tomatoes
- 4 1/2 pounds squid
- 2 tablespoons bread crumbs
- 1 fistful parsley leaves, chopped
- 2 tablespoons grated caciocavallo cheese
- 2 tablespoons pine nuts, chopped
- 1 to 2 tablespoons lemon juice
- 1 egg, beaten with a pinch of salt
- 1/2 teaspoon piece hot pepper flakes
- 1/2 cup oil-cured black olives, pitted
- 1 cup dry white wine
- salt

Dry white wine. Recommended:
- Bianco del Vesuvio
- Bianco dei Colli Maceratesi

1 Soak the raisins in lukewarm water. Chop one of the garlic cloves with the celery and basil leaves. Sauté the garlic-celery-basil mixture in 3 tablespoons olive oil, add the chopped tomatoes and simmer for 20 minutes.

2 Detach the tentacles from the heads of the squid and remove the beak from the tentacles. Discard the heads and the contents of the body sacs, wash and dry the tentacles and sacs, and chop the tentacles into 1/4-inch pieces. Mince the remaining clove of garlic. In a skillet, heat the remaining tablespoon of olive oil. Add the minced garlic and the squid and sauté over medium heat for 5 minutes. Transfer the mixture to a bowl and add the bread crumbs, parsley, grated cheese, drained raisins, pine nuts, lemon juice, and beaten egg. Mix well. Fill the squid sacs two-thirds full with the stuffing, and sew the openings with white thread. Prick the sacs with a needle.

3 Place the stuffed squid in the tomato sauce with the hot pepper, olives, wine, and salt. Bring to a boil and then reduce heat and simmer for 40 minutes, turning the squid occasionally. Transfer to a serving platter or to individual plates, and serve.

Polpettone al pomodoro
(Meat Loaf in Tomato Sauce)

Preparation time
30 minutes

Cooking time
1 hour

Difficulty
medium

Serves 6
- 4 slices day-old bread
- 1 pound ground beef
- 3 ½ ounces grated Parmesan cheese
- 2 eggs
- 1 fistful parsley leaves, chopped
- 1 clove garlic (optional) mashed
- 3 ½ ounces raw ham, sliced
- salt and pepper
- 2 ounces provolone cheese, cut into strips
- 2 eggs, soft-boiled and peeled
- 9 tablespoons extra virgin olive oil

For the sauce
- 5 tablespoons extra virgin olive oil
- 1 clove garlic slightly crushed
- 1 16-ounce can tomato purée
- 4 basil leaves, torn
- salt and pepper

Full-bodied red wine.
Recommended;
- Taurasi
- Barbaresco

1 Soak the bread in 1 cup water in a bowl. Squeeze the excess water from the bread and place it in a mixing bowl with the ground beef, Parmesan cheese, raw eggs, parsley, garlic, salt, and pepper. Blend all the ingredients well, first with a fork, then with your hands, squeezing between your fingers. It should be very well mixed.

2 Place a sheet of waxed paper or aluminum foil on the work table and sprinkle it with flour. Place the meat mixture on top, spreading it with your hands until it is about ¾-inch high. Cover the surface with the slices of raw ham and the strips of provolone, and place the two whole soft-boiled eggs in the middle.

3 Raise one side of the paper and slide your hands underneath so that it rolls onto itself, forming a loaf. Make sure that the ham, cheese, and eggs are folded inside and do not fall out.

4 Heat 4 tablespoons oil in a skillet and when it is hot, add the loaf and brown it, turning it carefully. As soon as a golden brown crust has formed around it, remove it and keep it warm.

5 To make the sauce: In a Dutch oven, heat the remaining oil. Add the garlic and sauté until golden. Remove the garlic from the pot, add the tomato purée, and bring it to a boil. Add the meat loaf, basil, salt, and pepper, and cook over low heat for about 45 minutes. Turn the meat loaf occasionally. Remove the meat loaf from the pan, and place it on a warm serving platter. Slice it thickly and pour the tomato sauce on top. Serve immediately.

Pomodori con il riso
(Rice-Filled Tomatoes)

Preparation time
30 minutes plus
resting time

Cooking time
45 minutes

Difficulty
easy

Serves 4
- 8 medium round tomatoes
- 6 basil leaves
- 1 clove garlic
- 1 cup cooked rice
- 2 heaping tablespoons grated Parmesan cheese
- salt and pepper
- 6 tablespoons olive oil

Light red wine.
Recommended:
- Capri Rosso
- Rosso Canosa

1 Wash the tomatoes and cut off and reserve the tops. Carefully scoop out the tomatoes with a spoon, reserving the pulp. Salt the insides and turn them over to drain. Pass the tomato pulp through a food mill into a mixing bowl.

2 Wash and dry the basil leaves and chop them with the garlic. Add the basil and garlic to the tomato pulp together with the rice, Parmesan cheese, salt, and pepper. Mix well and set aside for an hour.

3 Preheat the oven to 375°F. Oil a baking dish. Dry the insides of the tomatoes with paper towels, place them in the baking dish, and fill them with the rice mixture. Drizzle the oil over the tomatoes, replace their tops, and bake them for about 45 minutes, until the tomatoes are soft. Transfer them to a serving platter 10 minutes after they have been removed from the oven, or serve them at room temperature.

Peperoni al gratin
(Gratinéed Peppers)

Preparation time
30 minutes

Cooking time
20 minutes

Difficulty
medium

Serves 4 to 6
- 4 large sweet peppers
- salt
- bread crumbs
- 1 handful parsley leaves, chopped
- 1 clove garlic chopped
- 1 teaspoon dried oregano
- 2 tablespoons capers, rinsed and drained
- ½ cup oil-cured olives, pitted and chopped
- 8 tablespoons extra virgin olive oil

Dry white wine.
Recommended:
- Greco di Tufo
- Frascati

1 Thoroughly char the peppers over a flame, then place them in a plastic bag. When they are cool, remove and discard the stem, seeds, and inner filaments. Peel the peppers and cut them into strips.

2 Preheat the oven to 400°F. Oil a baking dish and arrange a layer of peppers on the bottom. Salt them slightly and sprinkle them with half of each of the following: bread crumbs, parsley, garlic, oregano, capers, and olives. Drizzle half the oil over all, then repeat the process with the remaining ingredients. Bake for 20 minutes. The peppers are good both hot and cold.

CAMPANIA

Eggplant, Positano-style

SPECIALTIES

Antipasti
Alici a scapece, Insalata di mare, Pizza.

First courses
Minestra maritata, Migliaccio, Pasta e fagioli, Risotto alla pescatora, Sartù di riso, Spaghetti alla puttanesca, Spaghetti alle cozze, spaghetti alle vongole, Zuppa di cozze, Zuppa di soffritto.

Entrées
Agnello con i lampasciuni, Baccalà in cassuola, Coccio all'acquapazza, Pollo alla diavola, Polpo alla luciana, Purpetielli affogati, Salsicce con le pepacelle.

Desserts
Babà, Pastiera, Sfogliatelle, Struffoli, Susanielli, Torta caprese, Zeppole di san Giuseppe.

TYPICAL RESTAURANTS

Da Gemma
Via Frau' Gerardo Sasso 9, Amalfi
Tel. 089/871345, Closed Wednesday
Prices: Lire 75,000

Paranza
Via Dragone 2, Atrani
Tel. 089/871840, Closed Tuesday
Prices: Lire 70,000

Antica Trattoria Martella
Via Chiesa Conservatorio 10, Avellino
Tel. 0825/31117, Closed Sunday evening and Monday
Prices: Lire 60,000

Pergola
Via Nazionale, Capaccio
Tel. 0828/723377,
Closed Wednesday
Prices: Lire 55,000

Hostaria di Bacco
Via G. B. Lamia 9, Furore
Tel. 089/874006-874583
Closed Friday
Prices: Lire 60,000

Focolare
Via Cretaio 68, Ischia
Tel. 081/980604, Closed Wednesday
Prices: Lire 60,000

Melograno
Via Mazzella 110, Cava dell'Isola, Ischia
Tel. 081/998450
Prices: Lire 70,000

Peppina
Via Bocca 23, Ischia
Tel. 081/998312, Closed Wednesday
Prices: Lire 50,000

Trattoria di Pietro
Corso Italia 8, Melito Irpino
Tel. 0825/472010, Closed Wednesday
Prices: Lire 35,000/45,000

Da Sica
Via Bernini 17, Neapel
Tel. 081/5567520, Closed Thursday
Prices: Lire 40,000

La Cantina di Triunfo
Riviera di Chiaia 34, Naples
Tel. 081/668101, Closed Sunday and

official Holidays
Prices: Lire 60,000

La Chiacchierata
Piazza Matilde Serao 37, Naples
Tel. 081/411465, Closed Sunday
Prices: Lire 45,000

Mattonella
Via Nicotera 13, Naples
Tel. 081/416541
Closed Sunday evening
Prices: Lire 40,000

La Caveja
Via Santissima Annunziata 10
Pietravairano
Tel. 0823/984824
Closed Sunday evening and Monday
Prices: Lire 50,000

Donna Rosa
Via Montepertuso 97-99, Positano
Tel. 089/811806
Prices: Lire 50,000

Cucina Flegrea
Via Monteruciello 20, Pozzuoli
Tel. 081/5247481
Closed Wednesday
Prices: Lire 60,000

WINES
White
Aversa Asprinio, Bianco dei Campi
Flegrei, Capri, Castel San Lorenzo,
Cilento, Falanghina, Falerno del
Massico, Fiano d'Avellino, Greco di tufo,
Guardia Sanframondi, Ischia, Lacryma
Christi, Sant'Agata dei Goti, Solopaca,
Vesuvio.

Rosé
Taburno

Red
Aglianico, Capri, Castel San Lorenzo,
Cilento, Falerno del Massico Primitivo,
Falerno del Massico Rosso, Guardia,
Sanframondi, Ischia, Lacryma Christi
del Vesuvio, Per' e Palummo, Piedirosso,
Rosso dei Campi Flegrei, Sant'Agata dei
Goti, Solopaca, Taburno, Taurasi,
Vesuvio.

Dessert wine
Falanghina di Sant'Agata dei Goti
passito, Moscato di Castel San Lorenzo,
Per' e palummo passito.

CHEESES
Caciocavallo, Mozzarella di bufala,
Cacioricotta, Provola affumicata,
Pecorino, Burrino, Cacioforte, Casu
peruto, Provolone, Quagliata, Scamorza.

SHOPPING FOR TYPICAL PRODUCTS

Wines
Sant'Agata
Contrada Sant'Agata, Centola (Salerno)

Manzoni
Corso Garibaldi 244, Salerno

Cold Meats
La Tradizione
in Seiano, Via R. Bosco 931, Vico Equense
(Neapel)

Mario Iacullo
Contrada Anghiglio, Ricogliano (Salerno)

Cheeses
Caseificio Granese
Piazza Matteotti 4, Montella (Avellino)

Cremeria d'Angelo
Via Galiani 4, Neapel

Caseificio Belfiore
Via Belvedere 35, Agerola (Salerno)

Caseificio Fratelli Beneduce
Via Romani 6, Madonna dell'Arco
(Neapel)

Skewers of mozzarella

Pasta

Pasta may not have originated in Italy (in fact, it was probably invented in the Far East) but Italians certainly have come up with the best ways to cook and season it. So much so that it has become the country's food par excellence, its gastronomical banner. And the Mediterranean diet has been copied the world over because it is synonymous with healthy eating.

By pasta, we mean the mixture of wheat flour and water or eggs that makes spaghetti, tagliatelli, rigatoni, and so forth. There are two types of pasta:
• the pasta made from soft flour and eggs, usually homemade (industrial products use durum wheat);
• the pasta made from durum wheat and water which, if factory-made, is sold in dry form.

THE ORIGINS OF PASTA

There can really be no history of pasta because there are no historical sources. We know only that its origins are remote. Indeed, there is an Etruscan fresco that depicts what appear to be implements for kneading and cutting pasta. However, it is only a trace; nothing remains from Roman times.

Pasta was produced in China as far back as the first century A.D., and after the year 1000 it is known to have been sold in shops. As for Italy, a Genoese notary document of 1200 lists in its inventory a container (barisella) full of pasta, most probably the dry type. According to this

source, Marco Polo was not the first to import pasta from China, since his journey took place several decades later.

It seems that pasta, like rice, arrived in Sicily thanks to the Arabs. Since the word 'macaroni' was used for the first time in the above-mentioned Genoese document, people believed that pasta first made its appearance in Liguria. It is more likely that Liguria and Sicily were introduced to pasta independently through different channels. But though these two regions vie over who was the first to make it, it was Naples that became the undisputed capital of pasta when the pasta-makers of Amalfi moved to Torre Annunziata from 1840 until the outbreak of the First World War. Dry pasta is particularly characteristic of southern Italian cooking. Before the unification of Italy in 1870, the north was composed of 'rice-eaters' and the south of 'pasta-eaters.'

BUYNG PASTA

Considering that pasta is sold in packages for the most part, the only advice to be given is to make sure that the package is intact, and to check its expiration date.

THE CREATION OF THE FORK

Once, when spaghetti was eaten with the hands, the local aristocrats had to abstain from this very popular food, at least at official banquets. And their fork with its three long prongs proved to be more of a weapon than an eating implement. During the reign of Ferdinand II, a ravenous spaghetti eater in private, one of his chamberlains, Gennaro Spadaccini, invented a fork with four shorter prongs for His Majesty so that it was possible to eat long pasta even at formal dinners.

SERVING SUGGESTIONS

These pages contain a cross-section of pastas and sauces from the different Italian regions. Below is a brief description of some other creative pasta recipes.

Season spaghetti that has been boiled, rinsed under cold water, and drained with cold sauces made without the usual sautéed garlic and onion; for example, cold cooked peppers, tomatoes with oil and basil, caviar, fish eggs or bottarga (dried tuna or mullet roe), shellfish, blanched bean sprouts, etc.

Cook two ounces of white beans in a little water, add cut-up slices of swordfish and shelled langoustines and cook until done. Mix in some butter, and season pappardelle *with the sauce.*

Cook a pound of onions slowly in butter, adding a little water from time to time. Add abundant grated cheese (grana, fontina, emmenthal, or bitto). Remove from the heat and stir in an egg yolk so that the cheese will be creamy and not stringy. Season pennette rigate *with this sauce and a grinding of fresh black pepper.*

Sauté a diced eggplant in garlic and oil for three minutes. Add salt and a handful of small, cleaned squid, and as soon as the squid start to become opaque, remove them. Cover the eggplant and cook it until it is creamy. Add the squid for the last minute of cooking and then remove from the heat

and add a tablespoon or two of oil. Use this sauce to season thin spaghetti *or* linguine.

*In general, different sauces are used with egg pastas and dry pastas. The thinner pastas (*capellini, fedelini, spaghettini, bavettine*) do well with lighter sauces or ones made with fish or shellfish. This type of pasta lends itself to being served cold in salads. Spaghetti, vermicelli, and bucatini go well with more flavorful sauces: alla carbonara, all'amatriciana, savory vegetables, thick tomato sauces, flavorful stewed fish. The long dry pastas, of any size, are not suitable for Bolognese meat sauce or other similar sauces. Short pasta goes with any kind of sauce, even meat. If it is a particularly thick pasta like* rigatoni, *do not serve it with a delicate sauce.*

Egg pasta can be combined with seafood sauces. However, it is best when prepared with meat-based sauces such as Bolognese meat sauce, wild hare sauce, or sauces made with mushrooms or truffles. It is also delicious just with butter and cheese. The latter is considered a last-resort seasoning, but when the ingredients are fresh, of good quality and abundant, it makes a very tasty dish.

THE RIGHT WINE
When the condiments are delicate, choose white wines like Gavi, Erbaluce, Vermentino di Sardegna, Locorotondo or Alcamo.

IN SEARCH OF PASTA

Good-quality pasta can be found anywhere in Italy. A factory that makes very good fresh pasta is the Pastificio Dota di Torre del Greco (Via Nazionale 1078, Salerno). As for egg pastas or filled pastas, try the excellent products of La Sfogliatella (Via Lame 28/30, Bologna).

CALABRIA
AND
BASILICATA

Unique and unmistakable tastes

At first sight it may seem somewhat rash to associate Calabria, a region with more than four hundred miles of coastline bordering on two seas, the Ionian and the Tyrrhenian, with Basilicata, a region compressed between Campania, Apulia, and Calabria with hardly any coastline at all. And yet, from a gastronomic point of view, these two regions have many points in common, starting from their 'cult' of pork. This is expressed by a love of antipasti based on a variety of cold cuts: *capocollo*, *soppressata*, *coppa* and *salame*, the latter often fiery given the amount of hot pepper, fennel seeds, and other aromatic herbs used in its preparation. And the famous long sausage known in Italy by the name of *lucanica* or *luganica* originated in Lucania, which was the ancient name of Basilicata.

A view of Tropea in Calabria.

The traveler looking for ancient peasant traditions will have no trouble in finding food suitable for individuals of strong character in this distant corner of southern Italy. This is a gastronomy in which formal elegance willingly gives way to a taste for simple, nourishing dishes with unique and unmistakable flavors. A typical example is the Calabrian *murseddu*, beef tripe and pluck sautéed with onions, tomato, and red wine

The *ciaudedda*, a typical dish from Basilicata.

which, according to tradition, should be eaten first thing in the morning at the tavern before setting off for a hard day's work in the fields. In addition to preserved pork products, residents of Calabria and Basilicata take pleasure in eating homemade pasta: the Calabrian *maccaruni*, a sort of macaroni rolled around a knitting needle, is similar to the *minuich* of Basilicata. Both are usually served with either a thick tomato sauce or a rich meat sauce made without tomatoes, and covered with grated pecorino cheese.

Another typical dish is pasta with legumes seasoned with garlic, hot red pepper, lard and pork rind, because pork should never be left out of any dish. On any trattoria menu you will always find dishes like *làgane* and chickpeas (or beans or lentils); the *làgane* are broad egg noodles and they are always homemade.

If you would like to discover the differences between the two regions, the best place to start your journey is at Tropea in Calabria, preferably at the beginning of July. Not only will you see one of the most beautiful towns on the Tyrrhenian coast, but you will also be able to attend the Fair of the Blue Fish and the Red Onion, where you can sample *alici a beccafico* (anchovies that have been split open and filled with bread crumbs, grated pecorino cheese, oregano, parsley, and

garlic), or *alici a braciolette*, anchovies baked with bread crumbs and fresh tomatoes.

In addition to anchovies, Calabria offers its visitors a wide range of cooked and preserved fish: pilchard, mackerel, needlefish, tuna, and swordfish, which arrive in the Straits of Messina between April and September. Swordfish can be cooked in a variety of ways, but the best recipe of all has to be *alla ghiotta,* in which thin slices of fish are covered with fresh bread crumbs, olives, pepper, and capers, rolled up and fried in oil, and then simmered with tomatoes.

Before leaving the Straits, take time to see the famous bronzes of Riace at the National Museum of Magna Grecia in Reggio Calabria. Fished up from the sea in 1972 along the Riace coast, these two six-foot warriors are among the most beautiful and best-preserved bronze statues of Hellenic art that have ever been found.

While at Reggio, you can treat yourself to some of the local products, such as tomatoes

or eggplant preserved in oil, stuffed olives, or the unusual *mustica* (or *rosamarina*). These are newly hatched whitefish that are dried in the sun on wooden boards, covered with hot red pepper and then preserved in oil; they are eaten as a spread on bread like caviar, or are added to special sauces. On the Ionian coast between Calabria and Basilicata is the vast archeological area of Metaponto. Once an important city of Magna Grecia, Metaponto has a temple dedicated to Apollo, a theater, the vase-makers' quarter, a necropolis, and a short distance away, the sixth-century B.C. temple to Hera, also known as the Tavole Palatine, of which fifteen Doric columns are still standing.

The province of Matera is famous for its Sassi, a conglomerate of grottoes, houses, and shelters dug out of spurs of calcareous rock, truly an unforgettable setting. Gastronomically speaking, this area is known for its Apulian traditions, that is, for a diet rich in cheeses and vegetables. They make delicious mozzarella, excellent fresh and aged pecorino, caciocavallo, and different types of ricotta.

One of the vegetarian specialties is *ciambotta*: fried potatoes, eggplant, and peppers which are then stewed with tomatoes and garlic. Another is *ciaudedda*, a very popular country dish made with fresh fava beans, potatoes, onions, artichokes, and bacon.

Tomatoes drying in the sun in Calabria.

A fourth-century B.C. clay statue found in a tomb in the necropolis of Metaponto.

Làgane e ceci
(Egg Noodles and Chickpeas)

Preparation time
30 minutes plus
soaking time

Cooking time
40 minutes

Difficulty
easy

Serves 4
- ³/₄ cup dried chickpeas
- 4 cups flour, sifted
- 4 eggs
- 6 tablespoons extra virgin olive oil
- 2 cloves garlic
- 1 hot red pepper
- salt
- 1 tablespoon chopped parsley (optional)

Light red wine.
Recommended:
- Aglianico del Vulture Giovane
- Rosso di Velletri

1 Soak the chickpeas in cold water for at least 24 hours, changing the water after the first 12 hours. Boil them in a pressure cooker for 30 minutes. When they are done, add salt and leave them uncovered for 5 minutes. Drain the chickpeas and set aside.

2 Make a mound with the flour with a well in the center. Add the eggs and work the mixture together until it is smooth and elastic. Using a pasta machine, roll and cut the pasta into strips 1 ¼ inches wide. Spread them out on a floured cloth to dry.

3 In a skillet, heat the oil. Add the garlic and red pepper and sauté until tender. Remove them

from the skillet and discard. Add the drained chickpeas and cook them for a few minutes.

4 Cook the noodles in boiling salted water, and drain them when they are *al dente*. Toss with the sauce.

Làgane is a type of fresh pasta. It is often used in soups prepared with dried legumes, which are made throughout central and southern Italy. The type of flour used and the width of the pasta (from ¹/₂ inch to 1 ¹/₄ inches) vary from region to region.

Alici alla reggina
(Baked Anchovies)

Preparation time
30 minutes

Cooking time
30 minutes

Difficulty
medium

Serves 4 to 6
- 2 pounds fresh anchovies
- 2/3 cup bread crumbs, plus more for pan
- 2 fistfuls parsley leaves, chopped
- 1 clove garlic chopped
- 1/2 cup brine-cured green olives, pitted and chopped
- 1 tablespoon capers, rinsed and drained
- 5 tablespoons extra virgin olive oil
- salt and pepper

Dry white wine.
Recommended:
- Bianco di Nicastro
- Bianco della Valdinievole

1 Remove the heads from the anchovies, open them along the belly, gut them and remove the backbone. Rinse them and dry with paper towels.

2 In a mixing bowl, combine bread crumbs, parsley, garlic, olives, and capers. Drizzle the oil over the mixture and mix well.

3 Preheat the oven to 325°F. Oil a 9-inch baking dish and coat it with bread crumbs. Arrange a layer of opened anchovies on the bottom, season with salt and pepper, and top with a layer of the bread crumb mixture. Continue to make layers until all the ingredients are used up. Sprinkle the surface with bread crumbs and a little oil, and bake for about 30 minutes. When a golden brown crust has formed, remove the dish from the oven and serve.

Involtini di salsiccia
(Sausage Rolls)

Preparation time
30 minutes

Cooking time
30 minutes

Difficulty
easy

Serves 4
- 4 tablespoons extra virgin olive oil
- 1 clove garlic, slightly crushed
- 1 15-ounce can tomato purée
- salt and pepper
- 8 to 12 leaves Savoy cabbage
- 1 pound spicy fresh sausage with fennel seeds

Light red wine.
Recommended:
- Sant'Anna di Capo Rizzuto
- Velletri Rosso

1 In a saucepan, heat the oil. Add the garlic and sauté until it begins to color. Remove the garlic and add the tomato purée, salt, and pepper to the pan. Reduce the heat and let the sauce simmer.

2 Blanch the cabbage leaves in boiling water. Drain and dry them. Place them on a work surface, remove the central rib, and fold the leaves in half along the rib.

3 Break the sausage meat up and sauté it in a dry skillet over medium heat. When it has lost some of its fat but is not too dry, about 8 minutes, divide it among the cabbage leaves. Close them and tie them with kitchen string. Place the sausage rolls in the tomato sauce and cook them over moderate heat for about 20 minutes, or until they are tender. Remove the string and serve the rolls in their sauce.

Calzoni alla moda di Melfi
(Stuffed Pastry, Melfi Style)

Preparation time
50 minutes plus
soaking time

Cooking time
1 hour 10 minutes

Difficulty
medium

Serves 6 to 8
For the filling
- ³/₄ cup dried chickpeas
- 1 pound chestnuts in shells
- salt
- 1 bay leaf
- ¹/₄ cup unsweetened cocoa
- ¹/₄ cup sugar
- 1 pinch cinnamon
- 1 to 2 tablespoons aromatic liqueur

For the pasta
- 4 cups flour
- salt
- ¹/₂ cup sugar
- 4 eggs
- 1 egg yolk
- 3 ¹/₂ ounces lard, cut into pieces
- white dessert wine
- lard or oil for frying

Light dessert wine.
Recommended:
- Malvasia di Rapolla Amabile
- Moscato d'Asti

1 Soak the chickpeas for 24 hours. Make a cut in the chestnut shells and boil them in the pressure cooker, adding a pinch of salt and the bay leaf, for 20 minutes. Drain the chestnuts and set aside, then cook the chickpeas for 30 minutes. Drain the chickpeas and set aside.

2 Peel the chestnuts and pass through a food mill with the drained chickpeas. Sift in the cocoa and add the sugar, cinnamon, and liqueur. Mix well and set aside.

3 Sift the flour onto a wooden board with a pinch of salt and the sugar. Make a mound with a well in the center. Break the eggs into the hollow, add the egg yolk and lard, and work together. Add wine if necessary to obtain a compact, amalgamated dough. Roll the dough out and divide it in two. Distribute teaspoonfuls of filling 2 inches apart on one sheet of the dough. Cover with the other sheet and press the dough closed around the fillings. Cut the dough into squares. Fry these in 2 inches of hot lard. When they are golden brown, drain, and serve immediately.

CALABRIA AND BASILICATA

SPECIALTIES

Antipasti (Appetizers)
Capicollo, Lampascioni in agrodolce, Mustica, Soppressata, Vecchiarelle infumicate.

First courses
Cavatelli, Ciambotta, Ciaudedda, Fusilli al ragù, Làgane e ceci, Orecchiette alla materana, Strascinati.

Entrées
Alici a beccafico, Cuturidd, Frittole, Mugnulatidd, Murseddu, Pesce spada alla ghiotta, Stigghiolata, Ventriceddi ripieni.

Desserts
Cassatredde, Giurgiulena, Mustazzuol, Pitta n'chiusa, Sanguinaccio.

TYPICAL RESTAURANTS

Pezzolla
Via roma 21, Accettura
Tel. 0835/675008, Closed Saturday
Prices: Lire 30,000/40,000

Vecchio Luma
Località Sarnelli, Avigliano
Tel. 0971/87080, Closed Friday
Prices: Lire 30,000/40,000

Becco della Civetta
Vicolo I Maglietta 7, Castelmezzano
Tel. 0971/986249, Closed Tuesday
Prices: Lire 40,000/50,000

Osteria del Gallo
Largo Nazionale 2, Marsicovetere
Tel. 0975/352045, Closed Tuesday
Prices: Lire 35,000

Terrazzino sui Sassi
Vico San Giuseppe 7, Matera
Tel. 0835/332503874583
Closed Tuesday evening
Prices: Lire 35,000/50,000

Trattoria Lucana
Via Lucania 48, Matera
Tel. 0835/336117,
Closed Sunday
Prices: Lire 30,000/40,000

La Fattoria sotto il Cielo
Contrada Petrucco, Pignola
Tel. 0971/420166, Closed Wednesday
Prices: Lire 40,000/50,000

Antica Osteria Marconi
Viale Marconi 233-235, Potenza
Tel. 0971/56900
Closed Monday and Sunday evening
Prices: Lire 35,000

Da Peppe
Corso Garibaldi 15, Rotonda
Tel. 0973/661251,
Closed Monday
Prices: Lire 40,000/60,000

Luna Rossa
Via Marconi 18, Terranova di Pollino
Tel. 0973/93254,
Closed Wednesday
Prices: Lire 50,000

Ciambotta Calabrese

Fattoria
Via Magna Grecia 83, Catanzaro
Tel. 0961/780064-782809,
Closed Monday
Prices: Lire 45,000

Al Ficodindia
Viale Kennedy, Crucoli
Tel. 0962/34637,
Closed Monday
Prices: Lire 30,000/45,000

La Capricciosa
Via Angelo Viscardi, Firmo
Tel. 0981/940297
Closed Monday
Prices: Lire 35,000

Casina dei Mille
Strada Statale Ionica 106
Melito di Porto Salvo
Tel. 0965/787434
Closed Sunday evening
Prices: Lire 60,000

Casa Janca
Via Riviera Prangi Pizzo
Tel. 0963/264364, Closed Wednesday
Prices: Lire 35,000

Il Setaccio Osteria del Tempo Antico
Contrada Santa Rosa 62, Rende
Tel. 0984/837211, Closed Sunday
Prices: Lire 30,000/40,000

WINES
White
Bianco di San Vito di Luzzi, Cirò,
Melissa, Scavigna.

Rosé
Rosato di San Vito di Luzzi, Savuto,
Scavigna.

Bucatini from Maratea

Red
Aglianico del Vulture, Cirò, Donnici,
Lamezia, Melissa, Pollino, Rosso
di San Vito di Luzzi, Sant'Anna
di Isola di Capo Rizzuto, Savuto,
Scavigna.

Dessert wine
Greco di Bianco.

CHEESES
Caciocavallo, Caciocotto, Cacioricotta,
Casieddu, Paddraccio, Pecorino, Provola,
Provolone, Ricotta affumucata, Ricotta
salata, Scamorza.

SHOPPING FOR TYPICAL PRODUCTS
Wines
Il Buongustaio
Piazza Vittorio Veneto 1, Matera

Cold Meats
Salumificio del Colle
Contrada Colle del Carroso
Mormanno (Cosenza)

Lucana Salumi
Via Gramsci 127, Picerno (Potenza)

Cheeses
Caseificio Pian della Spina
Via Pian della Spina
Filiano (Potenza)

La Fattoria sotto il Cielo
Contrada Pedrucco
Pignola (Potenza)

Lanzo
Via Daniele 10-12, Catanzaro

Fratelli Gentile
Via Bellavista 76, Carlopoli (Catanzaro)

SICILY

A baroque cuisine

Poached slices of tuna with a parsley pesto.

For an idea of what Sicilian gastronomy is like, just take a look at a Sicilian cart. These days, the carts parade only at local festivals, but they were once precious instruments of work used for transporting wine or stones or vegetables. They can be seen and admired in the Pitré Museum in Palermo, where a whole section of the museum is dedicated to them. The artistically carved wheels of the carts, covered with statuettes, friezes, and arabesques; the sides of the carts with their painted tales of saints and knights; and the gorgeous trappings, ornaments, and plumes are of an almost mind-boggling magnificence. And so is the Sicilian cuisine: full of color, mouth-watering, replete with surprising details, almost exaggerated in its workmanship: it is a synthesis of all the civilizations that have left their mark on this region.

Here, wild fennel, pine nuts, and raisins have become fixed ingredients in a typical dish like pasta with sardines, a reconciliation between the local resources and the gastronomies of the Greeks, Arabs, and Spanish. The Sicilian pasta dishes are so rich in ingredients that they are a meal in themselves. At Ragusa, for example, macaroni is seasoned with a tomato sauce, finely chopped veal, chicken livers, peas, *caciocavallo* (the local cheese, similar to a sharp provolone), and, as if this were not enough, it is all

poured into a mold lined with slices of fried eggplant. Of course, they could never do without eggplant in Sicily, for that would mean giving up *pasta alla Norma* (named after one of the masterpieces of the famous composer from Catania, Vincenzo Bellini) and *caponata*, a vegetable composition that includes fried eggplant, celery, tomatoes, onions, capers, pine nuts, raisins, and olives, to which some even dare to add potatoes and slices of fried peppers.

This exaggerated dish is in perfect harmony with the baroque style that characterizes so many Sicilian cities. Catania, with its marvelous Via Crociferi built entirely out of black lava; Acireale, with its cathedral, palaces and Basilica of Ss. Peter and Paul; Siracusa, Avola, and Noto, the richest of baroque gems. For those who love fish, the Festival of Santa Venera, the patron saint

Pasta alla Norma made with tomatoes, eggplant, and salted ricotta cheese.

of Avola, is held on August 15. At night, all the fishermen's boats are illuminated on the beaches, and delicious fish soups made with sea water are served.

Since it is always very crowded on the August 15 holiday, there is another Fish Fair on June 23 at Aci Trezza, where juicy lobsters, tender octopus, and savory sea urchins are on the menu. Obviously, Sicily's most typical dishes are based on fish. After all, it is an island. At Messina, the king of all

fish is the swordfish which, following its usual migratory route from the Sargasso Sea to the Mediterranean, crosses the Straits of Messina from April to September. Someone even has gone so far as to invent swordfish 'chops', which are nothing more than rolled up slices of swordfish stuffed with bread crumbs, basil, parsley, capers, provolone cheese, and eggs.

The western tip of the region is noted for tuna fishing. There, a labyrinth of chambered nets have been set up to bring the fish close to the shore for the *mattanza*, the tuna massacre, a cruel spectacle that people from all over come to watch. For those who prefer to eat, there is *spaghetti alla bottarga* (spaghetti with pressed and dried tuna roe) to sample, and a variety of other dishes using tuna. And around

Trapani, an Arab dish can always be found on the menu: couscous with meat, vegetables, or even fish.

However, the one area in which Sicily remains unrivalled is in its sweets, especially those made with almonds. Almonds are at the base of *pasta reale*, the royal dough that is shaped into beautiful miniature fruits. One really has to go to Agrigento at the end of the winter and see the astounding spectacle of the almond trees in blossom in the Valley of the Temples. Nowhere else in the world, not even in Greece, are there so many fine examples of ancient Greek temples. And the perfumed white blossoms of the almond trees seem to pay homage to those monuments. Sicilians use almonds to make *torrone*, or nougat, as well as a soft version filled with pistachio nuts and honey. And almonds are used to make Easter lambs, granita, and ice cream (which was invented on this island). And there is also the famous *cassata*, a triumph of sponge cake, ricotta cheese, and candied fruit; *cannoli*, thin cylinders of crisp pastry filled with ricotta cheese and pistachio nuts; or the *crispelle* of fried rice covered with honey which are made for St. Joseph's Day on March 19.

As a tribute to one of the most important fruits of Sicily, serve the special candied orange peel at the end of a meal together with a glass of the excellent Passito di Pantelleria.

Above: The Temple of Concordia at Agrigento with almond trees in the foreground. Left: Boats in the harbor of Aci Trezza.

Risotto alla marinara
(Rice with Seafood)

Preparation time
30 minutes

Cooking time
40 minutes

Difficulty
easy

Serves 6 to 8
- 1 pound mussels, cleaned
- 1 pound clams
- 1 strip lemon zest
- salt
- 1 pound shrimp
- 3 ¹/₂ ounces small squid, cleaned and chopped
- extra virgin olive oil
- 1 small carrot, chopped
- 1 onion, chopped
- 1 small stalk celery, chopped
- ¹/₂ cup dry white wine
- 6 tablespoons tomato purée
- 2 cups rice
- 10 basil leaves, torn
- hot red pepper flakes
- 4 tablespoons grated caciocavallo cheese

Dry white wine.
Recommended:
- Eloro Bianco
- Bianco dell'Elba

1 Heat the mussels and clams in a covered pot over high heat until they open. Remove them from their shells and strain their juices. Bring 6 cups water to a boil with lemon zest and salt, and drop in the shrimp for 30 seconds, until they are barely opaque. Skim them from the water and shell them. Add the strained juices of the mollusks to the shrimp water and keep at a boil.

2 In a Dutch oven, heat the oil over medium-high heat and sauté the carrots, onions, and celery and sauté until softened. Add the squid and sauté for 5 minutes. Add the wine. When it has evaporated, add the tomato purée and 1 cup of the boiling fish broth. Simmer, covered, for 10 minutes.

3 Cook the rice in boiling salted water for about 10 minutes. Drain it and add to the Dutch oven. Simmer until the rice is al dente, adding a ladleful of boiling fish broth when necessary, making sure that it is completely absorbed before adding another. Five minutes before the end of cooking, add the shrimp and the mollusks. Add the torn basil leaves, a little hot red pepper, and the grated cheese.

Cannelloni alla siciliana
(Sicilian-Style Pasta Rolls)

Preparation time
1 hour plus
marinating time

Cooking time
2 ½ hours

Difficulty
medium

Serves 6
- 1 pound beef rump or rumpsteak
- 8 bacon strips
- 1 onion, chopped
- 1 carrot, chopped
- 1 stalk celery, chopped
- 1 clove garlic, slightly crushed
- 1 bay leaf
- 6 whole cloves
- 10 whole peppercorns
- ⅓ cup red wine
- flour
- 3 tablespoons lard
- 4 tablespoons grated caciocavallo cheese
- salt and pepper
- 3 ¼ cups durum wheat flour
- 7 eggs
- 1 to 2 tablespoons olive oil
- 2 tablespoons butter

Light red wine.
Recommended:
- Etna Rosso
- Oltrepò Pavese Pinot Nero

1 Lard the meat with the bacon strips. Place the meat in a large bowl and add the onions, carrots, celery, garlic, bay leaf, cloves, and peppercorns. Pour on the wine, cover, refrigerate, and marinate for 12 hours, turning the meat occasionally.

2 Remove the meat from the marinade, reserving the marinade and vegetables. Dry the meat with paper towels, and flour it lightly. Heat the lard in a deep pot and brown the meat on all sides. Add salt, pepper, the marinade and vegetables, and cook, covered, for about 2 hours, turning the meat occasionally. When the sauce has thickened and the meat is done, grind the meat. Pass the vegetables through a food mill and mix them with the meat and 1 tablespoon of the grated cheese.

3 Sift the flour onto a board, and make a hollow in the center. Break 4 of the eggs into it, beating them slightly with a fork. Work the eggs and flour together with your fingers. When all the flour has been absorbed, knead the dough until it is smooth and elastic. Cover with a cloth and let it rest for 30 minutes, then roll it out into a fairly thin sheet and cut into 4 x 8-inch rectangles. In a large pot, bring abundant salted water to a boil and add oil. Drop in a few pasta rectangles at a time and boil for 6 minutes or until al dente. Remove them with a slotted spoon and place them on a napkin or towel.

4 Preheat the oven to 375°F. Butter a 9 x 13-inch baking dish. Place 3 heaped tablespoons filling along the center of each rectangle the long way, roll them up, and arrange them side by side in the baking dish. Cover them with the remaining grated cheese and dot them with the butter. Bake for 20 minutes. Beat the remaining 3 eggs with a pinch of salt and pour them over the pasta rolls. Increase the oven temperature to 425°F and cook until a golden brown crust has formed on top. Serve immediately.

Braciole di pesce spada alla siciliana

(Swordfish 'Chops' Sicilian Style)

Preparation time
30 minutes

Cooking time
25 minutes

Difficulty
medium

Serves 4
- 2 pounds swordfish
- 6 tablespoons extra virgin olive oil, plus additional
- 1 onion, chopped
- 6 tablespoons bread crumbs
- 2 tablespoons capers, rinsed, drained, and chopped
- 2 tablespoons grated Romano cheese
- 1 egg (optional)
- 8 bay leaves
- 2 tablespoons lemon juice, strained
- salt and pepper

Dry white wine. Recommended:
- Bianco dell'Etna
- Ribolla dei Colli Orientali del Friuli

1 Rinse and dry the swordfish and cut it into 12 rectangular slices weighing about two ounces each. Chop the trimmings.

2 In a skillet, heat 2 tablespoons of the oil. Add the swordfish trimmings and the onion and sauté until the onion is translucent, about 8 minutes. Remove from the heat and add the bread crumbs, capers, grated cheese, egg, if using, and enough oil to make a smooth mixture. Distribute the mixture on the swordfish rectangles, roll them up, and thread them onto 4 skewers with bay leaves in between them.

3 Combine the lemon juice with a pinch of salt. When the salt has dissolved, add pepper and 4 tablespoons oil slowly, beating constantly. Dip the skewers in this marinade.

Heat a nonstick frying pan and cook these 'chops' for 15 minutes, turning them frequently and basting them with the marinade. Serve immediately.

Frittedda
(Smothered Vegetables)

Preparation time
20 minutes plus
resting time

Cooking time
30 minutes

Difficulty
easy

Serves 4
- 6 artichokes
- lemon juice
- 4 tablespoons extra
  virgin olive oil
- 1 large onion,
  coarsely chopped
- $3/4$ pound fresh
  shelled fava beans
- $3/4$ pound fresh
  shelled peas
- salt and pepper
- $1/2$ cup wine
  vinegar
- 1 teaspoon sugar

Light red wine.
Recommended:
- Corvo Rosso
- Copertino Rosso

1 Remove the tough outer leaves from the artichokes, cut off the stem and the tops of the leaves, and trim the base. Cut them in half and remove the choke. Slice them thinly. Place them in a mixture of water and lemon juice.

2 In a saucepan, heat the oil with 2 tablespoons water. Add the onions and cook until they soften. Then add the artichokes and sauté for 3 minutes.

Add the fava beans, and lastly, the peas. Season with salt and pepper. Add 1 cup hot water, cover, and cook over medium heat for about 20 minutes.

3 When all the vegetables are tender and the water has evaporated, add the vinegar and the sugar. Cook over high heat, stirring constantly, until the vinegar has evaporated. Serve at room temperature.

Jelu i muluni
(Watermelon Gelatin)

Preparation time
30 minutes plus
resting time

Cooking time
5 minutes

Difficulty
easy

Serves 8 to 10
- 1 6-pound
  watermelon
- 4 packets unflavored
  powdered gelatin
  (3 tablespoons)
- 1 cup sugar
- 1 stick cinnamon
- salt
- ½ cup candied
  melon rind, diced
- 3 ½ ounces
  semisweet chocolate

1 Cut the watermelon into slices, removing and discarding the rind, seeds, and filaments. Strain the pulp into a heavy-bottomed pot: there should be about 8 cups.

2 Dissolve the gelatin in a few tablespoons of the strained watermelon pulp, making sure it is not lumpy. Slowly add it to the rest of the watermelon pulp. Add the sugar, cinnamon stick, and a pinch of salt.

3 Place the pot over low heat and bring the mixture to a boil, stirring constantly. Continue to cook it for 5 minutes.

4 Remove the cinnamon stick and add the diced candied rind. Wet individual molds and pour the watermelon mixture into them. Let them cool, and then refrigerate until serving time.

5 Shave the chocolate into pieces. Unmold the watermelon gelatins onto a cold serving platter and decorate with the pieces of chocolate.

Palermo is also famous for its delicious jasmine gelatin, which is made from an infusion of jasmine flowers.

Cassata

(Ricotta Cake)

Preparation time
1 ½ hours plus
cooling time

Cooking time
5 minutes

Difficulty
difficult

Serves 10 to 12
- 1 cup granulated sugar
- 1 vanilla bean
- 5 ounces bittersweet chocolate
- 1 pound mixed candied fruit
- 1 1-pound sponge cake
- 1 pound, 12 ounces ricotta cheese
- cinnamon
- ¼ cup shelled pistachio nuts; coarsely chopped
- 2 tablespoons Maraschino liqueur
- 3 tablespoons apricot jam
- ¼ cup superfine sugar
- 1 ½ cups confectioner's sugar
- 2 to 3 tablespoons orange water
- green food coloring

1 In a small saucepan, mix the granulated sugar with the vanilla bean and 3 tablespoons water. Cook over low heat until the sugar has dissolved. Cool.

2 Break or cut the chocolate into ¼-inch pieces, and dice the candied fruits, setting aside the best ones for the decoration. Line the bottom of a 10 x 1 ¼-inch springform pan with waxed paper.

3 Cut the sponge cake into ½-inch slices. Line the bottom and sides of the cake pan with the slices, taking care to cover the pan completely.

4 Strain the ricotta cheese directly into a mixing bowl and beat it with a wire whisk until it is light and creamy. Remove the vanilla bean from the sugar, and add the sugar, a pinch of cinnamon, the pieces of chocolate, and the diced candied fruit

to the ricotta. Lastly, add the pistachio nuts and Maraschino liqueur.

5 Fill the cake pan with this mixture, level it out, and cover it with the remaining slices of sponge cake. Refrigerate for at least 12 hours. In the meantime, mix the apricot jam with the powdered sugar and place this mixture over low heat, stirring constantly. Heat it until a thread forms when you take a little between your thumb and index finger and open and close them. Unmold the cassata onto a plate and brush it with the glaze.

6 Melt the confectioner's sugar over low heat. Pour it onto a marble surface, add the orange water and a few drops of coloring and blend it with a spatula until it is creamy. Spread this glaze over the top and sides of the cassata. Decorate the cake with the remaining candied fruit. Refrigerate until serving time.

SICILY

SPECIALTIES

Antipasti
Arancini di riso, Caponata, Scacce ripiene, Tonno in agrodolce.

First courses
Cuscus alla trapanese, Gattò di patate, Maccheroni con i broccoli arriminati, Pasta alla Norma, Pasta con le sarde, Spaghetti ai ricci di mare, Spaghetti alla bottarga, Timballo di maccheroni.

Entrées
Ammucca ammucca, Braciole di pesce spada, Coniglio alla stimpirata, Falsomagro, Involtini di pesce spada, Panata alla palermitana, Sarde a beccafico.

Desserts
Cannoli, Cappidduzzi, Cassata, Cubaita, Gelo d'anguria, Pasticcio di San Giuseppe.

TYPICAL RESTAURANTS

La Brocca d'u cinc'oru
Corso Savoia 49a, Acireale
Tel. 095/607196-7648155
Closed Sunday evening and Monday
Prices: Lire 45,000

Leon d'Oro
Via Emporium 102, Agrigento
Tel. 0922/414400, Closed Monday
Prices: Lire 50,000

Don Ciccio
Via del Cavaliere 87, Bagheria
Tel. 091/932442, Closed Wednesday and Sunday
Prices: Lire 55,000

Cortese
Viale Sicilia 166, Caltanissetta
Tel. 0934/591686, Closed Monday
Prices: Lire 55,000

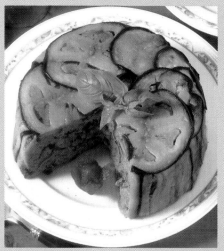

Eggplant pie

Ghicchirichi
Contr. Ogliastrello Castelmola, Castelmola
Tel. 0942/28201, Closed Wednesday
Prices: Lire 35,000

Al Gabbiano
Via Giordano Bruno 128, Catania
Tel. 095/537842, Closed Sunday
Prices: Lire 50,000

La Lampara
Via Pasubio 49, Catania
Tel. 095/383237, Closed Wednesday
Prices: Lire 40,000

Trattoria Casalinga
Via Biondi 19, Catania
Tel. 095/311319, Closed Sunday
Prices: Lire 40,000

La Brace
Via XXV Novembre 10, Cefalù
Tel. 0921/23570, Closed Monday
Prices: Lire 50,000

Villa Miraglia
Bosco della Miraglia, Cesarò
Tel. 095/696585
Prices: Lire 50,000

Monte San Giuliano
Vicolo San Rocco 7, Erice
Tel. 0923/869595, Closed Monday
Prices: Lire 55,000

Egadi
Via Colombo 17, Favignana
Tel. 0923/921232
Open from May to September
Prices: Lire 65,000

Fattoria delle Torri
Vicolo Napolitano 17, Modica
Tel. 0932/751286
Closed Monday
Prices: Lire 55,000

Ai Cascinari
Via d'Ossuna 43-45, Palermo
Tel. 091/6519804
Closed Monday
Prices: Lire 45,000

Capricci di Sicilia
Via Istituto Pignatelli 6, Palermo
Tel. 091/327777
Closed Monday
Prices: Lire 55,000

Da Rosario
Via Giacomo Cusmano 25, Palermo
Tel. 091/6112330-322992
Closed Sunday
Prices: Lire 55,000

I Grilli
Largo Cavalieri di Malta 2, Palermo
Tel. 091/334130, Closed Monday
Prices: Lire 55,000

Osteria Fratelli Lo Bianco
Via Emerico Amari 104, Palermo
Tel. 091/585816, Closed Sunday
Prices: Lire 20,000/25,000

Santandrea
Piazza Sant'Andrea 4, Palermo
Tel. 091/334999, Closed Tuesday
Prices: Lire 55,000

Al Fogher
Contrada Bellia 1-SS 117 bis
Piazza Armerina
Tel. 0935/684123, Closed Monday
Prices: Lire 55,000

Antica Macina
Via Giusti 129, Ragusa
Tel. 0932/248096-621287, Closed
Monday
Prices: Lire 60,000

Eremo della Giubilana
Contrada Giubiliana, Ragusa
Tel. 0932/669119, Closed Monday
Prices: Lire 45,000

Veneziano
Via Romano 8a, Randazzo
Tel. 095/7991353-921418
Closed Sunday evening and Monday
Prices: Lire 35,000/40,000

Hostaria del Vicolo
Vicolo Sammaritano 10, Sciacca
Tel. 0925/23071
Closed Sunday evenings
and Monday
Prices: Lire 60,000/75,000

Vecchio Fienile
Strada Provinciale 18, 4 km, Scicli
Tel. 0932/930377, Closed Wednesday
Prices: Lire 40,000

Archimede
Via Gemmellaro 8, Syrakus
Tel. 0931/69701, Closed Sunday evening
Prices: Lire 40,000/50,000
Darsena

Pignulata di Messina

Riva Garibaldi 6, Syrakus
Tel. 0931/66104
Closed Wednesday
Prices: Lire 35,000/45,000

Trattoria del Porto
Via Ammiraglio Staiti 45, Trapani
Tel. 0923/547822
Closed Monday
Prices: Lire 50,000

Mamma Lia
Via San Giacomo 1, Ustica
Tel. 091/8449594
Prices: Lire 40,000/50,000

WINES
White
Bianco d'Alcamo, Etna, Grecanico.

Rosé
Eloro, Etna, Nardo.

Red
Cerasuolo di Vittoria, Eloro, Etna,
Faro.

Dessert wine
Malvasia delle Lipari, Marsala, Moscato
di Noto, Moscato di Pantelleria, Moscato
di Siracusa, Passito di Pantelleria.

CHEESES
Caciocavallo, Cascavaddu, Guastedda
Pecorino, Piacintinu, Primusali, Provula,
Ragusano, Ricotta, Tumazzu.

SHOPPING FOR TYPICAL PRODUCTS
Wines
Azienda Agricola Poggio di Bortolone
Contrada Bortolomi 19, Chiaramonte
Gulfi

Enoteca Picone
Via Marconi 36, Palermo

Cold Meats
Cooperativa La Collina
Via Umberto 1, Sant'Angelo di Brolo

Da Filippo
Via Stabile 19, Palermo

Cheeses
Giorgio Cannata
Via Marchesa Tedeschi 32, Modica

Casa del formaggio
Corso Italia 330, Ragusa

Gelato (ice cream)

Although the origins of this extraordinary gastronomical invention are very ancient, it only became popular after the process of refrigeration had been perfected. The Italians, and in particular the Neapolitans and Sicilians, have created a culture of ice cream that includes a thousand flavors and colors which can satisfy the whims of one and all.

The ancient Greeks and later the Romans, but even before them the Chinese, loved to make cold drinks with snow and ice. Before refrigeration, a cold drink in the summer was a dream for anyone except a king or queen. They were able to have the winter snow packed in cold cellars to cool beverages and create the ancestors of today's sherbets and granita.

The ice cream most similar to what we eat today was created in the sixteenth century, probably by a Florentine architect by the name of Bernardo Buontalenti. It was introduced to France by Catherine de' Medici when she married Henry II, the King of France. Indeed, when that noblewoman moved to Paris, she took along her own Florentine ice-cream makers and pastry chefs. They created water ice creams, or rather sherbets, by using a new technique. Real ice cream dates back to the middle of the seventeenth century, when an English pastry chef invented an ice cream based on cream and eggs. For a long time its formula remained a secret so that only Charles I of England and a few other privileged souls were able to enjoy that delicacy. Ice cream became popular some thirty years later

thanks to the Sicilian nobleman Francesco Procopio dei Coltelli, who opened the Café Procope in Paris where it was possible to eat delicious sherbets and ice creams, and which became famous in Europe as a meeting place for writers, artists, and men of letters.

CHARACTERISTICS

Eating ice cream represents a moment of pure delight, particularly in the summer, yet at the same time ice cream is a valuable source of nourishment. Its ingredients – milk, cream, and eggs – are rich in protein. The fruit or, in some cases, vegetables that may be added can provide vitamins. It is, however, important to distinguish between ice creams, be-

cause they are not all alike. Some are based on cream (and known internationally as ice cream) and others on milk (ice milk), while sherbets have a fruit base. Ice creams with a high fat content are made with cream, milk, egg yolks, sugar, and a flavoring ingredient (coffee, chocolate, vanilla, nuts, etc.). Milk ices are low in fat and include any fruit cream made from concentrated fruit juice or syrup mixed with milk. The absence of cream and eggs makes them lighter and more digestible. Lastly, sherbets are the most refreshing of all. They are really not ice cream in the true sense of the word since they are made with fruit (or vegetable) juice and sugar, and contain no fat.

222

SERVING SUGGESTIONS

Ice cream is often served in the middle of the afternoon, or in the evening to crown an important dinner. When it is served as a dessert at the end of a meal, the low temperature of ice cream causes a greater flow of blood to the stomach, thus facilitating digestion.

Sherbet often substitutes for ice cream as a dessert, particularly because it is lighter. In the past (but even nowadays), a lemon sherbet was served between the courses of a meal to freshen the palate and prepare the stomach for the following courses. One can do the same thing with an unusual vegetable sherbet (for example, made with celery, tomato, or carrot).

At the end of a dinner, serve a pear sorbet to which you have added two tablespoons of pear brandy.

Heat a croissant in the oven, cut it in half horizontally, and fill it with vanilla or chocolate ice cream. Replace the top, and serve it with a fork and spoon.

Serve cut-up fruit in a bowl together with ice cream of the same flavor.

Arrange seasonal salad greens on individual plates, and in the middle of each place a scoop of a mixed vegetable sherbet in the center of a concave leaf.

THE RIGHT WINE

Wine is not served with ice cream. With fruit sherbets, on the other hand, serve champagne or a demi-sec spumante.

IN SEARCH OF ICE CREAM

The tradition of ice cream parlors exists for the most part in Campania and Sicily. In Naples, do not miss the Gelateria Bilancione (Via Posillipo 238/b) and taste their fior di latte and hazelnut flavors in particular. If you are in Palermo in August or September, try the very rare jasmine ice cream that they make at Sebastiano Compagno (Via Roma 15), where there is also a huge choice of other flavors. In Bagheria, try the 'Bagheria' ice cream that they make with citrus fruits at the Gelateria Anni 20 (Via Giovanni XXIII 116). And in the north, the Pasticceria Strumia (Via Vittorio Emanuele 9, Sommariva Bosco (Cuneo)) is well known for ice creams based on Piedmontese wines, one of which is a delicate Moscato ice cream.

SARDINIA

The sea and pastoral traditions

It is said that the real Sardinia shows itself from October to December, and not in the touristic and rather artificial area of the famous Costa Smeralda, but rather in the heart of an agricultural and pastoral world that is still populated by people who love their land and keep the ancient traditions alive. And the Sardinian gastronomy certainly does consider the needs of its shepherds before anything else by producing an infinite variety of breads, among which the *fresa* and the *pane carasau* take pride of place. After all, is there anything easier to transport than bread? And all the better if it is unleavened, as is the case with *pane carasau*, since it lasts amazingly well and is as thin as a sheet of music (*carta da musica*, which is another name for this bread).

A land of pastures cannot help but offer meat and cheeses, and since there are many more sheep than cows, there is a vast array of fine pecorino cheeses: the *casu marzu* which, though excellent in taste, may not be appreciated by those with weak stomachs since it is filled with wriggling larvae and the *fiore sardo*, which can be eaten fresh or aged, like most good pecorino cheeses.

Cow's milk cheese is reserved for children in the form of the amusing *gioghittus de casu*,

little dolls and animals made of cheese which turn food into toys that brighten one's day.

Certainly the most interesting product of this pastoral gastronomy is suckling pig, which is roasted *carraxiu*, that is, in a pit on a bed of myrtle branches and leaves which in turn cover a layer of embers, with another layer of myrtle and embers placed on top of the pig. Since Sardinia is the kingdom of myrtle, why not also use it to cook hens or other fowl? A very interesting recipe is that for *tacula*, in which bunches of thrushes or blackbirds are steamed and then placed in canvas bags that contain myrtle leaves so that on cooling they will absorb the fragrance of that aromatic plant. Tacula is a particular specialty of Cagliari, which is a good departure point for exploring the southwestern area of Sulcis-Iglesiente,

Sulcis-Iglesiente, following in the steps of the ancient Phoenicians and the prehistoric civilization that left those extraordinary constructions, the *nuraghi*. After a visit to Cagliari and the National Archeological Museum, which possesses a remarkable collection of nuraghic statuettes, you can go to Nora, an ancient Phoenician city which later became subject to Carthage and then to Rome. Heading north, there are magical places that are worth visiting, such as the necropolis of Montessu, the nuraghe *Su Casteddu*, and the Roman temple of Antas.

No mention has been made of the sea, and yet there is nothing like it in all of Italy, not only for the transparency of its waters, but also for the beauty of its wind-sculpted coastline. And nowhere else does the sea offer such a plentitude of fish of all types, from the superb lobsters, which are served either boiled or roasted with a simple dressing of oil, salt, and lemon juice to the humble red mullet, not to mention the gilthead, sole, sea bass, cuttlefish, tuna, and gray mullet. From the latter two come another great local specialty, *bottarga*, or dried mullet or tuna eggs. Mullet bottarga is the more delicate and is usually eaten sliced and seasoned with a little oil and lemon juice. Another exceptional dish is the *cassòla*, a fish soup which the local population maintains only the fishermen can cook well. At Santa Teresa Gallura, one of the most fascinating places on the northern coast, and in particular at Capo Testa,

the white granite rock has been sculpted by the wind into works worthy of great artists. Another good reason for a visit in early September is the gastronomical fair dedicated to such products of the sea as lobster, eel, and octopus, all of which are accompanied by the excellent local Vermentino wine.

To complete this itinerary through nature, a visit should be paid to Alghero, or rather to the nearby Capo Caccia, where the griffin vultures, those majestic birds with a wingspan of more than eight feet, and peregrine falcons still take refuge.

After a splendid walk, indulge in an excellent plate of pasta with an Alghero sauce made of clams, olives, capers, garlic, and parsley, and a good white Nuragus wine to accompany it.

When a bottle of Vernaccia or Malvasia makes its appearance, it means that the time has come to sample Sardinian sweets. First and foremost among them is the *seadas* (or *sebadas*), a specialty from Oliena in the province of Nuoro, a fresh, slightly acid cheese that serves as a filling for sweet, fried ravioli served with bitter honey.

The Roman temple of Antas near Iglésias.

Bronze nuraghic statuette from the National Archeological Museum at Cagliari.

227

Angiulottos de casu
(Ravioli Filled with Cheese)

Preparation time
30 minutes plus resting time

Cooking time
10 minutes

Difficulty
medium

Serves 6
- 4 cups durum wheat flour
- 1 tablespoon extra virgin olive oil
- 1 pound fresh pecorino cheese or ricotta cheese made from sheep's milk
- 1 pinch saffron
- 2 to 3 eggs
- salt and pepper
- ¹/₂ cup grated aged pecorino cheese
- ¹/₂ cup butter, melted

Dry white wine.
Recommended:
- Vermentino di Gallura
- Trebbiano di Romagna

1 Sift the flour into a mound and make a well in the center. Add the oil and enough lukewarm water to make a firm dough. Cover it with a cloth and let it rest for 30 minutes.

2 Grate the pecorino cheese into a bowl and mix in the saffron and 1 or 2 eggs. Add salt, if necessary, and pepper.

3 Roll out the dough. Beat 1 egg in a bowl with a pinch of salt and 1 tablespoon water, and brush the dough with it. Divide the dough in half. Distribute the cheese filling on the dough at intervals. Cover with the other half of dough, and press the your fingers. Cut into square ravioli.

4 Cook the ravioli in boiling salted water. Drain them and sprinkle with grated cheese.

Zuppa di aragoste
(Lobster Soup)

Preparation time
20 minutes

Cooking time
30 minutes

Difficulty
medium

Serves 4
- 2 1-pound lobsters
- ½ cup extra virgin olive oil
- 1 fistful parsley leaves, chopped
- 2 cloves garlic
- 2 cups chopped plum tomatoes
- 1 teaspoon coarse sea salt
- salt and pepper
- 4 slices country bread

Aromatic white wine.
Recommended:
- Vermentino di Gallura
- Alto Adige Riesling Italico

1 Rinse the lobsters under cold water, and split them in half. Remove the black filament along the tail and the sandy sac. Chop 1 garlic clove.

2 In a saucepan, heat the oil. Add the chopped garlic and parsley and sauté. Add the lobsters and cook until the shells become red. Remove the lobsters and keep them warm.

3 Mash the tomatoes and add them to the saucepan. Cook over medium heat for 10 minutes. Dissolve the sea salt in a ladleful of boiling water and add it to the tomatoes. Boil over high heat for 5 minutes. Return the lobsters to the saucepan, cover, and cook for another 10 minutes. Taste and adjust salt and pepper.

4 Halve the remaining garlic clove and rub the slices of bread with the cut sides. Toast the bread in the oven or under a hot grill. Place a slice of bread in each soup plate and add soup and half a lobster. Serve immediately.

Pudda e martaucci
(Bay-Scented Chicken)

Preparation time
20 minutes plus
resting time

Cooking time
1 ¹/₂ hours

Difficulty
easy

Serves 6
- 1 3-pound stewing
  hen
- 1 onion, peeled
- 1 carrot, peeled
- 1 stalk celery
- a few sprigs parsley
- salt
- 40 bay leaves

Light red wine.
Recommended:
- Monica di
  Sardegna
- Lacrima di Morro
  d'Alba

1 Wash and dry the chicken, put a pinch of salt inside, and tie it up. Bring abundant water to a boil in a large pot and add the onion, carrot, celery, and parsley. Add salt and the chicken. Cover and simmer for 1 ¹/₂ hours. The chicken must be well-cooked.

2 Prepare a bed of bayleaves on a serving platter. Drain the chicken and put it on the platter, then cover the chicken with more bay leaves. Put a plate with a weight on it on top of the chicken and leave it for 12 hours at room temperature so that the fragrance of the bay leaves can penetrate the flesh. Then remove the chicken from the leaves, cut it into pieces and serve.

Bay leaves can be found in the spice section of the supermarket.

Seadas

(Sweet Fried Ravioli)

Preparation time
30 minutes plus resting time

Cooking time
15 minutes

Difficulty
medium

Makes 14 to 15 seadas
- 2 ½ cups flour
- salt
- 2 eggs
- ¼ cup butter, cut into pieces and softened
- ¾ pound fresh pecorino cheese
- finely grated zest of 1 lemon
- finely grated zest of 1 orange
- vegetable oil for frying
- ¼ cup honey
- juice of 1 orange, strained

Dessert wine or a sweet Passito. Recommended:
- Vernaccia di Oristano
- Vin Santo della Valdinievole

1 Sift the flour onto a board. Add a pinch of salt, the eggs, and the butter. Work all the ingredients together until they form a smooth, firm dough. Shape the dough into a ball, place it in a bowl, cover with a cloth, and let it rest in a cool place for about 30 minutes.

2 Grate the pecorino cheese on the side of the grater with large holes. Mix it with the lemon and orange zests.

3 Roll out the dough into a ⅛-inch sheet and cut it into circles 4 inches in diameter. Put a teaspoon of filling on each circle, fold it in half, and seal the edges well with your fingers.

4 Heat 1 inch of oil in a skillet and when it is very hot, add a few seadas at a time and fry them until they are golden brown on both sides. Drain them on paper towels. Transfer them to a serving platter and keep them warm.

5 Heat the honey in a double boiler, and mix it with the orange juice. Pour it over the hot seadas and serve immediately.

The *seadas*, also called *sebadas* or *sevadas*, are traditionally served with *ranzigu*, a honey which comes from the pollen of the strawberry tree and has a characteristic bitter taste.

SARDINIA

Island fish soup

SPECIALTIES

Antipasti (Appetizers)
Bottarga di muggine in insalata,
Peisceddu scabecciaus, Tataliu.

First courses
Angiulottos de casu, Culingiones,
Culurgiones ogliastrini, Maccarrones
furriaos, Malloreddus alla campidanese,
Pane frattau, Pilau, Zuppa barbaricina,
Zuppa gallurese.

Entrées
Aragosta alla catalana, Burrida, Cassola,
Cordula arrosto, Ghisau, Pecora in
umido, Procetto arrosto, su mathamene,
Tacula.

Desserts
Gueffos, Pabassinos, Pardulas, Seadas.

TYPICAL RESTAURANTS
La Singular
Via Arduino 45, Alghero
Tel. 079/982098, Closed Monday
Prices: Lire 35,000

Golgo
in Golgo, Baunei
Tel. 0337/811828
Prices: Lire 55,000

Il Caminetto
Via Battisti 8, Cabras
Tel. 0783/391139, Closed Monday
Prices: Lire 55,000

Crackers
Corso Vittorio Emanuele 195, Cagliari
Tel. 070/653912, Closed Wednesday
Prices: Lire 30,000/40,000

Lillicu
Via Sardegna 78, Cagliari
Tel. 070/652970
Closed Sunday
Prices: Lire 50,000/65,000

Da Pasqualino
Via Roma 99, Calasetta
Tel. 0781/88473,
Closed Tuesday
Prices: Lire 50,000

Desogos
Via Cugia 6, Cuglieri
Tel. 0785/39198, Closed Monday
Prices: Lire 40,000

Ispinigoli
Landstraße 125, km 210, Dorgali
Tel. 0784/94293-95268
Prices: Lire 55,000

Da Riccardo
Via Nazionale 4, Flussio
Tel. 0785/34752, Closed Tuesday
Prices: Lire 50,000/60,000

Pan di zucchero
Via Centrale 365, Iglesias
Tel. 0781/471114, Closed Monday
Prices: Lire 50,000/60,000

Su Talleri
Corso Umberto I 228, Macomer
Tel. 0785/71699, Closed Sunday
Prices: Lire 55,000

Pisturri
in Pisturri, Magomadas
Tel. 0785/35530
Prices: Lire 35,000

Il Rifugio
Vicolo del Pozzo 4, Nuoro
Tel. 0784/232355,
Closed Wednesday
Prices: Lire 40,000

Ci Kappa
Via Martin Luther King 2-4, Oliena
Tel. 0784/288024, Closed Monday
Prices: Lire 50,000

Monte Maccione
in Monte Maccione, Oliena
Tel. 0784/288363
Prices: Lire 35,000/50,000

Ai Monti del Gennargentu
in Settiles, Orgosolo
Tel. 0784/402374
Prices: Lire 60,000

Craf
Via de Castro 34, Oristano
Tel. 0783/70669, Closed Sunday
Prices: Lire 55,000/60,000

Da Zia Giovanna
Via Sulis 11-Via Aspruni 35, Padria

Tel. 079/807074, Closed Saturday
Prices: Lire 30,000

Da Nino
Corso IV Novembre 26, Sorgono
Tel. 0784/60127, Closed Sunday
Prices: Lire 40,000

Cibò Qubó
Via Merceddì 193, Terralba
Tel. 0783/83730, Closed Tuesday
Prices: Lire 50,000

Antica Trattoria del Vico
Vicolo Martiri 10, Teulada
Tel. 070/9270701, Closed Tuesday
Prices: Lire 60,000

Da Lenin
Via San Gemiliano 19, Tortoli
Tel. 0782/624422, Closed Sunday
Prices: Lire 55,000

Lo Spiedo d'Ogliastra
Via Zinnias 23, Tortoli
Tel. 0782/62385
Prices: Lire 30,000

WINES
White
Malvasia di Cagliari, Nuragus,
Trebbiano d'Arborea, Vermentino
di Gallura.

Rosé
Carignano del Sulcis, Mandrolisai.

Red
Campidano di Terralba, Cannonau,
Carignano del Sulcis, Girò, Mandrolisai,
Monica.

Dessert wine
Girò di Cagliari liquoroso, Malvasia

Spinu

di Bosa, Malvasia di Cagliari liquoroso,
Monica di Cagliari liquoroso, Moscato
di Cagliari, Moscato di Gallura,
Moscato di Temio Pausania, Moscato
di Sorso Sennori, Nasco di Cagliari,
Vernaccia di Oristano.

CHEESES
Bonassai, Caciotta, Casu Ascedu,
Casu Becciu, Casu Spiattatu,
Dolce Sardo, Fiore Sardo, Fresa,
Ircano, Pecorino.

SHOPPING FOR TYPICAL PRODUCTS

Wines
Il Ghiotto
Piazza Civica 23, Alghero

Fratelli Mutzu
in Sa Serra, Buddusò

Azienda Zedda Piras
Via Clusa 125, Cagliari

Enoteca Biuoni
Via Aldo Moro 119, Olbia

Cold Meats
Il Ghiotto
Piazza Civica 23, Alghero

Salumificio Ma. Gi. Ca.
In Is Bangius, Marrubiu

Cheeses
Il Ghiotto
Piazza Civica 23, Alghero

Caseificio Cuozzo
Via Cagliari 23, Oristano

TYPICAL PRODUCTS
Bottarga (dried fish roe)

Made from fish eggs, bottarga is a seafood specialty that is especially appreciated by those who like strong-tasting foods. As its popularity grows, it is being included more and more often in new creations from the kitchen.

CHARACTERISTICS

Bottarga is an artisan product made from the ovaries of fish which have been salted, pressed, and left to dry for a period of four or five months.

In theory, bottarga can come from any fish that has comestible eggs. However, in practice, the most popular bottarga is that from the gray mullet (muggine or cefalo). It looks like a square salami and has a characteristic nut color that tends toward pink or amber. It smells much like sea urchins, and has a strong taste that should, however, not be too salty.

Dried tuna roe is also available on the market. It has a stronger taste and is inferior in quality to that of the mullet. The rare and highly prized bottarga di spigola (sea bass) is very delicate in taste.

STORING BOTTARGA

Bottarga can be kept for months wrapped in aluminum foil on the lowest shelf of the refrigerator.

When buying vacuum-packed bottarga, check the expiration date.

One way to maintain its flavor and keep it soft is to put it in a jar and cover it with oil. Keep it in the refrigerator for 20 days, at which time the bottarga can be eaten, while the strained oil, excellent for seasoning spaghetti or salads, can be kept for months in the refrigerator.

BUYING BOTTARGA

• Bottarga must be dry in appearance but not dried out. It should be firm, not hard, to the touch. Do not buy it if it is very hard or tough.

• Do not buy bottarga that is brown or very dark in color since it may be old and hard.

• Bottarga should have its particular odor, and not smell like anchovies preserved in oil.

• Whole bottarga vacuum-packed in a plastic bag and marked with an expiration date is the most reliable.

• Grated bottarga is usually of inferior quality and very salty.

• Sometimes there is a small hole in the middle of the bottarga. This is due to the fact that during the drying process they are often hung in pairs with a stick run through them to keep them apart.

234

SERVING SUGGESTIONS

Bottarga provides a special touch to any antipasto, an individual note when seasoning a pasta, and a pleasant surprise to salads. In short, it adds a new and unusual taste that will please connoisseurs and gourmets alike. Use a knife for slicing bottarga or, even better, a truffle shaver. When grating it, use a serrated knife.

Slice the bottarga and serve it with tomatoes cut in wedges or slices with a little oil.

Slice, crumble, or grate the bottarga and place it in a bowl with a garlic clove. Cover it with olive oil and let it sit for an hour before using it to season pasta.

Slice the bottarga and arrange it on a carpaccio of fish with a little olive oil and lemon juice.

Serve slices of bottarga on sliced smoked salmon.

Add a teaspoon of grated bottarga to a soft-boiled egg.

Garnish a green salad – dressed with oil, lemon juice, and very little salt – with sliced bottarga.

MISTAKES TO AVOID

Bottarga must never be cooked; it should be used as it is on dishes that are ready to be served.

It is not to be used in any preparation with grated cheese, since it does not combine well with cheeses, especially aged ones.

THE RIGHT WINE

The ideal wine is Vernaccia di Oristano, but any smooth white wine like Vermentino goes well with bottarga.

When the bottarga is being served at an elegant dinner, then a Spumante Classico Brut is recommended. A dry sherry would be the preferred foreign wine.

IN SEARCH OF BOTTARGA

Bottarga is made along the entire Mediterranean coast from Provence to Tunisia to Sicily. However, the most significant production is in Sardinia, where the region's brackish lagoons provide an ideal habitat for gray mullet. The best purchases are to be made at the fisheries of Alghero, Oristano, and Carloforte. You can also find homemade bottarga in Sardinia; these are to be consumed within a short time since they have been left in a saline solution for a few hours and then

hung outdoors, without pressing, until they have dried.

General Index

Recipe Index by Course